1000
Mediterranean
Meals

1000
Mediterranean
Meals

EVERY RECIPE YOU NEED
FOR THE HEALTHIEST WAY TO EAT

CHARTWELL
BOOKS

Brimming with creative inspiration, how-to projects, and useful information to enrich your everyday life, Quarto Knows is a favorite destination for those pursuing their interests and passions. Visit our site and dig deeper with our books into your area of interest: Quarto Creates, Quarto Cooks, Quarto Homes, Quarto Lives, Quarto Drives, Quarto Explores, Quarto Gifts, or Quarto Kids.

© 2020 Quarto Publishing plc

This edition published in 2020 by Chartwell Books,
an imprint of The Quarto Group
142 West 36th Street, 4th Floor
New York, NY 10018 USA
T (212) 779-4972 F (212) 779-6058
www.QuartoKnows.com

Conceived, designed, and produced by The Bright Press, an imprint of The Quarto Group
The Old Brewery, 6 Blundell Street, London N7 9BH, United Kingdom
Tel 00 44 (0)20 7700 6700

Publisher: James Evans
Art Director: Katherine Radcliffe
Editorial Director: Isheeta Mustafi
Managing Editor: Jacqui Sayers
Senior Editor: Caroline Elliker
Editorial Assistant: Chloe Porter
Designer: Ginny Zeal
Photographers: Ian Garlick, Ria Osborne

Image credits:
Shutterstock: Wiktory 82; Louno Morose 238
Stockfood: Rua Castilho 29; Oliver Brachat 75; Barbara Bonisolli 97

Recipe contributors: Rebecca Baugniet; Carol Beckerman; Judith M. Fertig; Valentina Harris; Maria Segura; Wendy Sweetster

10 9 8 7 6 5 4 3 2 1

Chartwell titles are also available at discount for retail, wholesale, promotional, and bulk purchase. For details, contact the Special Sales Manager by email at specialsales@quarto.com or by mail at The Quarto Group, Attn: Special Sales Manager, 100 Cummings Center, Suite 265D, Beverly, MA 01915, USA.

This book provides general information. It should not be relied upon as recommending or promoting any specific diagnosis or method of treatment for a particular condition, and it is not intended as a substitute for medical advice or for direct diagnosis and treatment of a medical condition by a qualified physician. Readers who have questions about a particular condition, possible treatments for that condition, or possible reactions from the condition or its treatment should consult a physician or other qualified healthcare professional.

ISBN: 978-0-7858-3871-5

Library of Congress Control Number: 2020936780

Printed in Singapore

contents

The Mediterranean diet

It is a well-known fact that the Mediterranean diet incorporates all the traditional healthy living habits of people from the countries bordering the Mediterranean Sea. It includes lots of vegetables, legumes, whole grains, breads, fruits, nuts, seeds, and olive oil, as well as plenty of fish, poultry, and small amounts of red meat.

Health benefits

All food that falls under the general heading of Mediterranean is fresh, unprocessed, unrefined, and usually low in saturated and trans fats. The Mediterranean diet is considered to be one of the healthiest ways of eating, with statistics of heart disease and obesity generally recorded as being much lower in those countries where this sort of regime is followed, when compared to other more northern countries.

Recent news that eating a Mediterranean diet during pregnancy might ward off childhood allergies and asthma just adds to the list of studies suggesting this style of eating has a lot to offer. Living longer and having lower risks of heart disease, cancer, diabetes, and possibly birth defects have all been linked to eating a healthy Mediterranean diet.

Everything in moderation

Of course, there is no one "Mediterranean" diet. There are twenty-one countries that border the Mediterranean Sea. Diets vary between these countries and also between regions within a country. Many differences in culture, ethnic background, religion, economy, and agricultural production result in different diets. But the common Mediterranean dietary pattern has these characteristics:

- high consumption of fruits, vegetables, bread and other whole grains, potatoes, beans, nuts, and seeds
- olive oil as an important monounsaturated fat source
- dairy products, fish, and poultry consumed in low to moderate amounts, and little red meat
- eggs consumed up to four times a week
- alcohol consumed in low to moderate amounts

Healthy and tasty

Mediterranean food is not just really good for you, it is also really delicious to eat and pretty to look at. It encompasses the culinary traditions and cultures of all the countries that border the Mediterranean waters. This is convivial food that suits the climate and the pace of life, consisting largely of lots of little dishes made out of tantalizing and delicious local specialties—from grilled fish to delicate filled pastries, tasty stews, and fresh produce combined into salads. This is food that will enliven even the most jaded palate, where the key is always variety to satisfy even the hungriest diner.

This book contains many different recipes from all around the Mediterranean, recipes that are traditional and classical as well as new, innovative ideas, chosen because they taste delicious, are relatively simple to reproduce at home, and look simply wonderful on the table— generally bright and colorful, reminiscent of the warm and welcoming Mediterranean.

CHAPTER 1

Antipasti, Meze & Tapas

The custom of serving a selection of small plates of food to begin a meal, or instead of a meal, is very much a part of the Mediterranean culture. Called antipasti, meze, or tapas depending upon the country, many of these dishes use similar basic ingredients, albeit in very different styles.

THE ORIGINAL SMALL PLATES

What could be more evocatively Mediterranean than to take refuge from the sun with a fortifying drink and to nibble at some fresh, tastebud-tingling, grilled asparagus wrapped in jamón serrano? Tradition holds that this style of eating originated from the custom of using a slice of bread or ham used as a lid to keep insects out of drinks, hence the speculation that "tapas" is derived from the verb tapar, "to cover."

However it started, small plates are now a staple of the Mediterranean bar experience, where mouthfuls of delicious treats, mostly on toasts or carvings of bread, are served with traditional toppings like morcilla and piquillo peppers or pâtés and cured meats with capers.

AN EVOLUTION OF STYLES

The notion of perfect and delicious little bar snacks has now taken wing from its humble beginnings, developing into a worldwide gastronomic delight perceptively different from the usual restaurant experience. Still essentially Mediterranean in its compositions of herbs, seasonings, and ingredients, small plates have become more luxurious and decadent while still maintaining the feel of convivial food.

Now that the popularity of small plates has become a worldwide trend, it is possible to observe an evolution in its styles. It has become feasible to take almost any popular meal, minimize it down to a single tasting-sized portion, and presto, a new dish has sprung from the void.

FOOD FOR SHARING

The dynamic of sharing food has created an amazing assortment of small dishes, specially styled as a focal point, around which a group can sit and chat, scooping off mouthful-sized portions as the mood takes them. Such examples of this are Grilled Lamb Cutlets with Burnt Butter, Rosemary & Capers (see page 36), and Deep-fried Stuffed Giant Olives (see page 31). Can you imagine a more enticing shared delight than a party enjoying these wonderful dishes in good company with excellent wine?

In addition to small plates, this style of eating can also incorporate large servings of food to be shared—such as Beef Carpaccio with Anchovy Mayo & Crispy Garlic (see page 35), or the traditional Portuguese pork stew Cataplana (see page 33). Certainly it's more fun to have lots of plates on the table and sample a little from each than to have just one large meal to oneself.

Antipasti, meze and tapas is all about sharing in so many ways. They are not just food genres, they are a means for gathering and convening, of celebrating, talking, and sharing something that is just a little bit special. So gather your family and friends, chill the wine, and get ready to indulge in these small plates of wonder.

EQUIPMENT

One of the many joys of eating in this way is that very little specialty equipment is essential. Here are just a few pieces that will make your home experience a little more authentic.

Small earthenware dishes: Earthenware is the perfect material for serving small dishes. You can bake with it, and it keeps your food hot and in individual portions.

Ovenproof ceramic dishes: As an alternative to earthenware, you can have a selection of dishes made from glazed ceramic—anything from the size and depth of a ramekin to a shorter wider variety.

Wooden boards: As charcuterie is such a major part of Mediterranean cuisine , having a beautiful wooden board for serving cold meats on is a must.

Wooden kebab skewers: What easier way of making tasty mouthfuls than serving dishes as kebabs. Small skewers, maybe long enough to fit two or three pieces of meat, fish, or vegetables, are perfect.

Toothpicks: Useful for picking up your olives and using as skewers, a box of toothpicks will never go unused.

Mortar & pestle: When dealing with spices and aromatics, having a good sturdy mortar and pestle around to pound flavor into food is essential.

Roasted Almonds & Seeds

Makes 2⅔ cups (250 g)

2 cups (150 g) whole almonds, with skin
⅓ cup (55 g) pumpkin seeds
⅓ cup (55 g) sunflower seeds

4 tbsp. olive oil
1 tsp. dried chili pepper flakes
½ tsp. cumin seeds

1 tbsp. sea salt
1 tsp. freshly ground black pepper

1 Preheat the oven to 350°F (180°C). Mix all the ingredients together in a bowl.

2 Transfer to a large roasting pan. Cook for 20–25 minutes, turning at regular intervals until the almonds are deep gold.

3 Drain on paper towels and add a little more salt if desired. Serve warm.

WITH SPICES
Prepare the basic recipe, replacing the cumin and chili pepper flakes with ¼ teaspoon cayenne pepper and ½ teaspoon paprika.

WITH CURRY POWDER
Prepare the basic recipe, replacing the cumin and chili pepper flakes with 1 teaspoon curry powder.

WITH RAISINS
Prepare the basic recipe, replacing half the seeds with 2 tablespoons golden raisins.

WITH WALNUTS & APRICOTS
Prepare the basic recipe, replacing the almonds with walnut halves, and half the seeds with 2 tablespoons chopped dried apricots.

Hummus

Serves 4–6

1 x 16 oz. (450 g) can chickpeas or
  garbanzo beans
¼ cup (50 ml) water or vegetable stock

3–5 tbsp. lemon juice (depending on taste)
1½ tbsp. tahini
2 cloves garlic, crushed

½ tsp. salt
1–2 tbsp. olive oil
chopped fresh parsley, to garnish

1 Drain chickpeas, reserving liquid from can. Combine chickpeas, water or stock, lemon juice, tahini, garlic, and salt in blender or food processor. Add ¼ cup (50 ml) of reserved liquid from chickpeas. Blend for 3–5 minutes on low speed until thoroughly mixed and smooth.

2 Place in serving bowl, and create a shallow well in the center of the hummus. Add olive oil in the well.

3 Garnish with chopped parsley. Serve immediately with warm or toasted pita bread. If preferred, cover and refrigerate until required, and add the final oil and parsley garnish just before serving.

WITHOUT TAHINI
Prepare basic recipe, omitting tahini. When the hummus is smooth and creamy, add 1 teaspoon ground cumin.

WITH ARTICHOKE
Instead of the basic recipe, combine chickpeas, tahini, and 1 x 14-oz. (400-g) drained can of artichoke hearts in food processor. Slowly blend in lemon juice, garlic, and olive oil. If it is too thick, gradually add water or vegetable stock. Season with salt and pepper.

WITH ROASTED GARLIC
Instead of basic recipe, mix chickpeas, water or stock, lemon juice, and salt in blender or food processor. Add about 6 cloves of roasted garlic, olive oil, and ½ teaspoon dried oregano. Add extra olive oil, ½ teaspoon at a time, if the hummus is too thick.

WITH KALAMATA OLIVE
Prepare basic recipe, adding a handful of chopped, pitted Kalamata olives and a large pinch of dried oregano. Omit parsley garnish.

Tzatziki

Greek tzatziki, traditionally served as an appetizer, can be left on the table as an accompaniment for other foods throughout the meal. The key to the best tzatziki is the thick creamy texture that allows it to be eaten alone, as a dip, spread, or condiment.

Serves 4–6

1 tbsp. olive oil
2 tsp. lemon juice
2 cups (450 ml) thick
    Greek yogurt
4–10 garlic cloves (or to
    taste), finely chopped

1 cucumber, peeled and
    finely diced or coarsely
    grated
chopped fresh parsley, to
    garnish

1   Combine the olive oil and lemon juice in a mixing bowl by whisking gently together. Fold the yogurt into the mixture slowly, making sure it is fully mixed in.

2   Add the garlic, according to taste, and the cucumber. Stir until evenly distributed.

3   Garnish with a little chopped parsley. Serve well chilled.

WITH MINT
Prepare the basic recipe, adding about 3 tablespoons finely chopped fresh mint leaves to the mixture with the cucumber.

WITH DILL
Prepare the basic recipe, adding about 3 tablespoons finely chopped fresh dill to the mixture with the cucumber.

WITH CHILI
Prepare the basic recipe, adding ¼ teaspoon finely chopped dried red chili to the mixture with the cucumber for a little added spice.

WITH ROASTED GARLIC
Prepare the basic recipe, adding gently roasted, peeled garlic cloves instead of fresh garlic for a softer, sweeter flavor.

Eggplant Dip with Walnuts

The combination of the walnuts and the stinging sharpness of the vinegar used in this recipe gives this Greek dip, called *melitzanosalata me karythia*, a nice tart taste that goes wonderfully with wedges of pita bread, raw vegetables, and salty cheeses.

Serves 4–6

4½ lbs. (2 kg) eggplant
3 cloves garlic
⅓ cup (75 ml) extra-
    virgin olive oil
3 tbsp. red wine vinegar
1 tsp. salt

½ tsp. freshly ground
    black pepper
½ bunch fresh flat-leaf
    parsley, finely chopped
7 tbsp. coarsely chopped
    walnuts

1   Preheat oven to 375°F (190°C). Remove stem from eggplants, rinse, and pat dry. Place whole eggplants on a cookie sheet and bake for just over an hour. Remove from the oven and cool.

2   As soon as they can be handled, remove skin (it will come off easily by hand) and place the pulp in a fine strainer to drain for about 15 minutes, or until it stops dripping.

3   Combine eggplant pulp with remaining ingredients in a food processor and process until blended. Alternatively, once the eggplant pulp has drained, chop finely, mash with a fork, and stir in all the other ingredients until well blended, adding the oil and vinegar alternately. Serve chilled or at room temperature.

WITH PINE NUTS
Prepare the basic recipe, but replace the walnuts with pine nuts and halve the amount of vinegar.

WITH LEMON JUICE
Prepare the basic recipe, but omit the walnuts and replace the vinegar with 1½ tablespoons fresh lemon juice.

WITH CHILI
Prepare the basic recipe, but halve the amount of vinegar and stir in 1 finely chopped fresh red or green chili to the finished dip.

WITH CILANTRO
Prepare the basic recipe, but halve the amount of vinegar and omit the walnuts. Instead, stir about 4 tablespoons finely chopped cilantro into the finished dip.

Sicilian Marinated Olives

This way of flavoring olives is very traditional in Sicily, where it is known as *olive cunsati*. The longer the olives are left in their marinade, the stronger the flavor they will take on, but they can be equally delicious served almost immediately after being dressed. Add a handful of these olives to any dish of cured meats for an easy antipasto.

Serves 4–6

14 oz. (400 g) green
   olives, preserved in
   brine
2 tbsp. chopped fresh dill
4 cloves garlic, peeled
   and crushed
15 fresh mint leaves
sea salt

4 oz. (125 g) small inner
   stalks celery with
   leaves, chopped
6 tbsp. extra-virgin olive
   oil
8 tbsp. red wine vinegar
½ red chili pepper, seeded
   and finely chopped

1   Drain the olives, then put them into a heavy-duty plastic bag and loosely tie closed. Place the bag on a worktop and, with a rolling pin, lightly crush the olives (it is more a matter of cracking them), then transfer the olive pulp out of the bag and into a bowl.

2   Add the dill, garlic, mint, and a pinch of salt, then cover with water. Let soak for a minimum of 1 hour or a maximum of 3 days.

3   Drain, then add the celery, olive oil, and vinegar, and finally the chopped chili. Stir it all together thoroughly and serve, or let stand until required.

WITH ORANGE & ROSEMARY
Drain and rinse a jar of black olives preserved in brine. Mix with juice of 1 large orange, 2 tablespoons chopped fresh rosemary, and olive oil to cover. Let stand until required.

WITH CHILI & GARLIC
Drain and rinse a jar of black or green olives preserved in brine. Mix with 2–4 chopped dried red chilies, 2–3 crushed garlic cloves, and olive oil to cover. Let stand until required.

WITH LEMON & FETA
Drain and rinse a jar of green or black olives in brine. Mix with juice of 1 lemon; thinly peeled skin of lemon, chopped finely; 2 tablespoons chopped parsley; 2 tablespoons crumbled feta; and olive oil to cover. Let stand until required.

WITH LEMON & CILANTRO
Drain and rinse a jar of green olives in brine. Mix with the juice of 1 large lemon, 3 tablespoons chopped cilantro, and olive oil to cover. Let stand until required.

Charcuterie with Pickled Garlic & Caper Berries

This is the absolute cornerstone of tapas, a simple but vital centerpiece. It can be easily presented on a wooden board (olive wood is wonderful) at the center of the table and you'll be fighting everyone off to get to it.

Serves 4

8 slices dried chorizo
8 slices Serrano ham
8 slices Spanish ham
8 slices Spanish air-dried
   sausage
½ cup (75 g) pickled
   garlic
½ cup (75 g) pickled
   caper berries
drizzle of really good-
   quality Spanish extra-
   virgin olive oil

1 Lay your different charcuterie meats elegantly on a board.

2 Scatter with the pickled garlic and caper berries.

3 Drizzle with olive oil and serve with warm crusty bread.

WITH RED PEPPERS & ARUGULA
Prepare the basic recipe, replacing the garlic and caper berries with 3 thinly sliced roasted red peppers (canned peppers are fine) and decorating the board with dressed arugula leaves.

WITH SALAMI
Prepare the basic recipe, replacing the hams with several varieties of Italian salami.

WITH PÂTÉ
Prepare the basic recipe, replacing the hams with several varieties of pâtés.

WITH MORTADELLA, TRUFFLE CHEESE & PISTACHIOS
Prepare the basic recipe, replacing the hams with mortadella sausage and truffle cheese. Omit the garlic and caper berries and serve with peeled pistachio nuts sprinkled over the sausage.

Pan-fried Pimientos de Padrón

Serves 4

1½ cups (350 g) Spanish green peppers
(preferably pimientos de Padrón)

2 tbsp. light olive oil
½ tsp. sea salt

1 Wash the peppers thoroughly in cold water and pat dry.

2 Place a large lidded skillet over high heat, add the olive oil, and heat until almost smoking. Add the peppers, cover, and cook for 4–5 minutes, turning occasionally, until blistered and slightly charred.

3 Drain the peppers on paper towels, sprinkle generously with the sea salt, and serve.

WITH GARLIC SALT
Prepare the basic recipe, replacing the sea salt with garlic salt.

WITH SPICES
Prepare the basic recipe, adding ½ teaspoon ground cumin to the oil before cooking.

WITH CORIANDER
Prepare the basic recipe, adding ½ teaspoon ground coriander to the oil before cooking.

WITH CHORIZO
Prepare the basic recipe, adding 1 chopped chorizo sausage to the oil and frying for 1 minute before adding the peppers

Gildas

Serves 4

4 oz. (125 g) best-quality anchovy fillets
marinated in olive oil

⅔ lb. (300 g) guindilla (or large chilies), cut
into smaller pieces if necessary
½ lb. pitted green olives

1 Curl up each anchovy and thread it onto a cocktail pick, along with 2 or 3 chilies and 1 olive.

2 Stack the gildas onto a serving plate and serve immediately.

WITH BLACK OLIVES
Prepare the basic recipe, replacing the green olives with pitted black olives.

WITH CAPER BERRIES
Thread a caper berry onto the cocktail pick along with the other ingredients.

WITHOUT CHILI
Omit the chili and simply alternate olives and anchovies on the pick.

Falafel

Falafel is very popular in the Middle East as a fast food. Vendors sell it on the street corners in Cairo and in many other towns and cities. As a main dish, it is served as a sandwich, stuffed into pita bread with lettuce, tomatoes, and tahini. As an appetizer, it is served on a salad, or with hummus and tahini. Falafel is a great favorite among vegetarians.

Serves 4

1 cup (200 g) dried chickpeas or 1 x 16-oz. (450-g) can chickpeas, drained
2 cloves garlic, chopped
1 large onion, chopped
3 tbsp. chopped fresh flat-leaf parsley
1 tsp. ground coriander
1 tsp. ground cumin
sea salt and freshly ground black pepper to taste
2 tbsp. all-purpose flour
canola or vegetable oil for deep-frying

1 Place dried chickpeas in a bowl, covering with cold water. Allow to soak overnight.

2 Drain the chickpeas, rinse with fresh water, place in pan with fresh water, and bring to a boil. Allow to boil for 5 minutes, then let simmer over a low heat for about an hour. Drain and allow to cool. (Omit these steps if using canned chickpeas.)

3 Combine drained chickpeas, garlic, onion, parsley, coriander, cumin, salt, and pepper in medium bowl. Add flour. Mash chickpeas, combining all ingredients together into a thick paste. (You can also combine ingredients in a food processor.)

4 Form the mixture into small balls, about the size of ping-pong balls. Slightly flatten. Fry in 2 inches of canola oil over medium to high heat until golden brown (5–7 minutes). Drain thoroughly on paper towels and serve hot.

WITH BEANS
Prepare basic recipe, replacing chickpeas with cannellini or navy beans.

WITH LENTILS
Prepare basic recipe, replacing chickpeas with lentils.

WITH CHILI
Prepare basic recipe, adding 1 teaspoon chili powder with the other spices.

WITH LEMON
Prepare basic recipe, replacing the spices with 2 teaspoons finely grated lemon zest for a different kind of flavor.

Grilled Asparagus Wrapped in Jamón Serrano

Jamón Serrano is a dry-cured ham, rather like prosciutto. The combination of the slightly metallic flavor of the asparagus and the sweet saltiness of the ham makes for a deliciously tantalizing plateful.

Serves 4

12 medium-thick asparagus, trimmed and washed
2 tbsp. extra-virgin olive oil

12 thin slices jamón Serrano
freshly ground black pepper

1 Preheat a griddle pan until piping hot or preheat the oven to 350°F (175°C). Brush the asparagus very lightly with olive oil.

2 Wrap each asparagus stem in the ham and oil lightly on the outside, then cook on the griddle pan or on a cookie sheet in the oven until the edges of the ham are lightly colored and the asparagus is tender enough to be pierced easily with the tip of a knife.

3 Remove from the pan and arrange on a plate. Sprinkle with a little more oil and black pepper and serve.

WITH PARMA HAM
Prepare the basic recipe, replacing the Serrano ham with slices of Parma ham.

WITH MANCHEGO
Prepare the basic recipe, sprinkling the finished dish with a few shavings of Manchego cheese.

WITH MOZZARELLA
Prepare the basic recipe, but line the slices of ham with thin strips of mozzarella before wrapping the asparagus.

WITH PARMESAN
Prepare the basic recipe, covering the wrapped asparagus with freshly grated Parmesan before grilling or baking. Cook until the cheese becomes golden and slightly crisp.

Marinated Manchego with Peppers & Cumin

Marinating cheese might seem odd, but smooth manchego is complemented deliciously by the piquant cumin and peppers.

Serves 4

1 tsp. cumin seeds
½ cup (120 ml) extra-virgin olive oil
sea salt and freshly ground black pepper

12 slices Spanish manchego cheese
1 cup (85 g) roasted red peppers (jarred, if
    desired), cut into strips

1 Heat a small dry skillet and toast the cumin seeds for 30 seconds or until they become aromatic. Whisk the seeds into the olive oil with some salt and pepper.

2 Arrange the cheese slices in an airtight storage container. Pour in the cumin dressing and sprinkle with the pepper strips. Toss to mingle all the ingredients, then refrigerate overnight.

3 Let stand at room temperature for 1 hour before serving in a deep bowl with all the marinade.

WITH CAPER BERRIES & ANCHOVIES
Prepare the basic recipe, replacing the toasted cumin seeds and roasted red peppers with 1 tablespoon caper berries and 4 anchovy fillets.

WITH BASIL & TOMATOES
Prepare the basic recipe, replacing the toasted cumin seeds and roasted red peppers with 1 tablespoon chopped basil and ½ cup (185 g) chopped cherry tomatoes.

WITH THYME & GARLIC
Prepare the basic recipe, replacing the cumin seeds and roasted red peppers with 1 teaspoon chopped fresh thyme and 2 finely sliced garlic cloves.

WITH WINE & TARRAGON
Prepare the basic recipe, omitting the cumin seeds and roasted red peppers and adding 1 teaspoon chopped fresh tarragon, 4 tablespoons white wine, 1 tablespoon white wine vinegar, 1 finely chopped garlic clove, and 1 teaspoon chopped fresh thyme.

Salt Cod-stuffed Piquillo Peppers

Punchy and piquant, piquillo peppers are a regular feature in Spanish cooking. These scarlet beauties are often found pickled or canned, which makes them a fantastic item to keep in your pantry. When stuffing the peppers, handle them with the utmost care as the skins tear easily, which will ruin their ability to contain the salt cod mixture.

Serves 4

¾ cup (250 g) dry salt cod
1 bay leaf
1 potato, a floury variety such as russet, peeled, boiled, and mashed
2 cloves garlic, crushed and finely chopped
zest and juice of 1 lemon

½ cup (120 ml) extra-virgin olive oil, plus extra for greasing and drizzling
salt and freshly ground black pepper
4 jarred piquillo peppers (or any other whole red peppers in a jar)

1 Soak the salt cod in cold water 24 hours in advance, changing the water halfway through.

2 Preheat oven to 350°F (180°F). Place the soaked salt cod in a large pan with cold, fresh water to cover, add the bay leaf, and bring just to the boiling point. Remove pan from heat, set aside, and rest for 5–10 minutes. Remove salt cod from the pan and let cool.

3 When the fish is cool enough to handle, remove any skin or bones and flake the flesh. In a large bowl, mix the fish, potatoes, garlic, and lemon zest and juice together, mashing vigorously with a fork. Add oil bit by bit, slowly beating it into the mixture until absorbed. Season with salt and freshly ground pepper.

4 Fill the peppers with the fish mixture, taking care not to tear the flesh. Place the filled peppers in a lightly oiled baking pan and bake for about 20 minutes, until filling is heated through. Drizzle with olive oil and serve immediately.

WITH SHRIMP
Prepare the basic recipe, replacing the salt cod with the same amount of cooked shrimp.

WITH GOAT CHEESE
Prepare the basic recipe, omitting the salt cod and garlic. Replace with a stuffing of the mashed potato combined with ½ cup (125 g) goat cheese, ½ teaspoon dried red pepper flakes, 2 finely sliced scallions, and 1 teaspoon freshly chopped mint.

WITH CRABMEAT
Prepare the basic recipe, omitting the salt cod. Replace with a stuffing of the mashed potato combined with ¾ cup (100 g) white crabmeat, 1 chopped chili, ½ bunch finely chopped fresh cilantro, and the juice of 1 lime.

WITH HAM & RICE
Prepare the basic recipe, replacing the salt cod and potato stuffing with 1 cup (100 g) cooked rice mixed with ¼ cup (125 g) chopped ham and 1 teaspoon paprika.

Boquerones

Boquerones are tiny butterflied anchovies, in a very acidic marinade that serves to cure the fish as well as add flavor. This recipe can only be done with fresh fish, so the smallest sardines will do if anchovies are not available.

Serves 4

1⅓ cups (500 g) fresh anchovies or small sardines, 4–5 inches long, preferably from Spain
1 tsp. sea salt
¾ cup (175 ml) white wine vinegar
2 tbsp. fresh lemon juice
3 cloves garlic, crushed
½ small bunch fresh parsley, finely chopped

1 Using your fingers, butterfly the anchovies. Run your finger along the backbone, separating the flesh from the bone as your finger gently slides down to the tail. Then lift out the bones in one piece. Starting with the head, you simply peel the bone away from the flesh — backbone, tail, and all. You are left with a whole, clean, butterflied fillet.

2 Place the anchovies in an airtight container, skin-side down, and sprinkle them lightly with sea salt. You may need to do this in layers.

3 Mix the vinegar, lemon juice, garlic, and parsley. Pour the mixture over the fillets. Give the container a shake to cover all the fish with the marinade. Cover the container and refrigerate for 2 days. The fish will marinate and turn white.

4 Serve piled on a board or plate with a trickle of the marinating liquid.

WITH SOUR CREAM & DILL
Prepare the basic recipe. Before serving, drain the marinated anchovies. Gently mix in 2 tablespoons sour cream and 1 tablespoon chopped fresh dill.

WITH TOMATOES & SCALLIONS
Prepare the basic recipe, adding 2 finely chopped tomatoes and 2 finely sliced scallions to the marinade. Mix gently.

WITH RED PEPPER
Prepare the basic recipe, adding 1 finely chopped red bell pepper and ¼ teaspoon cayenne pepper to the marinade.

WITH GHERKINS & CAPERS
Prepare the basic recipe, adding 4 finely chopped small gherkins and 1 tablespoon capers to the marinade.

Artichoke & Manchego Rice Cakes

These unusual little croquettes contain artichoke in the rice mixture, and break open to reveal a melting cheese center. Manchego is made from sheep's milk and has a tart flavor that goes wonderfully with the delicate taste of artichokes.

Serves 6

2 large globe artichokes
4 tbsp. butter
1 small onion, finely chopped
1 garlic clove, finely chopped
4½ oz. (140 g) long-grain rice

2 cups (450 ml) hot chicken stock
2 oz. (50 g) grated fresh Parmesan cheese
sea salt and freshly ground black pepper
5 oz. (140 g) Manchego cheese, very
    finely diced

3–4 tbsp. fine cornmeal
olive oil, for frying
fresh flat-leaf parsley, to garnish

1   Remove and discard stalks, leaves, and chokes to leave just the heart of each artichoke. Chop finely.

2   Melt the butter in a pan and gently fry the chopped artichoke hearts, onion, and garlic for 5 minutes until softened. Stir in the rice and cook for about 1 minute. Keeping the heat fairly high, gradually add the stock, stirring occasionally until all the liquid has been absorbed and the rice is cooked—this should take about 20 minutes. Season well, then stir in the Parmesan cheese. Season to taste with salt and pepper.

3   Transfer the mixture to a bowl. Let cool, then cover and chill for at least 2 hours.

4   Spoon about 1 tablespoon of the mixture into the palm of one hand, flatten slightly, and place a few pieces of diced Manchego cheese in the center. Shape the rice around the cheese to make a small ball. Flatten slightly, then roll in the cornmeal, shaking off any excess. Repeat with the remaining mixture to make about 12 cakes.

5   Shallow-fry the rice cakes in hot olive oil for 4–5 minutes, until they are crisp and golden brown. Drain on paper towel and serve hot, garnished with flat-leaf parsley.

WITH MOZZARELLA
Prepare the basic recipe, replacing the Manchego with mozzarella for a milder-tasting rice cake.

WITH SCAMORZA
Prepare the basic recipe, replacing the Manchego with smoked Scamorza (matured mozzarella) for a much more complex taste.

WITH ASPARAGUS
Prepare the basic recipe, replacing the artichokes with about 10 chunky asparagus spears, chopped.

Grilled Zucchini with Pesto

The slightly smoky flavor of the grilled zucchini is perfect with the freshness of the pesto, the piquancy of the garlic, and the lovely fresh intensity of the fresh basil.

Serves 6

12 medium-sized zucchini, ends trimmed
1¼ cups (300 ml) extra-virgin olive oil
2 cloves garlic, lightly crushed
2 large handfuls fresh basil leaves

2 tbsp. pine nuts
sea salt and freshly ground black pepper
fresh basil leaves to garnish

1 Slice the zucchini lengthwise into ¼-in. (½-cm) thick, long strips. Sprinkle the slices with salt and place them in a colander to drain for about an hour.

2 Wash and dry all the slices, then brush with a little of the olive oil and grill in a griddle pan, under the broiler, or on the barbecue until softened and slightly charred.

3 Meanwhile, make the pesto by pounding the garlic, basil leaves, and pine nuts together in a mortar and pestle, gradually adding the remaining oil until the right texture has been reached. Alternatively, you can mix everything together in a food processor.

4 Arrange the grilled zucchini on a platter, spoon the pesto on top, garnish with the basil leaves, and serve at once.

WITH GRILLED PEPPERS
Prepare the basic recipe, replacing the zucchini with 6 quartered and seeded bell peppers. Omit the salting step.

WITH GRILLED EGGPLANT
Prepare the basic recipe, replacing the zucchini with 4 large eggplant, sliced lengthwise into ¼-in. (½-cm) thick slices.

WITH MINT & PARSLEY PESTO
Prepare the basic recipe, replacing the basil in the pesto with mint and parsley and omitting the garlic.

WITH ALMOND PESTO
Prepare the basic recipe, replacing the pine nuts in the pesto with almonds.

Gibraltarian Swiss Chard Pie

Torte de acelga is traditionally eaten on Good Friday in Gibraltar, a day on which, according to Catholic tradition, no meat is consumed. It is very similar to other versions of this kind of pie or savory cake enjoyed in other parts of the Mediterranean.

Serves 6–8

6 bunches fresh Swiss chard
1 x 15-oz. (425-g) package ready-made pie pastry
oil, for greasing
6 eggs
1 cup (60 g) soft bread crumbs

1 cup (130 g) grated cheese of your choice
3 tbsp. chopped fresh flat-leaf parsley
2 tsp. minced garlic
sea salt and freshly ground black pepper

1 Preheat oven to 300°F (150°C). Remove the stems from the Swiss chard leaves for use in another recipe. Boil the leaves, drain very well, and chop finely.

2 Roll out the pastry and lay it in an oiled 8-in. (20 cm) deep pie pan, reserving enough pastry to top the pie later.

3 Beat the eggs, then add bread crumbs, cheese, parsley, garlic, and seasonings. Add egg mixture to the chopped Swiss chard and mix well.

4 Fill the pastry shell with this "relleno" or filling and cover the pie with the saved pastry, sealing the edges well. Cook in the oven for about 30 minutes or until the pie is crisp and golden on top. Serve hot or cold.

WITH SPINACH
Prepare the basic recipe, replacing the Swiss chard with about 3 lb. (1½ kg) fresh spinach.

WITH ASPARAGUS
Prepare the basic recipe, replacing the Swiss chard with about 1 lb. (450 g) fresh asparagus.

WITH ARTICHOKE
Prepare the basic recipe, replacing the Swiss chard with about 12 fresh artichoke bases, quartered.

WITH PEA
Prepare the basic recipe, replacing the Swiss chard with about 1½ lb. (700 g) peas.

Middle Eastern Fritters

The flavor of these very simple little chickpea fritters, known as *sambusac*, will vary according to the spice mixture you add to your filling.

Serves 6

1 lb. (450 g) all-purpose flour
1 tsp. sea salt
1 package active dry yeast
4 tbsp. olive oil
1 large onion, chopped

2 cloves garlic, chopped
1 x 16-oz. (450-g) can chickpeas, drained
mixture of ground spices (cumin, coriander, allspice, cinnamon, chili powder, white pepper, etc.), to taste

1 large bunch fresh cilantro or parsley, chopped
about 4 cups (950 ml) canola or vegetable oil, for frying

1 Mix the flour, sea salt, and yeast with enough warm water to make a pliable dough. You will need up to 2 cups (450 ml) lukewarm water to achieve the right texture. Knead thoroughly for about 15 minutes.

2 Use some of the olive oil to lightly coat a large bowl, then add the dough, cover with a sheet of oiled plastic wrap or a lightly floured cloth, and leave in a warm place for about an hour.

3 While the dough is rising, fry the onion and garlic with the remaining olive oil until just translucent, then add chickpeas and your chosen spices. Mash together to make a sort of paste. Remove from heat, add chopped cilantro or parsley, season to taste, and set aside.

4 Divide the risen dough into about 15 pieces and flatten each one into a small 6-in (15-cm) circle. Place a generous tablespoonful of the chickpea mixture into the center of each circle and fold over the edges to make a semicircular parcel. Fry these in canola oil that is 4 in. (10 cm) deep until crisp, flipping over once or twice during the cooking process. Transfer onto paper towel to drain, turn over, and drain again. Serve hot or cold.

WITH LENTILS
Follow the basic recipe, replacing the chickpeas with canned lentils.

WITH CRANBERRY BEANS
Follow the basic recipe, replacing the chickpeas with canned cranberry beans.

WITH CHILI PEPPERS
Follow the basic recipe, adding 2 dried red chili peppers to the onion and garlic. Fry together gently until the onion and garlic are cooked, then discard the chili peppers and continue with the rest of the recipe.

Patatas Bravas

Patatas bravas simply translates as brave potatoes. They are sliced fried potatoes smothered in a rich tomato sauce with a hint of smoky spiciness.

Serves 4

about 1 lb. (450 g) waxy potatoes (such as Yukon Gold), well scrubbed
about 2 cups (450 ml) mild olive oil or sunflower oil for deep-frying

for the tomato sauce
3 tbsp. olive oil
1 small onion
1 clove garlic, peeled
1 small dried red chili
½ tsp. smoked paprika

4 large ripe plum tomatoes, chopped
2 tsp. tomato paste
½ cup (120 ml) water
sea salt and freshly ground black pepper
fresh flat-leaf parsley, to garnish (optional)

1 Cut the potatoes into even-sized chunks. Add them to a large pan half-filled with the oil and heat gently over a low flame until small bubbles rise to the surface. Cook the potatoes like this —almost poaching them in the oil—for around 12–15 minutes, until they are just tender. Then, increase the heat and deep-fry the potato pieces until golden brown.

2 While the potatoes are cooking, prepare the sauce. Heat the oil in a small saucepan. Finely chop the onion, garlic, and chili, and gently fry in the hot oil for 3–4 minutes, until softened but not colored. Stir in the paprika and cook for a few seconds more. Add the tomatoes to the pan. Stir in the tomato paste and water. Cook over low heat for about 10 minutes until the tomatoes are well softened, stirring occasionally. Season to taste with salt and pepper.

3 Lift the potatoes out of the oil with a slotted spoon and drain on paper towels. Put into a warmed dish, add the tomato sauce, and serve.

WITH AÏOLI
Prepare the basic recipe, but serve with a garlicky aïoli on the side in place of or along with the spicy tomato sauce.

WITH CHORIZO
Prepare the basic recipe, adding 6 slices sliced and fried chorizo on top of the dish.

WITH PIQUILLO PEPPERS
Prepare the basic recipe, adding 2 chopped piquillo peppers (jarred roasted red peppers) to the sauce at the end of cooking.

WITH BLOOD SAUSAGE
Prepare the basic recipe, adding 1 Spanish blood sausage, chopped and fried, to the cooked potatoes just before covering with the sauce.

Mushroom, Tomato & Mozzarella Ciabatta

Serves 2

1 large ciabatta loaf
3 tbsp. extra-virgin olive oil
1 garlic clove, halved
5 fresh ripe tomatoes, chopped

4 tbsp. wild mushrooms preserved in olive oil, drained
6 oz. (175 g) buffalo mozzarella, torn into pieces

4 oz. (125 g) fresh arugula
sea salt and freshly ground black pepper

1 Preheat the broiler. Using a sharp knife, split the ciabatta in half, then cut each half in half again, lengthwise, to give 4 bases. Brush with a little olive oil. Slide under the broiler for 2 minutes until lightly toasted, then rub with the garlic while still warm.

2 Sprinkle the bases evenly with the tomatoes. Top each with some of the mushrooms (halved or quartered if large) and scatter the mozzarella on top. Season, then broil for 2–3 minutes until lightly golden and bubbling.

3 Top with arugula leaves, then drizzle with a little more olive oil to serve.

WITH SMOKED SCAMORZA
Prepare the basic recipe, replacing mozzarella with slices of smoked Scamorza for a much stronger flavor.

WITH SUN-DRIED TOMATO
Prepare the basic recipe, replacing mushrooms with marinated sun-dried tomatoes.

WITH PESTO
Prepare the basic recipe, omitting the mushrooms and spreading the garlic- rubbed ciabatta with a thin layer of pesto before adding the tomatoes and the mozzarella and broiling.

Fried Chorizo & Potatoes

Serves 4

vegetable oil for deep-frying
1 large red-skinned potato, peeled and really thinly sliced

2 raw chorizo sausages, sliced thin
½ tsp. sea salt

1 Fill a deep saucepan to half full with vegetable oil and heat to 350°F (180°C). In the hot oil, fry the potato slices in batches for 1–2 minutes until golden. Remove with a slotted spoon and drain on paper towels.

2 Repeat with the slices of chorizo, allowing the slices to turn golden and become crisp. Drain on paper towels.

3 Sprinkle the potatoes and the chorizo with salt and serve immediately.

WITH PARSNIPS
Prepare the basic recipe, replacing the potato with 2 medium parsnips.

WITH CUMIN POTATOES
Prepare the basic recipe. Serve with a generous sprinkling of cumin.

WITH BEETS
Prepare the basic recipe, replacing the potato with fresh beets. Serve with a dip of crème fraîche (or soured cream) mixed with 1 tablespoon freshly chopped chives.

WITH ROSEMARY POTATOES
Prepare the basic recipe, replacing the salt with rosemary salt.

Deep-fried Stuffed Giant Olives

Along the sunny Adriatic coastline of the Marche, these deliciously addictive little mouthfuls are called *olive all'Ascolana*, named after the town of Ascoli Piceno.

Serves 8–10

60 giant (queen) green olives preserved in brine
4 oz. (125 g) pork fat
¼ cup (50 ml) extra-virgin olive oil
5½ oz. (165 g) ground pork
¼ lb. (115 g) ground beef
1 tbsp. tomato paste, diluted in a little cold water
3 chicken livers, chopped
3 tbsp. soft white bread crumbs
3 tbsp. beef stock
1 egg, beaten
1¾ oz. (50 g) Parmesan, grated
pinch grated nutmeg
sea salt and freshly ground black pepper
5 tbsp. all-purpose flour
2 eggs beaten with a splash of milk
3–4 tbsp. fine dry bread crumbs
oil for deep frying
lemon wedges, to garnish

1 Pit all the olives carefully with an appropriate instrument to keep them whole and as neat as possible. Set aside.

2 Fry the pork fat with the oil and the ground pork and beef until the meat is well browned, then add the tomato paste. Mix together and cook for about 20 minutes, then add the chicken livers and cook for another 10 minutes. Cool and chop finely with a heavy knife, or put mixture into a food processor and process until smooth.

3 Add the soft bread crumbs, stock, beaten egg, and Parmesan. Season to taste with nutmeg, salt, and pepper. Carefully fill each olive with this mixture. Roll the olives in flour, then in beaten egg and milk, and then in bread crumbs.

4 Deep-fry in piping hot oil until golden brown, drain on paper towel, and serve hot or cold with the lemon wedges.

WITH CHICKEN
Prepare the basic recipe, replacing the ground pork and beef with the same amount of ground chicken.

WITH TURKEY
Prepare the basic recipe, replacing the ground pork and beef with the same amount of ground turkey.

WITH LEMON ZEST
Prepare the basic recipe, but omit the chicken livers and nutmeg and add 2 teaspoons finely grated lemon zest.

Cataplana

Cataplana is a traditional Portuguese pork stew with garlic, wine, and clams, which is cooked in a special type of dish. Don't fear, though, it works perfectly well in a good Dutch oven or cast-iron pan with a lid.

Serves 4

5 cloves garlic, chopped
1 tbsp. sweet paprika
½ tsp. chili powder
sea salt
⅔ cup (150 ml) olive oil
5½ oz. (165 g) pork fillet, cut into ½-in. (12-mm) cubes

1 onion, finely chopped
1 cup (250 ml) dry white wine
½ lb. (225 g) quahog clams in the shell, scrubbed
2 tbsp. chopped fresh parsley
squeeze of lemon juice

1 Place the garlic, paprika, chili powder, salt, and half the olive oil in a food processor, and process to a paste. Marinate the pork in this mixture for at least 4 hours, or preferably overnight, stirring occasionally so all the meat gets a good coating.

2 Heat 3 tablespoons of the remaining olive oil in a wide saucepan with a well-fitting lid. Add the pork and all its marinade and cook over high heat for 5 minutes, stirring from time to time. Transfer the meat and sauce to a bowl and set aside.

3 Add the rest of the oil to the pan, and fry the onion over medium-high heat for 5 minutes. Add the wine and bring to a boil for 1 minute.

4 Return the pork to the pan, along with all the juices, stir well, then add the clams and replace the lid. Cook for 3–5 minutes, until the clams open. Discard any clams that do not open, stir through the parsley and a squeeze of lemon juice, and serve immediately.

WITH CHORIZO
Prepare the basic recipe, adding 1 chopped, small semidry chorizo when cooking the onion.

WITH CHILI
Prepare the basic recipe, adding 1 chopped, small red chili when cooking the onion.

WITH SAFFRON
Prepare the basic recipe, adding a small pinch of saffron when cooking the onion.

WITH MUSSELS, CHORIZO & SAFFRON
Prepare the basic recipe, replacing the clams with mussels, and adding 1 chopped, small semidry chorizo and a small pinch of saffron when cooking the onion.

Beef Carpaccio with Anchovy Mayo & Crispy Garlic

This Italian classic has had a Spanish makeover with anchovy mayo and crisped garlic.

Serves 4

5 oz. (150 g) beef fillet, trimmed
2 egg yolks
1 heaping tsp. Dijon mustard
1 tsp. white wine vinegar

sea salt and freshly ground black pepper
8 anchovy fillets in oil, mashed to a paste
1¼ cups (300 ml) vegetable oil
juice of 1 lemon

3 tbsp. olive oil
5 large cloves garlic, sliced
good handful watercress or arugula leaves,
    dressed in lemon juice and olive oil

1 Wrap beef tightly in plastic wrap and place in freezer for ½ hour.

2 To make the mayonnaise, put the egg yolks in a deep bowl and add the mustard, vinegar, salt, pepper, and anchovies. Mix well. With a whisk, mix in the vegetable oil, a drop at a time. Once you've added about a quarter of the oil, the mixture will begin to thicken. Add the rest of the vegetable oil in a thin stream, whisking all the time, until you have a thick smooth mayonnaise. Finish by squeezing in the lemon juice. Chill until you are ready to serve.

3 To make the crispy garlic, heat the olive oil in a heavy pan over high heat until the surface of the oil shimmers. Add the garlic and let sizzle for about 30 seconds, until just crisp and light golden brown. Remove from the oil and drain on paper towels.

4 Remove the beef from the freezer and, with a very sharp knife, slice as thin as you can. Lay slices neatly on plates and top with mayonnaise, crisp garlic, and the dressed watercress or arugula.

WITH PARMESAN
Prepare the basic recipe, adding 2 tablespoons freshly grated Parmesan cheese to the mayonnaise and 2 tablespoons freshly shaved Parmesan cheese on top as a garnish.

WITH PARMESAN & BACON
Prepare the basic recipe, adding 3 ounces crisply fried and crumbled bacon and 2 tablespoons shaved Parmesan cheese as a garnish.

WITH EXTRA ANCHOVIES
Prepare the basic recipe, garnishing with an additional 12 marinated (pickled) anchovies.

CLASSIC BEEF CARPACCIO
Prepare the basic recipe, but omit the mayonnaise and drizzle with really good olive oil and a squeeze of lemon juice instead. Shave 2 tablespoons Parmesan cheese on top.

Grilled Lamb Cutlets with Burnt Butter, Rosemary & Capers

Lamb cutlets are a ready-made finger food, with their own holders making them a really fun addition to your tapas menu. This recipe shows off lamb at its best. Get a rack of lamb that's either middle neck, which is cheaper with more flavor, or the best end of neck, which is more delicate.

Serves 4

1 rack of lamb
sea salt and freshly ground black pepper
½ tbsp. olive oil
½ stick (55 g) sweet butter

1 small sprig fresh rosemary
1 heaping tbsp. capers (I prefer capers in
    vinegar to salted)
juice of ½ lemon

1 Carve the lamb into individual cutlets. If the cutlets are really thick, you can pound them with a meat mallet to thin them out a bit, but I like them about ½ inch thick. Season with salt and pepper and rub with the oil. Heat a griddle pan on high heat until smoking. Cook the cutlets for 2–3 minutes on each side, remove from pan, and let rest.

2 In a small saucepan, melt the butter and add the rosemary. When it starts to foam, it will start to turn a nutty color. Add the capers, fry for 30 seconds, and then pour in the lemon juice.

3 Remove pan from the heat and season with salt and pepper. Place the lamb in a serving dish and pour in the juices and burnt butter sauce.

WITH ANCHOVIES
Prepare the basic recipe, adding 4 canned anchovies to the butter while you are burning it.

WITH FENNEL
Prepare the basic recipe, omitting the rosemary and adding 1 teaspoon crushed fennel seeds to the foaming butter.

WITH GARLIC
Prepare the basic recipe, adding 1–2 crushed cloves of garlic to the pan with the butter.

WITH MINT
Prepare the basic recipe, replacing the rosemary with a few sprigs of fresh mint.

Cured Beef Rolls with Arugula

It is always best, if you can, to buy your bresaola (an air-cured beef) from a whole piece of meat, which is then sliced professionally in front of you. This will always taste better than buying bresaola in plastic package. The secret with cured meats is to try to eat them as soon as possible after slicing. This recipe for bresaola–arugula rolls is a really lovely way to enjoy this delicious specialty from the Valtellina area of Lombardy, in Northern Italy. Don't be tempted to make it too far in advance, or the dressing on the arugula leaves will cause them to wilt and lose their crispness.

Serves 6

2 handfuls arugula leaves
3 oz. (75 g) Parmesan,
    finely shaved
juice of ½ lemon,
    strained, or 2 tsp.
    best-quality balsamic
    vinegar
extra-virgin olive oil to
    taste
freshly ground black
    pepper
7 oz. (200 g) bresaola,
    thinly sliced
fresh chives
wedges of lemon, to serve

1 Gently mix together the arugula and Parmesan. Dress lightly with lemon juice or balsamic vinegar, olive oil, and pepper.

2 Wrap up a small amount in the bresaola slices to make neat little rolls and tie each one closed with chives.

3 Arrange the rolls on a platter and garnish with wedges of lemon to serve.

CURED BEEF & ARUGULA PLATTER
Omit Parmesan, lemon, and chives. Arrange the bresaola on a platter and cover with arugula. Whisk together olive oil and balsamic vinegar, season with salt and pepper, and drizzle over dish.

CURED BEEF & RED ONION PLATTER
Omit arugula, lemon, and chives. Arrange the bresaola on a platter and cover with thinly sliced red onion. Whisk the olive oil with balsamic vinegar, season, and drizzle over the dish. Serve the platter with chopped chives scattered on top.

CURED BEEF & CREAM CHEESE PLATTER
Omit lemon and chives. Wrap the bresaola around spoonfuls of creamy cheese such as robiola and arrange on top of the arugula. Scatter with Parmesan shavings. Whisk the olive oil with balsamic vinegar, season, and drizzle over the dish.

CURED BEEF & PINK GRAPEFRUIT PLATTER
Omit arugula, Parmesan, lemon, and chives. Arrange the bresaola on a platter and cover with fresh pink grapefruit segments. Remove any excess juice. Whisk olive oil with balsamic vinegar, season, and drizzle over dish.

Arugula, Pear & Parmesan Salad

This pretty salad has a lovely combination of flavors. The sweetness of the pears really highlights the peppery quality of the arugula, and the saltiness of the Parmesan brings the whole thing together.

Serves 6

4 handfuls arugula leaves
2 small, firm pears,
    peeled and sliced
3 oz. (75 g) Parmesan,
    thinly shaved

1 tbsp. balsamic vinegar
6 tbsp. olive oil
sea salt and freshly
    ground black pepper

1 Arrange the arugula leaves on each of 6 plates. Place the pear slices around and among the leaves. Scatter with Parmesan shavings. Sprinkle with balsamic vinegar.

2 Mix the olive oil with salt and pepper until emulsified. Sprinkle over the salad and serve immediately.

WITH PEACH
Prepare basic recipe, replacing the pears with slices of firm, carefully peeled peaches.

WITH NECTARINE
Prepare basic recipe, replacing the pears with slices of unpeeled, firm nectarines.

WITH GREEN MANGO
Prepare basic recipe, replacing the pears with sliced unripe mangoes for an Asian twist to this otherwise very Italian salad.

WITH CHERRY TOMATO
Prepare basic recipe, replacing the pears with quartered cherry tomatoes or cubed larger tomatoes for a less sweet salad.

WITH PEAR & PECORINO
Prepare basic recipe, replacing the Parmesan with pecorino.

CHAPTER 2

Soups
& Salads

Mediterranean soups are a popular way to start the meal, especially in bad weather or when fall evenings start to feel chilly. As summer arrives and the weather heats-up imaginative, refreshing, yet nourishing salads are an absolute must.

Some Mediterranean soups can be a meal in themselves, with plenty of nourishing beans, which makes them really filling. Soups are a fantastic way to eat a variety of vegetables, whether it's a delicate gazpacho, a satisfying meal-in-a-bowl or a chunky minestrone. If you're looking for wholesome and comforting, plain or complex, sophisticated or simple, you'll find it here.

This chapter contains many of the classic salads, as well as some more unusual examples of salads prepared in many of the Mediterranean countries during summer, when fresh produce is at its very best. Salads are incredibly versatile and come in a seemingly endless array of colors, shapes, and sizes. Whether you're looking for a side dish or a filling main meal, a healthy snack, a wholesome lunch, a luxurious and indulgent treat smothered with creamy dressing, there's always a salad that's just perfect for you.

GREAT GARNISHES
One of the joys of serving soups and salads is the wide choice of garnishes that can be added so easily just before serving, to add flavor, color or texture. You can choose from a sprinkling of herbs, or a drizzle of yogurt, crispy croutons, tangy salsas, crispy shallots or even a couple of ice cubes for a chilled soup. Whatever you decide on, with a little care it can transform a simple bowl dish into a gourmet treat. Garnishes should add flavor and texture, as well as the visual appeal that is so important for whetting the appetite and stimulating the taste buds.

Toasts: croutons, brushetta or crostini are all perfect accompaniments. Slices of ciabatta can be brushed with oil and grilled until crisp and golden. Make them plain, or rub one side with a cut clove of garlic. Sprinkle with herbs and ground black pepper, or top with seeded, chopped tomatoes or a spoonful or two of salsa. Another option is to spread the toasts with pesto and top with chargrilled vegetables; or add a dollop of sour cream or yoghurt on to bite-size crostini, and top with a twist of parma ham or salami.

Fresh herbs: A sprinkling of chopped fresh herbs can add a splash of color and a delicate aromatic flavor to a variety of soups and salads. Fresh mint is particularly good in Mediterranean-style salads, and fragrant basil works well with tomato-based dishes.

Lemon wedges: Bright and citrusy lemons are a staple of Mediterranean cuisine. Serve lemon wedges on the side and allow your diners to squeeze over as much or as little juice as they like to add zing.

TOPPING IDEAS
Toppings are perfect for spooning, swirling or floating. Experiment with textures and flavors to complement the dish. When selecting a topping, think about the main ingredients, how substantial they are, and whether they would benefit from being enriched by a complementary refreshing topping.

Yogurt and cream: Yogurt works particularly well spooned or swirled on top of chili-spiced soups. For swirling or drizzling, select thin yogurt or thin down the thicker types, such as strained Greek-style yoghurt, by stirring in a little milk. A swirl of heavy cream goes particularly well with tomato and squash soups.

Fish & ham: Slivers of anchovy can make an interesting finishing touch when scattered over just before serving. Wafer-thin strips of prosciutto can be used in the same way. For a crisp topping, try grilling a couple of slices of cured ham until brittle, then snip into pieces, and scatter over.

Finely chopped vegetables: Spring onions, bell peppers, cucumber and tomatoes all make enticing toppings for cold soups.

Nuts and seeds: These are highly nutritious and add a lovely crunch. Pumpkin and sunflower seeds are great sprinkled over most savoury salads, while tiny sesame and poppy seeds are good in grated carrot salads and coleslaw. Toast nuts and seeds in a dry frying pan first to bring out their flavor.

Gazpacho

This refreshing cold soup originated in Andalusia in Spain, where it is nicknamed *Andalusian liquid salad*. Cold soup is ideal for the summer months and occasions such as barbecues, and gazpacho is an ideal healthy starter because of the high proportion of vegetable ingredients. It is easily made and can be prepared hours prior to serving and stored in the fridge.

Serves 4

1 red bell pepper
1 green bell pepper
1 cucumber, peeled, halved, and seeded
½ onion
1 clove garlic, crushed
6 ripe tomatoes, seeded
1 x 14-oz. (400-g) can chopped tomatoes
¾ cup (175 ml) extra-virgin olive oil
4 tbsp. red wine vinegar
salt and freshly ground black pepper
¼ cucumber, peeled, seeded, and chopped
chopped fresh chives, for garnish
4 warmed crispy rolls, to serve

1 Blanch the peppers in boiling water for about 2 minutes to loosen the skin, then peel, remove the seeds, and core. Dice half of each pepper and half the cucumber and set aside.

2 Put the other pepper halves, onion, remaining cucumber, garlic, fresh and canned tomatoes, olive oil, and red wine vinegar into a blender or food processor and blend until a smooth liquid. Season with salt and pepper.

3 Pour the liquid into a large bowl and refrigerate for at least 1 hour.

4 Just as you are about to serve the soup, ladle portions into chilled bowls. Add the remaining chopped red and green pepper and chopped cucumber to each bowl. Garnish with the chopped chives and serve with the warm rolls.

WITH LEMON
Prepare the basic recipe, adding the juice of 1 lemon to the other ingredients in the food processor. Add a thin slice of lemon to the garnish.

WITH LIME
Omit the vinegar, and replace it with 4 tablespoons freshly squeezed lime juice for a very different, crisp citrus flavor.

WITH CROUTONS
Prepare the basic recipe, but instead of serving the soup with the warm roll, make some croutons with 3 slices of white bread, cut into cubes and fried in a little oil until crisp and lightly browned. Sprinkle these over each bowl of soup to serve.

WITH ALMONDS
Omit the peppers, onion, cucumber, and tomatoes. Replace them with 1 cup (225 g) blanched almonds and 2 cups (450 g) stale white bread (crusts removed), soaked until spongy in cold water and squeezed dry. Add an extra clove of garlic and a generous splash of white wine or sherry vinegar and proceed as above, adding just enough cold water to create a creamy soup consistency. Sprinkle with a few toasted slivered almonds to serve.

Provençal Soup

This very simple soup will remind you of the lazy hazy south of France—healthy, tasty, colorful— the simple pleasures of life in the sunshine! Serve with toasted rustic or farmhouse bread.

Serves 4

3 large potatoes
3 large tomatoes
3½ pints (2 liters) cold water
sea salt and freshly ground black pepper
2 tbsp. olive oil
2 onions, finely chopped

1 clove garlic, halved
4 baguette slices, toasted
2 tbsp. dried fines herbes de Provence (or a combination of tarragon, parsley, and chervil)

1   Peel potatoes and cut them in half. Blanch tomatoes for 15 seconds in boiling water, then drain, cool, and peel. Cut them in half and remove seeds.

2   Put potatoes and tomatoes in a large saucepan filled with the cold water. Season with salt and pepper and bring to a boil. Lower heat and let simmer, covered, for 1 hour.

3   Heat oil in a skillet on medium heat. Add onions and fry for 20 minutes over low heat, without burning them. Add 1 cup of liquid from the tomatoes and potatoes saucepan and simmer for 15 minutes. Put onion mixture into a blender.

4   Drain potatoes and tomatoes, reserving the liquid. Add them to the blender. Purée, adding as much liquid as necessary from the saucepan to achieve the desired consistency. Season to taste.

5   Rub garlic halves over the toasted bread slices. Put the slices on the bottom of soup bowls and add the soup. Sprinkle the chopped herbs on the top. Serve very hot.

WITH PESTO
Prepare the basic recipe, but instead of finishing off the soup with the dried herbs, put ½ teaspoon of pesto on top of each bowl of soup to serve.

WITH CROUTONS
Prepare the basic recipe, but instead of putting the garlicky bread slices on the bottom of the bowls, make some croutons with 3 slices of white bread, cut into cubes and fried in a little oil until crisp and lightly browned. Sprinkle these over each bowl of soup to serve.

WITH CELERY
Prepare the basic recipe, giving some extra flavor to the soup by adding 3 stalks celery, strings removed, to the potatoes and tomatoes. Instead of sprinkling the dried herbs on top of each serving, garnish with 1 finely chopped small celery stalk and a few celery leaves.

Tomato & Basil Soup

This refreshing cold tomato and basil soup makes a perfect lunch dish on a hot summer's day. It goes especially well with crostini and pesto.

Serves 4–6

½ onion, peeled
2 stalks celery, with leaves
1 carrot, peeled and finely diced

4 tbsp. olive oil
1 lb. (450 g) ripe fresh tomatoes
1 x 14-oz. (400-g) can plum tomatoes

2 pints (1 liter) chicken or vegetable stock
1 large bunch fresh basil
sea salt and freshly ground black pepper

1 Cut the onion in half and slice sideways. Slice the celery into thin half-moons. Place a large pan over low heat and add the oil. Heat gently and add the onions, carrots, and celery. Stir well. Cook gently until soft.

2 Core tomatoes, halve, and dice into chunks. Add chunks to the pan, and cook for a few minutes. Add the canned tomatoes and stir. Add just enough stock to cover, and stir again. Bring to a boil, cover, and turn down the heat to a simmer. Cook for 15–20 minutes.

3 Strip the leaves from the basil stalks, then tear the leaves in half with your fingers. Add half of the leaves to the soup. Stir, then replace the pan lid, and cook for 10 minutes. Once cooked, remove from the heat and allow the soup to cool for a few minutes before adding the remaining fresh basil. Stir, season with salt and pepper, and stir again.

4 Using a blender, blend the soup on high power for a couple of minutes until it takes on a smooth, velvety texture. If desired, add more stock for a thinner consistency. Chill for 2 hours before serving.

WITH CROUTONS
Prepare the basic recipe. Serve the cold soup with a scattering of croutons made from 3 slices of white bread, cut into cubes and fried in a little oil until crisp and lightly browned.

WITH PESTO
Prepare the basic recipe. Finish off each bowl of cold soup by stirring ½ teaspoon pesto through just before serving.

WITH FRIED BASIL LEAF GARNISH
Prepare the basic recipe. To finish off the soup, fry about 12 fresh, washed, and dried basil leaves in ½ in (1 cm) of oil for about 30 seconds or until just crisp and translucent. Float these on top of each bowl just before serving.

WITH ROASTED TOMATO
On a cookie sheet, drizzle olive oil over fresh tomatoes and roast gently in the oven until soft. Prepare the basic recipe using the roasted tomatoes.

Spanish Squash & Apple Soup

This delicious squash soup, called *crèma de calabaza* in its native Spain, is sharpened by the flavor of the apple, which cleverly takes away some of the dense, sweet flavor of the squash.

Serves 6

1 medium acorn squash, halved and cleaned
1 apple, peeled and roughly chopped
1 large onion, peeled and roughly chopped
1 potato, peeled and roughly chopped
2 carrots, peeled and roughly chopped
¼ carcass roast chicken (optional)
1 tbsp. Spanish sweet paprika

3 generous cups (850 ml) water
1 tsp. dried oregano
1 cup (250 ml) whole milk
sea salt and freshly ground black pepper to taste
6 slices crusty bread, toasted
1 apple, skin on and thinly sliced

1 Preheat the oven to 375°F (190°C). Put the halved acorn squash on a cookie sheet and bake for about 1 hour or until softened.

2 While the squash is baking, prepare the vegetables. Put the apple, onion, potato, and carrots in a large pan with the chicken carcass, paprika, water, and oregano. Simmer for about 40 minutes, adding more water if necessary. Remove and discard chicken carcass (if using).

3 Remove the softened squash from the oven and remove skin and any remaining seeds. Put the cooked flesh of the squash into the soup and stir in the milk. In a blender or food processor, purée the soup completely and return to the heat.

4 In a separate pan, soften the slices of apple in boiling water for 5 minutes. Season the soup to taste and serve in a warm soup tureen or individual bowls lined with the toasted bread, with a few of the softened apple slices for each serving.

WITH PEAR
Prepare the basic recipe, replacing the apple with a large ripe pear.

WITH APPLE PURÉE GARNISH
Prepare the basic recipe. To add more apple flavor, drop 1 teaspoon unsweetened cooked apple purée or chunky applesauce into the center of each bowl of soup just before serving.

WITH PUMPKIN
Prepare the basic recipe, replacing the squash with a small pumpkin.

WITH BACON
Prepare the basic recipe, then finish off the soup with 6 tablespoons crisply fried warm bacon cubes, scattered over the top just before serving.

Avgolemono

This classic and flavorful soup recipe originated in Greece and combines eggs and lemon with rice and chicken stock to create a lovely zesty taste.

Serves 10

2 cups (450 ml) milk
2 tbsp. cornstarch
6 egg yolks, beaten
3½ pints (2 liters) chicken stock
½ cup (210 g) long-grain rice
¼ cup (60 g) butter

2 tbsp. chopped fresh flat-leaf parsley
¼ cup (50 ml) fresh lemon juice (or more to taste)
finely grated zest of 1 lemon
salt and freshly ground black pepper

1 Stir the milk and cornstarch together until smooth. Beat in the egg yolks. Set aside.

2 Bring the stock to a boil in a large pot, and add the rice. Cook, covered, over low heat until the rice is puffy and tender, about 25 minutes.

3 Remove the soup from heat, and add the milk and egg mixture very gradually, stirring constantly to prevent lumps forming.

4 Put the soup back on the burner and continue to cook for a moment, stirring, until it thickens. Remove from the heat again and add the butter, chopped parsley, lemon juice, and finely grated lemon zest. Season to taste with salt and pepper, stir once more, and serve immediately.

WITH BASIL
Prepare the basic recipe, replacing the parsley with 2 tablespoons finely shredded fresh basil leaves and the finely grated lemon peel with 1 teaspoon pesto.

WITH SHREDDED CHICKEN
Prepare the basic recipe, but for a more substantial soup, add the finely shredded meat from 2 poached small chicken breasts to the soup with the milk and egg mixture.

WITH CHIVES
For a very slight onion flavor, omit the chopped parsley and replace with the same quantity of finely chopped fresh chives, washed and dried.

VEGETARIAN AVGOLEMONO
Prepare the basic recipe, replacing the chicken stock with a richly flavored vegetable stock. Make the stock by gently boiling together even quantities of celery, carrots, and onions with a few parsley stalks in about 5 pints (3 liters) of water for about 1 hour. Strain the resulting liquid and season to taste with salt and pepper before using.

Lebanese Mixed Bean Soup

This wonderfully filling and nourishing soup is called *makhluta* in Lebanese and uses just about every kind of bean available! To save time, you can use canned beans instead of the dried, which means you can eliminate the overnight soaking step.

Serves 6

½ cup (100 g) dried white
  kidney beans
½ cup (100 g) dried red
  beans
½ cup (100 g) dried
  chickpeas
¼ cup (60 g) dried black
  fava beans
¼ cup (60 g) dried big
  black lentils
3½ pints (2 liters) water
1 tbsp. vegetable oil

2 medium onions, finely
  chopped
¼ cup (60 g) coarse
  bulgur
¼ cup (60 g) short-grain
  rice
½ tsp. ground cumin
1 tsp. salt
4 tbsp. lemon juice
1 lemon, cut into wedges,
  to serve

1 Soak kidney beans, red beans, and chickpeas in water for 12 hours. Soak the fava beans separately in water for 12 hours.

2 Drain the beans. Put kidney beans, red beans, and chickpeas in a large pan. Add the lentils. Cover with the 2 quarts of water, set pan over high heat, and bring to a boil. Lower heat and cook for 30 more minutes.

3 Cook fava beans separately using the same method, but after cooking for 30 minutes, drain and discard the cooking liquid. Add drained fava beans to the other beans.

4 In a large stockpot, heat oil, add onions, and stir-fry until browned. Add the beans with the bulgur, rice, cumin, and salt. Cook over low heat, stirring occasionally, for 30 minutes or until rice is tender. Add lemon juice and cook over low heat for 5 more minutes. Serve hot, with lemon wedges.

WITH SPICES
Prepare the basic recipe, adding 2 small dried red chili peppers, finely chopped, to the oil and onions before adding the beans and the other ingredients.

WITH GARLIC
Prepare the basic recipe, replacing the onions with 6 minced garlic cloves.

WITH TOMATO
Prepare the basic recipe, adding 4 peeled, seeded, and roughly chopped fresh tomatoes to the oil and onions before adding the beans and the other ingredients.

Moroccan Chickpea Soup

This delicious soup looks wonderfully colorful and has a lovely citrus flavor that really brings it to life.

Serves 4–6

1 tbsp. extra-virgin olive oil
1 medium onion, chopped
2 celery stalks, chopped
2 tsp. ground cumin
2½ cups (600 ml) hot vegetable stock
1 x 14-oz. (400-g) can chopped canned tomatoes
1 x 14-oz. (400 g) can chickpeas, rinsed and drained
freshly ground black pepper
¼ lb. (115 g) frozen or fresh fava beans
zest and juice of ½ lemon
¼ tsp. sea salt
large handful fresh cilantro, chopped
flatbread, to serve

1 Heat the oil in a large saucepan, then fry the onion and celery gently for 10 minutes until softened, stirring frequently.

2 Add the cumin and fry for another minute. Turn up the heat and add the stock, tomatoes, and chickpeas, plus a good grinding of black pepper. Simmer for 8 minutes.

3 Add fava beans and lemon juice and cook for 2 minutes more. Season to taste, then top with a sprinkling of lemon zest and chopped cilantro. Serve with flatbread.

WITH PEAS
Prepare the basic recipe, replacing the beans with fresh or frozen peas.

WITH PARSLEY
Prepare the basic recipe, replacing the chopped cilantro with the same amount of flat-leaf parsley.

WITH CHICKEN
Prepare the basic recipe, adding 2 small and skinless chicken breasts, cooked and finely shredded, with the chickpeas to the soup for a much more substantial dish.

Looz Shorba

Serves 4

2 tbsp. sweet butter
½ cup (80 g) chopped onions
2 tbsp. all-purpose flour

1½ pint (1 l) boiling chicken stock
½ cup (45 g) ground blanched almonds
½ cup (120 ml) heavy cream

sea salt and freshly ground white pepper

1 Melt the butter in a saucepan, add the onions, and cook until soft but not browned.

2 Stir in the flour. When smooth, add the boiling stock, stirring briskly. Allow to simmer for a few minutes.

3 Stir in the ground almonds. Cook, simmering, for 20 minutes. Stir in the cream and allow to heat through. Season with salt and pepper to taste. Serve hot.

WITH ALMOND
Prepare the basic recipe, replacing the chicken stock with a richly flavored vegetable stock. Make the stock by gently boiling together even amounts of celery, carrots, and onions with a few parsley stalks for about 1 hour in about 3 pints (1¾ liters) water. Strain the resulting liquid and season to taste with salt and pepper before using.

WITH TOASTED ALMONDS
Prepare the basic recipe, sprinkling 1 tablespoon dry-roasted slivered almonds over each serving.

WITH ALMOND
Prepare the basic recipe, adding 2 small boneless and skinless chicken breasts, cooked and shredded, to the soup.

WITH SPICES
Prepare the basic recipe. Stir a tablespoon of hot chili oil through the soup in a swirl, to serve.

Lebanese Red Lentil Soup

Serves 8

3 pints (1¾ liters) chicken stock
1 lb. (450 g) red lentils
3 tbsp. olive oil
1 tbsp. minced garlic

1 large onion, chopped
1 tbsp. ground cumin
½ tsp. cayenne pepper
½ cup (100 g) chopped fresh cilantro

juice of ½ lemon
8 lemon wedges, to garnish

1 Bring the chicken stock and lentils to a boil in a large saucepan over high heat, then reduce heat to medium-low, cover, and simmer for 20 minutes.

2 Meanwhile, heat olive oil in a skillet over medium heat. Stir in garlic and onion, and cook until the onion has softened and turned translucent, about 3 minutes. Stir the garlic and onion into the lentils, and season with cumin and cayenne. Continue simmering until the lentils are tender, about 10 minutes.

3 Carefully purée the soup in a blender or with a handheld blender until smooth. Stir in cilantro and lemon juice before serving, and garnish each serving with a lemon wedge.

VEGETARIAN RED LENTIL SOUP
Prepare the basic recipe, replacing the chicken stock with a richly flavored vegetable stock. Make the stock by gently boiling together even quantities of celery, carrots, and onions with a few parsley stalks in about 3½ pints (2 liters) of water for about 1 hour. Strain the resulting liquid and season to taste with salt and pepper before using.

WITH CROUTONS
Prepare the basic recipe. Make some croutons with 3 slices of brown or white bread, cut into cubes and fried in a little oil until crisp and lightly browned. Sprinkle these over each bowl of soup before serving.

CHUNKY RED LENTIL SOUP
Prepare the basic recipe, but do not purée or blend the soup to make it smooth. Instead, serve it with the lentils as they are.

Summer Minestrone

The word "minestrone" means "big soup," and this soup is certainly a big one, packed with lots of different vegetables, beans, and pasta.

Serves 6

7 oz. (200 g) borlotti beans, canned or dried	2 zucchini, cubed
4 tbsp. olive oil	1 potato, peeled and cubed
1 onion, finely chopped	1 carrot, cubed
handful of fresh flat-leaf parsley, chopped	sea salt and freshly ground black pepper
10 oz. (280 g) mixed fresh green vegetables (e.g., spinach, cabbage, Swiss chard) chopped	7 oz. (200 g) short stubby pasta
	2–3 tbsp. pesto
	freshly grated Parmesan cheese, to serve

1 If using dried beans, soak overnight in cold water, drain, rinse, then boil fast in cold water for 5 minutes. Drain, rinse, and boil in fresh water or stock until tender but not falling apart. Do not add salt to the water until the beans are tender, as this will cause the skin to shrivel and harden. Drain beans, reserving cooking liquid.

2 Fry onion gently in the olive oil until soft. Add cooked (or canned and drained) beans and stir together thoroughly. Add parsley, green vegetables, zucchini, potato, and carrot. Fry together gently, using the water from the boiled or canned beans to moisten.

3 When the vegetables are beginning to soften, pour in the rest of the bean water (or in the case of canned beans, add vegetable stock instead) to cover thoroughly, turn the heat down, and simmer slowly for about 30 minutes, stirring regularly. Add more liquid if necessary, using vegetable stock or water.

4 When vegetables are thoroughly soft, season to taste and add pasta. Cook gently until pasta is cooked. Remove from heat, stir in pesto, and transfer into soup bowls or a tureen and serve, sprinkled with a little freshly grated Parmesan.

WITH RICE
Prepare the basic recipe, replacing pasta with 6 oz. (170 g) long-grain rice.

WITH CHICKPEAS
Prepare the basic recipe, replacing borlotti beans with dried or canned chickpeas.

WITH SQUASH OR PUMPKIN
Prepare the basic recipe, replacing the zucchini with the same quantity of peeled, seeded, and cubed winter squash or pumpkin.

COLD SUMMER MINESTRONE
Prepare the basic recipe, but allow the soup to cool and thicken before adding the pesto and serving at room temperature.

Warm Fish Soup on a Bed of Toasted Garlic Bread

This is the easiest recipe for making a really Mediterranean-tasting fish soup. You can add mussels, shrimp, and all manner of other fish or seafood if you wish, although the basic recipe calls only for filleted white fish, which makes it really easy to eat. The bread soaks up all the flavors and juices of the fish and is eaten at the end, once all the fish has gone.

Serves 6

3 lbs. (1½ kg) filleted fish of various kinds (e.g., cod, monkfish, haddock, plaice)
8 tbsp. olive oil
5 cloves garlic, finely chopped
1 dried red chili pepper
6 tbsp. chopped fresh flat-leaf parsley
3 handfuls cherry tomatoes, halved

sea salt and freshly ground black pepper
1¼ cups (300 ml) dry white wine
1 cup (250 ml) fish stock
12 thin slices ciabatta bread, toasted
1 clove garlic, peeled and left whole
2 tbsp. extra-virgin olive oil, to serve

1   Trim all the fish fillets carefully, cut them into equal-sized chunks, wash, and pat dry.

2   Heat the oil in a deep saucepan with the garlic, chili, 4 tablespoons of parsley, and tomatoes for about 5 minutes. Add all the fish and stir. Season with salt and pepper and add the wine and fish stock. Cover tightly and simmer very gently for about 15 minutes.

3   Meanwhile, toast the bread slices, rub each side with the garlic, and line a large, wide serving bowl with the bread.

4   Pour the hot fish soup all over the bread, drizzle with a little olive oil, sprinkle with the remaining parsley, and serve at once.

WITH MUSSELS
Prepare the basic recipe, adding a large handful of cleaned fresh mussels to the saucepan, after adding the fish, wine, and fish stock.

WITH SHRIMP
Prepare the basic recipe, adding about 10 shelled and deveined shrimp to the saucepan with the fish.

WITH SQUID
Prepare the basic recipe, adding 2 or 3 small squid, cleaned and cut into chunks, to the saucepan with the fish fillets.

SMOOTH FISH SOUP
Prepare the basic recipe, but when the fish is cooked, blend or process it to a smooth creamy texture before pouring it over the garlic bread.

Greek Salad

Serves 4–6

5 tbsp. extra-virgin olive oil
1½ tbsp. lemon juice
½ tsp. dried oregano
¼ tsp. sea salt

¼ tsp. freshly ground black pepper,
   plus extra to serve
3 ripe tomatoes, cut into wedges
½ red onion, thinly sliced into rings

½ cucumber, peeled and sliced
½ green bell pepper, cubed
¼ lb. (115 g) feta cheese, crumbled
16 Kalamata olives

1 To make the dressing, put the olive oil, lemon juice, oregano, salt, and pepper in a small jar with a screwtop lid. Shake to combine.

2 Put all the salad ingredients in a large bowl. Pour the dressing over the salad and toss gently to combine just before serving. Sprinkle the salad with a little freshly ground black pepper.

WITH GREEN OLIVES
Prepare the basic recipe, replacing the Kalamata olives with pitted green olives.

WITH GARLIC
Prepare the basic recipe, adding 1 minced clove garlic to the dressing before adding it to the salad ingredients.

WITH TOASTED PINE NUTS
Prepare the basic recipe, adding a handful of lightly toasted pine nuts to the salad to give it extra crunch.

WITH CAPERS
Prepare the basic recipe, adding a handful of rinsed and dried capers to the salad with the olives.

Pipirrana

Serves 6

6 eggs
6 small or medium potatoes, peeled and cubed
1 green bell pepper, seeded and diced
1 red bell pepper, seeded and diced
½ onion, chopped

1 large fresh tomato, chopped
1 small can tuna, drained
½ cup (60 g) green olives with pimento or
   anchovy, halved
¼ cup (50 ml) extra-virgin olive oil

2 tbsp. distilled white vinegar
1 tsp. salt or to taste

1 Place eggs in a saucepan, and cover with cold water. Bring water to a boil, then immediately remove from heat. Cover and let eggs stand in the hot water for 10–12 minutes. Remove from hot water, cool, and peel. Cut eggs into quarters, and set aside.

2 Meanwhile, bring a large pot of salted water to a boil. Add potatoes and cook until tender but still firm, about 15 minutes. Drain potatoes and transfer to a large bowl.

3 Toss with eggs, bell peppers, onion, tomato, tuna, green olives, olive oil, and vinegar. Season to taste with salt. Cool, refrigerate, and serve cold.

WITH WATERCRESS
Prepare the basic recipe, then toss 2 handfuls of fresh watercress leaves through the salad when it is cold.

WITH BLACK OLIVES
Prepare the basic recipe, replacing the green olives with black olives.

WITH CAPERS
Prepare the basic recipe, adding a handful of capers, drained and rinsed, to the salad with the eggs.

WITH PINE NUTS
Prepare the basic recipe, adding a handful of pine nuts to the salad with the eggs.

WITH CHICKEN
Prepare the basic recipe, replacing the tuna with 1 large skinless chicken breast, roasted, and shredded.

Salad Niçoise

This classic salad is synonymous with the south of France, combining salad ingredients, herbs, eggs, and olives to make a very pretty and delicious dish topped off with a lightly grilled fresh tuna steak.

Serves 4

3 tbsp. aged red wine vinegar
7 tbsp. extra-virgin olive oil
2 tbsp. chopped fresh flat-leaf parsley
2 tbsp. snipped fresh chives
2 cloves garlic, peeled and finely chopped
1 tsp. sea salt
1 tsp. freshly ground black pepper
1 lb. (450 g) fresh tuna loin or 4 x 6-oz. (175 g) tuna steaks, 1 inch thick

4 Little Gem lettuce hearts (or crisp long-leafed lettuce, quartered lengthwise)
1 red onion, finely sliced
4 fresh plum tomatoes, roughly chopped
8 new potatoes, cooked and quartered lengthwise
¼ lb. (115 g) extra-fine green beans, topped, cooked, and drained

6 anchovy fillets, cut lengthwise into thin strips
4 eggs, cooked for 6 minutes in boiling water from room temperature, halved
16 pitted black olives in brine, drained
8 fresh basil leaves, torn

1 Whisk together the red wine vinegar, olive oil, parsley, chives, garlic, salt, and pepper. Place the tuna in a shallow dish and cover with half of the dressing. Cover and chill for 1–2 hours to allow the fish to marinate. Toss tuna in the marinade from time to time.

2 Heat a ridged griddle pan under a hot broiler for 5 minutes. Remove the tuna from the marinade and place on the pan. Cook the tuna steaks for 2–3 minutes on each side, depending on how rare you like your fish. Cook the tuna loin (if using) for about 15 minutes or longer, turning frequently.

3 Lay the lettuce leaves on a large plate and add the onion, tomatoes, potatoes, haricots verts, and anchovies. Arrange the cooked tuna on top. Drizzle with the remaining dressing, then finish by adding the halved eggs, olives, and basil leaves.

QUICK & EASY
Prepare the basic recipe, replacing the fresh tuna with 2 small cans of tuna, drained and broken into chunks. Omit marinating the tuna, and just drizzle both the salad and the canned tuna with the dressing.

WITH QUAIL EGGS
Prepare the basic recipe, replacing the eggs with 12 quail eggs, lightly boiled for 2 or 3 minutes, then carefully shelled and halved.

WITH CAPERS
Prepare the basic recipe, adding about 12 capers, rinsed and dried, to the salad with the olives.

WITH CROÛTONS
Prepare the basic recipe, adding a handful of crisp croûtons to the salad with the olives and basil leaves.

Lebanese Fatoush Salad

This Middle Eastern salad, especially popular in Lebanon and Syria, consists of a chilled mixed salad tossed with small cubes of toasted bread. The texture of the toasted bread adds an unusual quality.

Serves 4

2 or 3 fresh ripe tomatoes, cubed
1 small cucumber, peeled, quartered lengthwise, and chopped
1 medium green bell pepper, seeded, ribbed, and diced
5 scallions, chopped

½ small head lettuce, shredded
2 tbsp. finely chopped fresh flat-leaf parsley
1 tbsp. finely chopped fresh mint or 1 tsp. dried mint
1 pita bread (or 2–3 slices of bread), toasted and cut into cubes

for the dressing
equal amounts of olive oil and lemon juice
sea salt and freshly ground black pepper to taste

1 Combine the vegetables, herbs, and bread in a large bowl. Make the dressing and pour it over the salad, toss well, and chill for 30–60 minutes before serving.

2 For an authentic Arabic flavor, the dressing should be made of equal parts of oil and lemon juice. However, you may prefer to use more oil—perhaps 2 to 3 parts of oil to 1 part lemon juice.

WITH PEACHES
Prepare the basic recipe, adding 3 cubed firm fresh peaches to the salad before tossing.

WITH MELON
Prepare the basic recipe, adding 2 slices melon, seeded and cubed to the salad before tossing.

WITH POTATOES
Prepare the basic recipe, adding 4 new potatoes, boiled and cubed, for a more substantial salad.

WITH RED BELL PEPPER
Prepare the basic recipe, replacing the green bell pepper with a very ripe red bell pepper.

WITH FETA
Prepare the basic recipe, adding 3 or 4 tablespoons crumbled feta cheese to the salad with the bread before adding the dressing.

Roasted Eggplant & Mint Salad

Serves 4

1 large eggplant
about 3 tbsp. extra-virgin olive oil
sea salt and freshly ground black pepper

⅓ lb. (150 g) feta cheese, crumbled
1 small clove garlic, finely chopped
handful fresh mint leaves, shredded

handful fresh cilantro leaves, shredded
squeeze of lemon juice

1 Preheat the oven to 425°F (220°C). Brush the eggplant slices on both sides with oil and season with salt and pepper. Place on a cookie sheet in a single layer. Roast for 15–20 minutes, turning, until golden. Allow to cool to room temperature.

2 Arrange the eggplant slices on a serving plate. Scatter the crumbled feta over the top, along with the garlic, mint, and cilantro. Add a squeeze of lemon juice and serve.

WITH SUN-DRIED TOMATO
Prepare the basic recipe, scattering the roasted eggplant slices with 8 chopped sun-dried tomatoes (from a jar, drained), the feta, and a handful of shredded basil leaves instead of the mint and cilantro.

WITH PARMESAN
Prepare the basic recipe, replacing the feta with the same amount of shaved Parmesan, and the mint and cilantro with freshly chopped flat-leaf parsley.

WITH RICOTTA
Prepare the basic recipe, replacing the feta with ⅓ lb. (150 g) ricotta and the cilantro with fresh flat-leaf parsley.

Spinach Salad with Yogurt

Serves 6

½ lb. (225 g) fresh spinach, washed and drained, or 10 oz. (275 g) frozen spinach

2 tbsp. fresh lemon juice
¼ tsp. salt
¼ tsp. freshly ground black pepper

1 tsp. finely chopped onions
1 cup (250 ml) plain yogurt

1 In a small saucepan, bring fresh spinach to a boil. Reduce heat to low and allow to cook for 10 minutes. (If using frozen spinach, follow package directions.) Drain spinach and allow to cool for 15 minutes. Chop into very small pieces. Place pieces in a piece of cheesecloth or heavy-duty paper towel and squeeze out excess water.

2 In a bowl, combine spinach, lemon juice, salt, pepper, and onions. Fold the yogurt in with other ingredients. Refrigerate and serve well chilled.

WITH RAISINS
Prepare the basic recipe, replacing the onions with 2 tablespoons raisins, soaked in enough cold water to cover for about 20 minutes, then drained and dried.

WITH TOASTED ALMONDS
Prepare the basic recipe, adding 2 tablespoons slivered almonds, lightly toasted, to the salad with the yogurt to add some nutty crunchiness.

WITH CHOPPED APRICOTS
Prepare the basic recipe, folding 8 fresh or dried apricots, chopped into small cubes, into the salad with the yogurt.

WITH TOASTED WALNUTS
Prepare the basic recipe, adding 2 tablespoons roughly chopped walnuts, lightly toasted, to the salad with the yogurt to add some crunch.

WITH POMEGRANATE SEEDS
Prepare the basic recipe, omitting the onions and adding 2 tablespoons fresh pomegranate seeds to the salad with the lemon juice.

Tomato & Olive Salad with Olive Paste

To make the olive pâté for this tomato and olive salad, just process a jar of pitted black olives, drained, with a little lemon juice, a clove of peeled garlic, chopped fresh parsley, and salt and pepper until smooth.

Serves 6

6 large tomatoes, peeled and cut into chunks
2 small cucumbers, peeled and cut into same size as tomatoes
2 large red onions, diced very small
3–4 tbsp. coarsely chopped fresh flat-leaf parsley
6 tbsp. chopped black olives

for the dressing
2 tbsp. black olive pâté (recipe above)
2 tbsp. lemon juice
6 tbsp. extra-virgin olive oil
sea salt and freshly ground black pepper

1 Put the tomatoes, cucumbers, and onions into a large bowl and mix together gently. Add the parsley and combine with the vegetables. Add the olives and mix well.

2 To make the dressing, combine black olive pâté, lemon juice, and olive oil. If the mixture is too sticky, add a little more olive oil and mix thoroughly. Add salt and pepper to taste.

3 Pour the dressing onto the vegetables and combine. The juices from the vegetables should help loosen the dressing as you mix it through the salad. Serve at once, with crusty bread.

WITH GREEN OLIVES
For a milder-tasting salad, use the same quantity of green olives and green olive pâté in place of the stronger-tasting black olives.

WITH CAPERS
Use capers in place of the olives. Dress the salad without the olive pâté, using olive oil and lemon juice instead.

WITH BELL PEPPERS
Exchanged half the quantity of tomatoes for red and green peppers, cut into small cubes.

WITH GARLIC
To make the salad taste subtly of garlic, omit the red onions and use 3 finely minced cloves of garlic, stirred into the dressing.

Neapolitan Roasted Pepper Salad

This is such a classic, delicious antipasto and incredibly addictive! Also delicious with mozzarella in a sandwich made with crusty bread.

Serves 6

6 large red and/or yellow bell peppers
3 cloves garlic, very finely chopped
large handful fresh flat-leaf parsley, chopped

8 tbsp. extra-virgin olive oil
sea salt and freshly ground black pepper

1 Preheat the oven to 400°F (200°C). Wash and dry peppers, then lay them on a rack or in a shallow metal pan in the oven for about 30 minutes, or until browned and soft.

2 Remove from oven and lay them in a deep tray on the counter. Cover the peppers with a large glass bowl so that they can steam as they cool, thus loosening their skins. As soon as the peppers are cool enough to handle easily, slip off their thin, papery skins and slide out their seeds. (Or you can wrap the roasted peppers in plastic wrap until cool, then peel and seed.)

3 Cut the prepared peppers in to wide slices and arrange, slightly overlapping, on a platter or in a shallow-sided bowl. Sprinkle with the garlic and parsley and then sprinkle with the olive oil and salt and pepper.

4 Mix gently to evenly distribute the seasoning, then let stand for an hour or more to allow the flavors to develop before serving.

WITH ANCHOVIES
Prepare the basic recipe, then sprinkle 6 drained and chopped anchovy fillets over the peppers with the garlic and parsley.

WITH OLIVES
Prepare the basic recipe, then sprinkle about 12 pitted and coarsely chopped green or black olives over the peppers with the garlic and parsley.

WITH FETA
Prepare the basic recipe, then add 3 tablespoons crumbled feta over the peppers with the garlic and parsley. Add a final dusting of dried oregano over the salad before serving.

WITH RED ONION
Prepare the basic recipe, replacing the garlic with 1 very finely sliced red onion.

Escalibada

This Spanish salad of grilled vegetables is served all over the Mediterranean in various different combinations.

Serves 6

2 red bell peppers
2 green bell peppers
2 medium-sized eggplant, thickly sliced
4 medium-sized tomatoes

for the dressing
1 tbsp. chopped fresh flat-leaf parsley
5 tbsp. extra-virgin olive oil

2 tbsp. red wine vinegar
1 clove garlic, mashed

1 Grill the peppers and eggplant over moderate heat on the barbecue. Pierce the skins of the eggplant to prevent skins from bursting, and grill them with the peppers for 15 minutes, turning several times. When the skins of the peppers are blistered and charred, remove from heat. Wrap in a towel and put in a paper bag. Set aside.

2 When the eggplant slices are tender, remove them from the grill and set aside (they will take a little longer to cook than the peppers). Score the skin of the tomatoes with a cross. Grill for 5 minutes, turning occasionally. Set aside.

3 When peppers are cool, remove what you can of the skin, remove the seeds, and slice. Peel tomatoes and slice. Arrange all the vegetables on a platter with the tomatoes in the center.

4 Toss together the dressing ingredients. Drizzle the dressing over the vegetables. Serve hot or at room temperature as a side dish or as a main course with bread.

WITH PESTO
Prepare the basic recipe, then drizzle a little fresh pesto over the salad just before serving.

WITH FETA
Prepare the basic recipe, then crumble 3 tablespoons feta cheese over the salad just before serving.

WITH PINE NUTS
Prepare the basic recipe, then scatter a handful of lightly toasted pine nuts over the salad just before serving.

WITH FENNEL
Prepare the basic recipe. Grill 2 fennel bulbs, sliced thickly through the base so that they remain intact, and add them to the salad with the bell peppers and eggplant. Increase the quantity of the dressing slightly to allow the fennel to be dressed.

WITH ZUCCHINI
Prepare the basic recipe. Grill 2 medium-sized zucchini, and add them to the salad with the bell peppers and eggplant. Increase the quantity of the dressing slightly to allow the zucchini to be dressed.

Baked Feta & Walnut Salad

This is a rustic Greek-style salad with baked feta cheese, walnuts, mixed salad greens, and thinly sliced fresh radish and zucchini, tossed with a tangy lemon-garlic dressing.

Serves 4

6 tbsp. extra-virgin olive oil
1 tsp. dried oregano
½ tsp. freshly ground black pepper
6–7 oz. (175–200 g) feta cheese, cubed
⅔ cup (80 g) shelled walnuts, halved

1 clove garlic, crushed
3 tbsp. fresh lemon juice
pinch sea salt
6 handfuls mixed salad greens of your choice
2 radishes, thinly sliced
1 zucchini, thinly sliced

1   Preheat the oven to 350°F (175°C). Mix 2 teaspoons of the olive oil with the dried oregano and black pepper in a bowl, then toss in the cubed feta cheese to coat well. Arrange the feta cubes on a cookie sheet lined with parchment paper or waxed paper. Bake for 10 minutes.

2   Place the walnuts on a separate cookie sheet and bake for 3 minutes, then roughly chop.

3   Put the remaining olive oil, garlic, lemon juice, and salt in a jar with a lid and shake to combine.

4   Put the salad greens, radish slices, and zucchini slices in a salad bowl and toss with half the dressing to coat. Scatter with the baked feta and walnuts and drizzle with the remaining dressing to serve.

WITH PINE NUTS
Prepare the basic recipe, replacing the walnuts with pine nuts.

WITH RED BELL PEPPER
Prepare the basic recipe, replacing the radishes with 1 medium-sized red bell pepper, seeded and cubed.

WITH ALMONDS
Prepare the basic recipe, replacing the walnuts with slivered or chopped almonds.

WITH BABY SPINACH
Prepare the basic recipe, replacing the mixed salad greens with baby spinach leaves.

Panzanella

This lovely, light Tuscan salad makes fantastic use of what was once a most precious commodity — stale bread. In Tuscany, this is essential summer eating, as it is light and delicious while still being filling enough to stave off hunger pangs.

Serves 6

8 slices rustic white
   bread, stale
4 fist-sized ripe, fresh
   tomatoes
1 large onion
1 large cucumber
handful of basil leaves,
   washed and dried

extra-virgin olive oil,
   to taste
red wine vinegar, to taste
sea salt and freshly
   ground black pepper

1 Soak the bread in cold water for about 15 minutes. Squeeze the bread dry in a clean cloth. Slice tomatoes, onion, and cucumber. Tear the basil into small pieces.

2 In a large bowl, mix the damp bread with the tomatoes, onion, cucumber, and basil. Dress with olive oil, vinegar, and salt and pepper to taste.

3 Mix together very well and let the salad stand for about 30 minutes before serving.

WITH FISH
Prepare basic recipe, adding some lightly grilled fillets of red mullet or hake, taking care not to break the fish up too much.

WITH TUNA
Prepare basic recipe, adding some canned tuna in olive oil, carefully drained, to the salad.

WITH MUSSELS
Prepare basic recipe, adding about 2 oz. (50 g) cooked and shelled fresh mussels to the salad. Use the strained, cooled, cooking liquid to soak the bread.

WITH BLACK OLIVES
Prepare basic recipe, adding about 20 large black olives, pitted and coarsely chopped, to the salad before dressing.

WITH CHICKEN
Prepare basic recipe. Grill 2 skinless chicken breasts until cooked through and well browned. Cool and slice into strips. Mix into the salad just before serving.

Insalata Caprese

This absolutely classic salad originates from the beautiful Italian island of Capri. It is truly unforgettable when made with the local richly flavored tomatoes, the soft and silky local buffalo mozzarella, and the intensely perfumed basil grown on the volcanic terrain.

Serves 6

2 handfuls (i.e. 2 very large, or 4 medium-sized, or 12 cherry tomatoes, or a mixture) firm ripe tomatoes, washed well

2 balls fresh mozzarella or 3 of buffalo mozzarella, drained
6 tbsp. extra-virgin olive oil

about 24 leaves fresh basil, torn into small sections
sea salt and freshly ground black pepper

1 Slice tomatoes and mozzarella into even-sized slices, cubes, or chunks. Put them into a salad bowl and toss together gently. Sprinkle with olive oil and mix together again. Add basil, torn into pieces. Sprinkle with salt and pepper to taste and mix again. Let stand for about 15 minutes before serving.

2 Alternatively, arrange the sliced tomatoes flat on a platter, cover each slice of tomato with a slice of mozzarella, and then scatter basil over slices before dressing with olive oil, sea salt, and freshly ground black pepper.

WITH AVOCADO
Prepare the basic recipe, adding slices of ripe avocado to make this salad into *insalata tricolore*.

WITH PARMA HAM
Prepare the basic recipe, adding some thin strips of freshly sliced Parma ham.

WITH ROASTED BELL PEPPERS
Prepare the basic recipe adding roasted bell peppers preserved in olive oil, or roast them yourself in a medium-hot oven or under the broiler. Their sweet flavor and soft texture works really well.

WITH GRILLED EGGPLANT
Prepare the basic recipe, adding a few slices of grilled eggplant to make the salad considerably more substantial. Use grilled eggplant preserved in olive oil or slice and grill it yourself. Before grilling, sprinkle slices with sea salt and place in a colander to drain, covered with a weighted plate. After an hour, rinse, dry, and brush with a little olive oil to grill.

WITH ARTICHOKE HEARTS
Prepare the basic recipe, adding a few chopped, well-drained, oil-marinated artichoke hearts.

Seafood Salad

This classic seafood salad is good served just warm, or it can be made a few hours ahead and served cold. Vary the choice of seafood according to personal taste or what is in season.

Serves 6

7 oz. (200 g) fresh squid, cleaned and cut into neat strips and rings
2 lbs. (900 g) fresh mussels, scrubbed and cleaned

1 lb. (450 g) fresh baby clams, scrubbed and cleaned
6 oz. (175 g) small fresh shrimp
4 large fresh shrimp

for the dressing
1 lemon, halved
6 tbsp. extra-virgin olive oil
3 tbsp. chopped fresh flat-leaf parsley
freshly ground black pepper
sea salt

1 Boil the squid in salted water for 25–30 minutes, or until tender. Drain and put in a large bowl. Steam the mussels and clams for about 8 minutes, discarding any that do not open.

2 Wash the small shrimp well and cover with cold water in a saucepan. Bring to a boil and cook for 1 minute, then drain and cool before shelling. Add to the bowl with the squid.

3 Remove the clams and mussels from their shells and put them in the bowl with the shrimp and squid. Toss together. Boil the 4 large shrimp for 2 minutes, then drain, devein, and cool. Set aside.

4 Squeeze the juice from half the lemon and slice the other half to use as a garnish. Add the juice to the mixed seafood with the oil, parsley, and pepper to taste. Add salt only after mixing. Serve garnished with the 4 large shrimp and lemon slices.

WITH FRESH CHILI
Prepare basic recipe, omitting all seafood but squid and doubling the amount of squid. Replace black pepper with very finely chopped fresh chili pepper. Mix the boiled squid with the dressing and serve with lemon slices.

WITH SHRIMP
Prepare basic recipe, omitting all seafood but the shrimp. Cook 14 oz. (400 g) peeled, deveined shrimp, mix with the dressing, garnish with lemon slices, and serve.

WITH SQUID & PANCETTA
Prepare basic recipe, omitting all seafood but the squid. Boil double the amount of squid until tender, then drain. Slice and mix with 3 oz. (75 g) fried pancetta cubes, then mix with the dressing and garnish with lemon slices.

WITH SCALLOP
Prepare basic recipe, replacing all the seafood with 12 large scallops. Sear the scallops with a little oil for 2–3 minutes per side, slice horizontally, and mix with the dressing. Garnish with lemon slices to serve.

CHAPTER 3
Breads
& Pizzas

Whether it's a thick crust pizza with layers of tomato sauce, melted cheese and delicious toppings, or a beautifully-baked tear and share focaccia , these pizza and bread recipes will please a crowd or satisfy a hungry family.

MAKING PERFECT DOUGH

You can do this on a lightly floured work surface or in a bowl. Place the flour and salt into a large bowl, and make a well in the center. Add the oil or butter to the middle, and pour in most of the yeast liquid. With a fork and a circular movement, gradually incorporate the dry flour from the inner edge of the well and mix into the liquid, and continue until you have used all the flour, and all the liquid if needed. When the dough comes together and becomes too hard to mix with your fork, lightly flour your hands and begin to pat it into a ball. Unless the recipe states otherwise, if the dough seems too wet, add a little more flour, and if it seems too dry, add a little more liquid. If short on time, or the dough is very sticky, use an electric stand mixer with a dough hook attachment.

HOW TO KNEADING DOUGH

Kneading the dough is crucial to the whole bread-making process. It develops the gluten and causes the dough to become smooth and elastic as you work it. It also teaches you about the feel of the dough. Do not be tempted to add more and more flour as you knead, as this will produce a loaf that is tough and dry. You could even use a touch of oil on the work surface instead of flour.

Take your ball of dough and roll it backward and forward, using your left hand to stretch it toward you and your right hand to push it away from you at the same time. Repeat this for 10 minutes until you have a smooth, springy, but soft dough that is quite elastic and no longer sticks to your hand. Work through the sticky phase until the dough develops a kind of smooth skin. To test if it is ready, you could try the stretch test: Pull off a piece of dough and stretch it. It should be elastic enough not to break quickly when stretched out.

Bread dough can be mixed and kneaded, wrapped in plastic wrap, and frozen for up to 1 month. Let it thaw and come to room temperature before you remove the plastic wrap, and prepare it for baking by either placing it in the prepared pans or on a cookie sheet. Cover and leave to rise until doubled in size, and bake.

RISING (PROOFING) THE DOUGH

This is going to sound complicated, but isn't really. You should place the dough in a lightly oiled bowl, turning the dough around to coat it completely with a thin coating of oil, to prevent a crust from forming on the surface of the dough. Cover the dough either with a slightly damp kitchen towel or with plastic wrap, and leave until the dough has just about doubled in size. The bowl should be big enough for the dough to rise without touching the cover, which would inhibit the rise. If you want the dough to rise quickly, put it somewhere warm, and if you want a fuller flavored loaf and have loads of time, leave it at room temperature or even overnight in the refrigerator. When it is ready, it will look puffed and soft. If touched with your finger, it should make an indentation that springs back out. If you over-proof the dough, crease marks will appear on the top of the dough, and it will begin to collapse. If this happens, you can reform the dough and leave it to rise a second time; the yeast will continue to feed and the dough will swell again.

PUNCHING DOWN (KNOCKING BACK) THE DOUGH

After rising once or twice, the dough usually needs to be punched down to deflate it. Transfer the dough to a lightly floured work surface and gently knead it again until all the air has been knocked out. Sometimes, all you need to do is roll the dough out to its required size. With very sticky dough recipes, you have to be careful not to knock the air out, but the recipe will explain the procedure.

BAKING THE BREAD

Professional bakeries use steam in their ovens to create the perfect crispy crust. You can replicate this at home by placing a large roasting pan in the bottom of your oven to heat up, then adding enough hot water to fill it two-thirds full at the same time you put the bread into the oven to bake. Do not open the oven door for at least 5 minutes, but after that, you can check if the pan needs more water. You can also spray the top of the bread with water just before you place it in the oven.

Pita Bread

Pita bread is served at just about every meal in the Middle East. It can be used for dipping, or to make delicious sandwiches in the pocket. In the Middle East, pita is made in brick ovens, where very high heat can be achieved. It is very hard to duplicate in a home kitchen, but this recipe, combined with high heat, comes close.

Makes about 10 pita breads, depending on size

1 package active dry or
    quick-rising yeast
½ cup (115 ml) warm
    water
1 tsp. granulated sugar

3 cups (340 g) all-
    purpose flour
1¼ tsp. salt
1 cup (240 ml) lukewarm
    water

1 Dissolve the yeast in warm water. Add sugar and stir until dissolved. Let sit for 10–15 minutes until mixture is frothy. Combine flour and salt in large bowl. Make a small depression in center and pour in yeast mixture. Slowly add the lukewarm water, and stir with wooden spoon or rubber spatula.

2 Place dough on floured surface and knead for 10–15 minutes. When dough is no longer sticky and is smooth and elastic, put it in large, oiled bowl. Turn dough over to coat other side with oil. Allow to sit in a warm place for about 3 hours, or until it has doubled in size. Once doubled, roll out in a rope, and pinch off 10–12 small pieces. Place balls on floured surface. Let sit, covered, for 10 minutes.

3 Preheat oven to 500°F (240°C) and move rack to very bottom of oven. Preheat cookie sheet also. With a rolling pin, roll out each ball of dough into a circle, about 6 in. (15 cm) across and ¼ in. (½ cm) thick. Bake in batches for 4 minutes until the bread puffs up. Turn over and bake for 2 minutes.

4 Remove each pita with a spatula from the cookie sheet. With spatula, gently push down puffiness. Repeat process with remaining pitas. Immediately place in storage bags to keep soft.

WITH HERBS
Prepare the basic recipe, adding 1 tablespoon dried mixed herbs to the dough.

WITH BLACK OLIVES
Prepare the basic recipe, adding 2 tablespoons chopped black pitted olives to the dough.

WHOLE-WHEAT PITA BREAD
Prepare the basic recipe, replacing the all-purpose flour with whole-wheat flour.

WITH CHILI PEPPERS
Prepare the basic recipe, adding 1 or 2 finely chopped dried chili peppers to the dough.

WITH SUN-DRIED TOMATOES
Prepare the basic recipe, adding 5 or 6 finely chopped sun-dried tomatoes to the dough.

Focaccia

Created in the little town of Recco on the Ligurian Riviera, this lovely oily and salty bread is perfect when split and filled with thinly sliced Parma ham and ripe tomatoes.

Makes 6 small, 3 medium, or 1 large focaccia

2 tsp. instant dry yeast
1 cup (240 ml) warm
    water plus 2 tbsp.
2 tbsp. sugar
3½–4 cups (400–450 g)
    white bread flour

1 tbsp. coarse salt
¼ cup (60 ml) olive oil,
    plus extra for greasing
    and sprinkling
polenta or cornmeal,
    for dusting

1   Preheat oven to 375°F (190°C). In the bowl of a standing mixer fitted with a dough hook, mix yeast with 1 cup (240 ml) warm water and sugar. Stir to dissolve. Let stand 3 minutes until foam appears. Turn mixer on low and slowly add the flour. Dissolve salt in the 2 tablespoons warm water and add to yeast mixture. Pour in olive oil. When dough starts to come together, increase speed to medium. Mix until dough is smooth and elastic, about 10 minutes.

2   Turn dough out onto work surface and knead a few times. Shape into ball and place in well-oiled bowl, turning to coat entire ball with oil so it doesn't form a skin. Cover with plastic wrap or damp towel and let rise in a warm place until doubled, about 45 minutes.

3   Coat a cookie sheet with a little olive oil and a sprinkling of polenta. Once dough is doubled in size turn it out onto work surface. Roll and stretch dough to an oblong shape about ½ in. (1 cm) thick. Lay dough on cookie sheet, cover with plastic wrap and rest for 15 minutes.

4   Remove plastic wrap and sprinkle top of dough with coarse salt and olive oil, making shallow dips in dough with your fingertips. Bake for 15 minutes, or until golden brown and crisp. Remove from sheet and cool before serving.

WITH FENNEL SEEDS
Prepare the basic recipe, then sprinkle top of focaccia with about 1 tablespoon fennel seeds before baking.

WITH ONIONS
Prepare the basic recipe, then spread top of focaccia with 2 very thinly sliced onions, olive oil, and salt and pepper before baking.

WITH ROSEMARY
Prepare the basic recipe, then sprinkle 1 teaspoon finely chopped fresh rosemary over the focaccia before making dents in surface with your fingers. Spread with olive oil and a sprinkling of salt before baking.

WITH GARLIC & THYME
Prepare the basic recipe, adding 1 tablespoon chopped fresh thyme to dough with the oil and water. Sprinkle 2 finely chopped garlic cloves over the surface before making dents with your fingertips, then spread with olive oil and a sprinkling of salt before baking.

Pesto Focaccia with Mozzarella

Focaccia is an Italian staple—serve it as a tear-and-share bread with dips,
use for sandwiches, or top with cheese, tomato and pesto.

Serves 6

2 cups (255 g) white bread flour
½ tsp. salt
2 tsp. garlic powder
2 tsp. Italian dried herbs
1 tsp. active dry yeast
¾ cup (180 ml) warm water
1½ tbsp. extra virgin olive oil + 1–2 tbsp.

coarse sea salt for sprinkling
rosemary sprigs

for the filling
5 Roma tomatoes, halved, and roasted with
  1 tbsp. olive oil in a hot oven
½ tsp. sugar

¾ cup (175 g) mozzarella cheese
salt and freshly ground black pepper to taste
4 tbsp. homemade pesto (see page 81)

1 Line a large cookie sheet with parchment paper, and lightly grease a 9 x 7-in. (23 x 18-cm) rectangular glass baking dish with a little olive oil. In a large bowl, combine the flour, salt, garlic powder, and dried herbs. Mix the yeast with ½ cup (120 ml) of warm water and stir to dissolve the yeast. Set aside for 5 minutes.

2 Make a well in the center of the flour, and add the yeast liquid and 1½ tablespoons olive oil. Turn the mixture around with either a plastic dough scraper or your hands. Gradually add the rest of the water until a sticky dough is formed. You may not have to use it all. Turn the dough out onto a lightly floured or oiled work surface. Knead the dough for about 10 minutes, until it is smooth and elastic. The dough will be wetter at first, but will form a smooth skin. Transfer to the oiled dish, cover with a paper towel, and leave to rise in a warm place for an hour or so.

3 Turn the dough out onto a lightly floured work surface, and stretch the dough into a rectangle. Carefully lift onto the cookie sheet, place in a greased plastic bag, and leave for about an hour, until doubled in size. Preheat the oven to 425°F (220°C). Remove the cookie sheet from the plastic bag and make deep dimples in the dough with your fingers. Drizzle the focaccia with 1–2 tablespoons olive oil and sprinkle with coarse sea salt. Push small rosemary sprigs into the dough. Bake for 15 minutes, or until golden brown.

4 Cool on a wire rack. Cut the focaccia into rectangles and lightly broil each cut side. In a small bowl, season the mozzarella cheese with salt and freshly ground black pepper. Spread each rectangle of focaccia with pesto and lay the mozzarella and tomatoes on top. Serve immediately.

WITH CHARBROILED EGGPLANT, FETA & SWEET POTATO
Prepare the basic recipe, omitting the mozzarella cheese. Slice focaccia in half lengthwise. Spread ½ cup (100 g) sweet potato purée over half of the focaccia and add sliced tomatoes, 6 oz. (175 g) crumbled feta cheese, and 4 slices chared eggplant to the other half on top of the pesto. Sandwich the 2 halves together.

WITH GOAT CHEESE & SALAMI
Prepare the basic recipe. Add 4 oz. (125 g) chopped goat cheese to the mozzarella cheese and tomatoes, and lay a few slices of salami on top.

WITH CHICKEN, AVOCADO & SWISS CHEESE
Prepare the basic recipe, omitting the mozzarella cheese. Place 1 avocado, pitted and sliced, on top of the tomatoes, then add 6 oz. (175 g) cooked sliced chicken, and sprinkle 4 oz. (125 g) shredded Swiss cheese on top.

WITH CREAM CHEESE, SMOKED SALMON & ARUGULA
Prepare the basic recipe, replacing the mozzarella cheese with cream cheese. Replace tomatoes with a layer of thinly sliced smoked salmon. Add 2 cups (50 g) arugula and omit pesto.

Farinata

Serves 6

2 cups (260 g) chickpea flour
2½ pints (1½ liters) water

sea salt and freshly ground black pepper
4 tbsp. olive oil

1 Put the chickpea flour in a bowl with the water and mix together thoroughly. Add the salt and pepper and half the oil. Let the batter stand for about 1 hour or even overnight, the longer the better.

2 Preheat the oven to 400°F (200°C). Use the remaining oil to grease a shallow, 12-in. (30-cm) square baking pan (or a similar size), and then pour in the batter. Bake for about 30 minutes, or until crisp on the outside and still soft in the middle.

3 You should end up with a wide sheet of farinata no more than 1¼ in. (3 cm) thick. It is best when served warm from the oven, though it is also quite good cold.

WITH STRACCHINO
Stracchino is a sour stretch-curd cheese that is delicious spread over squares of hot, freshly baked farinata, which are then rolled up and served.

WITH PARMESAN
Prepare the basic recipe, adding 2 or 3 tablespoons freshly grated Parmesan to the batter.

WITH ONIONS
Prepare the basic recipe, adding 1 finely chopped, lightly fried onion to the batter.

WITH OREGANO
Prepare the basic recipe, adding 1 tablespoon dried oregano to the batter.

Garlic Bread

Serves 4–6

1 head garlic
olive oil

sea salt
1 large loaf of good rustic bread

1 Preheat oven to 425°F (220°C). Crush the head of garlic and place it (skin and all) in the center of a large piece of aluminum foil (large enough to encase the loaf of bread). Drizzle with olive oil and season with sea salt.

2 Place the loaf on top of the garlic, fold the foil over to create a parcel, and bake for about 5 minutes (long enough to allow the garlic flavors to permeate the bread). Serve warm.

WITH BUTTER
Instead of the basic recipe, peel and mince all the garlic cloves. Mix with about 5 tablespoons sweet butter. Split the loaf in half, spread with the garlic butter, and wrap in the foil to bake at 425°F (220°C) for about 5 minutes.

WITH SMOKED GARLIC
Prepare the basic recipe, but replace the head of garlic with a head of smoked garlic, available from online suppliers.

WITH ROSEMARY
Prepare the basic recipe, adding a few sprigs of fresh rosemary to the garlic on the aluminum foil.

Lebanese Pizza with Za'atar

Za'atar, a Middle Eastern spice blend, is so versatile that it can be used on meats, vegetables, rice, and breads.

Makes 6

1 tbsp. roasted sesame seeds
¼ cup (30 g) ground sumac
2 tbsp. dried thyme
2 tbsp. dried marjoram
2 tbsp. dried oregano
1 tsp. coarse salt
1 tbsp. sugar or honey

1 cup (240 ml) warm water
2 tsp. active dry yeast
3 cups (350 g) all-purpose flour
1 tsp. salt
6 tbsp. olive oil
4 tbsp. za'atar
½ tsp. lemon juice

1 To make the za'atar, grind sesame seeds in food processor or with a mortar and pestle. Add the dried herbs and mix well. Store za'atar in a cool, dark place in a ziplock plastic bag or an airtight container. When stored properly, za'atar can be kept up to 6 months.

2 To make the dough, dissolve sugar or honey in warm water in small bowl. Sprinkle yeast over water and stir until it dissolves. Let mixture stand for 5 minutes, until a layer of foam forms. In larger bowl, combine flour and salt. Make a well in center and pour in a third of the oil and the yeast mixture. Mix flour into wet ingredients; add more water if it is too dry.

3 On lightly floured surface, knead dough for 15 minutes, until smooth and elastic. Shape dough into ball and put in a well-oiled bowl (using about half of remaining olive oil). Cover with moist towel and let rise in warm place until double (about 12 hours).

4 Preheat oven to 425°F (220°C). Roll out 6 equal circles of dough. In small bowl, mix za'atar with remaining oil and the lemon juice. Pour mixture equally onto dough circles and smooth it over surface. Bake for 8–10 minutes. Eat warm.

WITH SUN-DRIED TOMATOES
Prepare the basic recipe, then press 2 or 3 chopped sun-dried tomatoes into the surface before spreading on the za'atar and baking.

WITH OLIVES
Prepare the basic recipe, then scatter a handful of chopped, pitted olives over the pizza before spreading on the za'atar.

WITH FRESH TOMATO
Prepare the basic recipe, then scatter 6 chopped ripe tomatoes over the pizza before spreading on the za'atar.

Lebanese Flatbread

This soft flatbread is similar to pita bread in taste, but tends to be bigger and floppier in texture. In Arabic, it is called *khoubiz*.

Makes 8 flatbreads

6 cups (650 g) all-purpose flour, plus extra as needed
1 package active dry yeast
2 cups (475 ml) warm water

1½ tsp. salt
1 tsp. sugar
2 tbsp. oil, plus extra as needed

1 Sift flour into a large mixing bowl and warm in a low oven. Dissolve yeast in 4 cup warm water, then add remaining water and stir in salt and sugar. Remove about a third of the flour from bowl and set aside. Pour yeast mixture into center of remaining flour, then stir in some flour to make a thick liquid. Cover with cloth and leave in a warm place until frothy. Stir in rest of flour into bowl, adding 2 tablespoons oil gradually, then beat until smooth, either by hand for 10 minutes or with electric mixer using dough hook for 5 minutes.

2 Sprinkle some of the reserved flour onto a counter, turn out dough, and knead for 10 minutes, using more flour as required. When dough is smooth and satiny with slightly wrinkled texture, shape into a ball. Oil bowl, put in dough smooth-side down, then turn over so top is coated with oil. Stretch plastic wrap over bowl and leave in a warm place to rise until almost doubled, about 1 to 12 hours.

3 Preheat oven to 475°F (240°C). Punch down dough and turn out onto lightly floured worktop. Knead for 1–2 minutes, then divide into 8 equal pieces. Roll each piece into a ball, then into a 10-in, (25-cm) round, and place on lightly floured cloth. Cover with another cloth and leave for 20 minutes. Heat a large cookie sheet or flat griddle on the lowest shelf in an electric oven (in a gas oven select section with the most heat, probably near top). Place a round of dough on a lightly floured cookie sheet with a flat edge, then flatten and shape it evenly. Shake to ensure that it will slide off easily. Rub heated cookie sheet or griddle with wad of paper towel dipped in oil, then slide the flattened dough onto it.

4 Bake in hot oven for 4–5 minutes, until it puffs up like balloon. If you would like it browned on top, turn quickly and leave for a minute. Remove bread and wrap in a cloth to keep it warm and soft. Bake remaining loaves.

WITH CUMIN
Prepare the basic recipe, adding 1 teaspoon ground cumin to the yeast mixture with the sugar.

WITH ONION
Prepare the basic recipe, then sprinkle top of bread with finely chopped onion before sprinkling with a little more oil and baking as normal, onion side down first. Flip over after 2–3 minutes to bake on the other side.

WITH BACON
Prepare the basic recipe, then sprinkle top of bread with finely chopped bacon before sprinkling with a little more oil and baking as normal, bacon side down first. Flip over after 2–3 minutes to bake on the other side.

WITH GARLIC
Prepare the basic recipe, then cover top of bread with minced garlic, add a little oil, and bake as normal, garlic side down first. Flip over after 2–3 minutes to bake on the other side.

Black Olive Bread

You can vary the flavor of this bread with your choice of olive, so try Kalamata olives today and niçoise next week!

Makes 1 loaf

3½ cups (500 g) white
   bread flour
1 tbsp. active dry yeast
2 tbsp. sugar
1 tsp. sea salt
about ⅓ cup (60 g)
   chopped black olives

3 tbsp. olive oil, plus
   extra for greasing
1½ cups (350 ml) warm
   water
1 tbsp. polenta

1   In a large bowl, mix together flour, yeast, sugar, salt, olives, olive oil, and water. Turn out mixture onto a floured board. Knead until smooth and elastic, 5–10 minutes. Set aside in warm place and let rise about 45 minutes, until it doubles in size.

2   Punch down. Knead well again, for about 5–10 minutes. Let rise for about 30 minutes, until it doubles in size. Turn out and punch down the dough on a floured board. Place a bowl lined with a well-floured towel upside down over the dough. Let rise until doubled in size.

3   While dough is rising for the third time, put a pan of water in the bottom of the oven. Preheat oven to 500°F. Gently turn dough out onto a baking pan that has been lightly oiled and dusted with polenta. Bake loaf at 475°F (240°C) for 10–15 minutes. Reduce heat to 375°F (190°C) and bake for 30 more minutes, or until done.

WITH GREEN OLIVES
Prepare the basic recipe, replacing black olives with green olives.

WITH OREGANO
Prepare the basic recipe, adding 1 tablespoon dried oregano to the dough.

WITH GARLIC
Prepare the basic recipe, adding 2 minced cloves of garlic to the dough.

WITH ROSEMARY
Prepare the basic recipe, adding 2 teaspoons finely chopped fresh rosemary leaves to the dough.

WITH SUN-DRIED TOMATOES
Prepare the basic recipe, adding about 8 chopped sun-dried tomatoes to the dough.

Pesto & Sundried Tomato Loaf

Pesto can be used in so many ways, not least of all in a bread, paired with sundried tomatoes.

Makes 1 loaf

1 tsp. sugar dissolved in
   1⅔ cups (395 ml)
   warm water
4 tsp. active dry yeast
3¼ cups (415 g) white
   bread flour
¾ cup (90 g) whole wheat
   flour

½ tsp. salt
2 tbsp. olive oil
4 tbsp. pesto (see below)
3 tbsp. finely chopped
   sundried tomatoes
   (well drained if in oil)
2 tsp. red pepper flakes

1 Line a large cookie sheet. Dissolve the sugar in the warm water, sprinkle the yeast on top, and leave for 10–15 minutes until frothy. In the bowl of a stand mixer with a dough hook attachment, combine the flours and salt. Make a well in the center, add the yeast liquid and olive oil, and mix until a soft dough forms.

2 Knead for 5–8 minutes until the dough is soft, smooth, and elastic. Transfer to a large, lightly oiled bowl. Cover and put in a warm place for an hour or so, until doubled in size.

3 Turn the dough out onto a lightly floured work surface and roll into 4 balls. Leave to rest for 10 minutes. Roll each ball into a 6-in. (15-cm)-long rope, and place on the cookie sheet. Cut a deep groove into each rope, and spoon a little pesto and some chopped sundried tomatoes along each groove. Bring the dough up over the pesto and tomatoes, sealing the mixture inside. Beginning in the middle, braid the dough toward each end and tuck the ends together, forming a rough circle. Put in a warm place for about 45 minutes, until almost doubled in size.

4 Preheat the oven to 425°F (220°C). Brush with a little olive oil, sprinkle with crushed red pepper flakes, and bake for 10 minutes. Reduce the oven temperature to 325°F (170°C) and bake for 15 minutes or until golden brown. Remove from the oven and cool on a wire rack.

HOMEMADE PESTO
Put 2 oz. (50 g) basil leaves into a food processor and pulse to a pulp. Add 1 small clove of garlic and 2 oz. (50 g) toasted pine nuts, and blend until mixed through. Stir in ½ cup (120 ml) extra virgin olive oil and 1 oz. (25 g) grated Parmesan. This will keep for up to 2 weeks in a sterile jar in the fridge.

WITH BACON
Prepare the basic recipe. Add 4 slices bacon, cooked until crispy and crumbled, to the sundried tomato pieces in the grooves.

PESTO SWIRL LOAF
Prepare the basic recipe. After first rising, turn the dough out onto a lightly floured work surface and divide in half. Punch down and press each half into a rectangle about 8 x 8 in. (20 x 20 cm). Spread pesto on dough and roll up like a jellyroll. Place in two 1-lb. (450 g) loaf pans and set to rise again. Bake in preheated oven at 350°F (180°C) for 30–35 minutes.

WITH PARMESAN
Prepare the basic recipe, adding ⅓ cup (30 g) grated Parmesan cheese to the sundried tomatoes in the grooves.

Sausage, Pepper & Mushroom Pizza

This pizza sauce is so versatile. Use it for all the pizzas in this chapter, as well as serving with pasta or fish. It also freezes well so why not make double the quantity.

Makes 2 medium pizzas

for pizza sauce
1 tbsp. olive oil
1 large onion, finely chopped
2 cloves garlic, crushed
2 x 14-oz. (400 g) cans chopped tomatoes
1 vegetable or chicken stock cube
1 tbsp. Worcestershire sauce
1 tsp. sugar

8 tbsp. tomato paste
1 tsp. dried oregano
8 basil leaves, torn

for the topping
10 tbsp. pizza sauce
12 oz. (350 g) Italian sausage, cooked, crumbled, and drained

4 cups (400 g) sliced mushrooms, lightly sautéed and drained
1 bell pepper, deseeded, sliced thinly
4 cups (450 g) shredded Provolone cheese
2 portions pizza dough (see page 91)
fine cornmeal, for dusting

1 Make the pizza sauce. (This recipe makes more than you need, but it is so versatile, I like to keep some in the refrigerator or freezer.) In a medium saucepan over a medium heat, add the oil, and sauté the onion and garlic for about 5 minutes, until softened. Add chopped tomatoes with juice, stock cube, Worcestershire sauce, sugar, tomato paste, dried herbs, and torn basil leaves, and simmer until thickened. Season to taste with salt and freshly ground black pepper. Set aside to cool, and chill in refrigerator.

2 Heat oven to 450°F (230°C). Divide the pizza dough in half, and roll each piece into a circle about ¼ in. (6 mm) thick. Cut 2 pieces of aluminum foil slightly bigger than the pizza bases, brush them with a little olive oil, dust with fine cornmeal, and place the pizza bases on top.

3 Spread each pizza base evenly with 5 tablespoons pizza sauce and a quarter of the cheese, then sprinkle on half the crumbled sausage, half of the mushrooms and pepper, and the remaining quarter of cheese. Bake directly on the oven rack for 10 minutes, or until the base is crisp and the cheese has melted. Serve immediately.

WITH SLICED TOMATO & FOUR-CHEESE
Prepare the basic crust. Spread each pizza base with 4 tablespoons pizza sauce, and add 1 sliced tomato. Mix together 3 oz. (75 g) shredded mozzarella, 1 oz. (25 g) shredded Monterey Jack, and 1 oz. (25 g) shredded Asiago. Spread over the pizza, sprinkle with ½ oz. (15 g) shredded Pecorino, and drizzle with a little olive oil.

WITH PESTO, TOMATO & GOAT CHEESE
Prepare the basic crust. Spread each pizza base with 4 tablespoons pesto (see page 81), and add 3 sliced tomatoes, 4 oz. (125 g) diced goat cheese, and a drizzle of olive oil. Garnish with fresh basil leaves.

UPSIDE-DOWN PROSCIUTTO & CHEDDAR PIZZA
Prepare the basic crust. Spread each pizza base with 4 oz. (125 g) shredded cheddar cheese, 4 slices prosciutto, 2 tablespoons roasted bell pepper slices, and 2 tablespoons sautéed mushroom slices, and cover with about 8 tablespoons pizza sauce. Bake for an extra 5 minutes, making sure the crust is cooked.

HAM & MOZZARELLA BIANCO PIZZA
Prepare the basic crust. Spread each pizza base with 4 tablespoons béchamel sauce, and top with 4 slices Serrano ham and 4 oz. (125 g) shredded mozzarella.

Gluten-Free Flatbread

Makes 4 flatbreads

1½ cups (130 g) rice flour
¾ cup (85 g) tapioca flour
¼ cup (40 g) potato starch
½ tsp. xanthan gum

½ tsp. baking soda
½ tsp. salt
2 tsp. cumin seeds
¼ cup (50 ml) orange juice

¼ cup (50 ml) extra virgin olive oil + 6 tbsp. for frying
¼ cup (50 ml) rice milk
water as needed

1 In a large bowl, combine all the ingredients. Add 1 tablespoon of water at a time until the dough holds together. Turn dough out onto a floured surface and break into quarters. Mold each quarter into a ball and roll into an oval ½ in. (1.5 cm) thick. The dough will break easily and the edges will be rough, just pinch them a bit with your fingers.

2 In a large skillet, add 6 tablespoons extra virgin olive oil and heat for 5 minutes. When the oil is hot, but not smoking, add two of the flatbreads and fry for 3 minutes each side. Continue with the remaining flatbreads. Serve hot or warm.

WITH PARSLEY, THYME & FENNEL
Prepare the basic recipe, adding 1 tablespoon chopped parsley, 1 teaspoon dried thyme, and 1 teaspoon fennel seeds to the flour.

WITH ROSEMARY
Prepare the basic recipe, adding 1 tablespoon chopped fresh rosemary leaves to the flour.

WITH HUMMUS
Prepare the basic recipe and serve with a hummus dip. In a food processor, blend together one 14-oz. (400-g) can garbanzo beans, rinsed and drained, with olive oil and lemon juice to taste, and a little water if necessary. Add 2 finely chopped green onions, 2 skinned, deseeded, and chopped tomatoes, and ½ teaspoon paprika. Serve with flatbread.

Flatbread with Rosemary & Garlic Oil

Makes 8 flatbreads

1 portion pizza dough (see page 91)
extra virgin olive oil for brushing

a few rosemary sprigs, leaves only
coarse sea salt

1 Prepare the basic pizza dough recipe. Punch down and divide into 8 pieces. Roll each piece into an oval shape about 4 inch thick.

2 Heat a large skillet over a medium-high heat, brush with olive oil, and cook each flatbread for 3–4 minutes each side, until golden brown and slightly charred. Mix olive oil and rosemary leaves and brush over the flatbreads, sprinkle with salt, and serve immediately.

WITH SPICY CHILI PASTE
Prepare the basic recipe. Instead of olive oil and rosemary, spread on 1 teaspoon of chili paste as you take the flatbread out of the skillet. With a pestle and mortar, mix together 2 chopped cloves garlic, 1 large deseeded and chopped green chili, 2 teaspoons each of sesame seeds and ground coriander, and 2 tablespoons each of olive oil and freshly chopped cilantro.

WITH SESAME
Prepare the basic recipe, adding 2 tablespoons sesame seeds to the flour.

WITH RED ONION & TOMATO
Prepare the basic recipe, omitting the olive oil and rosemary. Fry 2 thinly sliced red onions in 1 tablespoon olive oil until softened. Add half to the flour in the bowl. Finely chop the leaves from 5–6 rosemary sprigs and add to onions. Add to the top of the flatbread with 6 oz. (175 g) cherry tomatoes as they come out of the skillet.

Bread with Polenta Flour

Adding polenta to bread dough gives the bread a slightly grainier texture, a lovely golden yellow appearance, and the bread will also last longer.

Makes 2 medium-sized loaves

2½ oz. (60 g) fresh yeast
1 cup (250 ml) warm
    water
pinch granulated sugar

2¼ cups (225 g) all-
    purpose flour
1¼ cups (210 g) polenta
sea salt
2–3 tsp. olive oil

1   Mix yeast and water together, then add sugar and about 2 tablespoons of the all-purpose flour. Place the yeast mixture in a warm place for about 30 minutes to activate. Pour polenta and remaining flour onto a work surface. When the yeast mixture is fizzing gently and has formed something of a head, like on a glass of beer, knead it energetically into the polenta and flour on the working surface. Add more water as required to make a very soft dough. Add salt and oil and knead hard for about 10 minutes.

2   Transfer the very soft, elastic, slightly shiny dough to a large floured bowl, cover with plastic wrap (oil the underside of the plastic lightly to prevent it sticking to the rising dough), and return it to warm place to rise again for about 2 hours or until doubled.

3   Preheat oven to 375°F (190°C). Pull dough into two sections with well-oiled hands. Shape into rough rounds or whatever shape you like—long and narrow, braided, or oval. Stroke surface gently with a handful of olive oil and water mixed together. Bake on oiled and polenta-scattered baking sheets for about 15 minutes, or a little more or less time based on the size of the loaf.

4   Tap the bottom of the bread and listen for a hollow ring to let you know it is cooked through. Cool on a wire rack to allow the steam to escape.

WITH RAISINS
Prepare basic recipe, kneading a handful of golden raisins (soaked in hot water for 20 minutes to allow them to swell, then drained) into the dough with the salt and oil.

WITH PINE NUTS
Prepare basic recipe, kneading a handful of pine nuts into the dough with the salt and oil.

WITH RICOTTA
Prepare basic recipe. When the dough has risen, spread it out flat and cover with a thin layer of fresh ricotta. Sprinkle with salt and pepper, fold in half, and let rise for about 30 minutes before stroking the surface with oil and water and baking.

WITH ROSEMARY & SAGE
Prepare basic recipe, kneading a generous handful of chopped fresh rosemary and sage into the dough with the salt and oil.

WITH SUN-DRIED TOMATO
Prepare basic recipe, kneading 2 handfuls of coarsely chopped sun-dried tomatoes into the dough with the salt and oil.

Parmesan & Garlic Breadsticks

Large, soft, chewy, and flavored with Parmesan and garlic, this is the best recipe for breadsticks ever and one you'll come back to time and time again.

Makes 12 breadsticks

1 tsp. + 1½ tbsp. sugar, divided
1½ cups (355 ml) warm water
2 tsp. active dry yeast
3½ cups (450 g) white bread flour

1 tsp. salt
2 tbsp. olive oil
½ cup (100 g) butter
1 tbsp. garlic salt, divided

⅓ cup (40 g) finely shredded Parmesan cheese, divided
1 tbsp. freshly chopped parsley, divided

1. Dissolve 1 teaspoon sugar in the warm water, sprinkle the yeast on top, and leave for 10–15 minutes until frothy. In the bowl of a stand mixer with a dough hook attachment, combine the flour, 1½ tablespoons sugar, and salt. Make a well in the center, pour in the yeast liquid, and add the olive oil. Mix until a soft dough forms. Knead for 5 minutes. Transfer to a large lightly oiled bowl and turn to coat it all over. Cover and put in a warm place for an hour or so, until doubled in size.

2. Preheat the oven to 400°F (200°C). In a small pan over a gentle heat, melt the butter and pour it onto a large jellyroll pan. Sprinkle the butter with garlic salt and Parmesan cheese.

3. Turn the dough out onto a lightly floured work surface, punch down, and knead for 1–2 minutes. Roll the dough out to a rectangle 12 x 16 in. (30 x 40 cm), and cut into 12 x 1-in. (2.5-cm) strips. Double the long strips of dough in half, and twist to form breadsticks. Roll each breadstick in the butter in the pan until completely covered. When all the breadsticks are arranged in the pan, sprinkle the tops with a little more garlic salt, Parmesan cheese, and parsley.

4. Bake for 12–15 minutes, until golden brown. Cool on a wire rack, and serve warm.

CRISPY BREADSTICKS
Prepare the basic recipe. Cut the dough into ½-in. (1.5-cm) strips instead of 1-in. (2.5 cm) strips. Bake for 40 minutes at 300°F (150°C), until they are crispy.

WITH BACON
Prepare the basic recipe. Cut 6 slices of bacon in half, so that they are about 5 in. (12.5 cm) long. Wrap 1 slice around each breadstick and bake on parchment-paper-lined cookie sheets at 350°F (180°C), until the bacon has browned. Roll in Parmesan cheese mixed with garlic pepper seasoning.

WITH PIZZA SEASONING
Prepare the basic recipe. Sprinkle the tops with pizza seasoning. Mix together 2 tablespoons oregano, 1 teaspoon dried basil, 1 teaspoon lemon pepper, and ½ teaspoon each of dried thyme, salt, fennel, onion powder, and paprika.

WITH JALAPEÑO
Prepare the basic recipe. Just before sprinkling with garlic salt, lay slices of jalapeño across the breadsticks, either fresh or from a jar.

Sundried Tomato & Olive Sticks

This dough is quite wet, so do not be tempted to add more flour during mixing.

Makes 16 breadsticks

4 cups (510 g) white bread flour	oil + extra for greasing
1 tsp. dried rosemary	4 oz. (125 g) pitted and chopped black olives
2 tsp. salt	
2 tsp. instant dry yeast	4 oz. (125 g) chopped sundried tomatoes (well drained if in oil)
1⅔ cups (395 ml) warm water	
3 tbsp. extra virgin olive	fine cornmeal, to dust

1   Grease a large, deep rectangular baking dish with a little oil, and line 2 or 3 large cookie sheets with parchment paper. In the bowl of a stand mixer fitted with a dough hook attachment, combine the flour and dried rosemary. Add the salt, yeast and water, and mix on a slow speed until the dough starts to come together. Knead at a slow speed for 5–8 minutes, until smooth and elastic.

2   Add the olive oil and continue to knead for another 2 minutes. Add the olives and sundried tomatoes, and mix until just combined. Transfer to the baking dish, cover, and put in a warm place for an hour or so, until doubled in size.

3   Sprinkle your work surface with fine cornmeal and turn the dough out. Try not to knock out the air; it will still be quite wet. Dust the top of the dough with flour and fine cornmeal. Pull the dough out gently to a rough rectangle, and starting at one of the long sides, cut the dough into about 16 strips. Stretch each piece until it measures about 9 in. (23 cm) in length.

4   Arrange on the cookie sheets about 1 in. (2.5 cm) apart. Put each cookie sheet inside a greased plastic bag, and put in a warm place for 30 minutes. Preheat the oven to 425°F (220°C). Remove the plastic bags and bake for 10–12 minutes. Cool on a wire rack.

WITH DATE & BLUE CHEESE
Prepare the basic recipe, replacing the olives with ⅓ cup (30 g) finely chopped dried dates. Add 2 oz. (50 g) crumbled blue cheese to the bowl with the flour.

WITH CURRY SEASONING
Prepare the basic recipe, omitting the olives. Add 2 teaspoons hot curry powder to the bowl with the flour.

WITH FAJITA SEASONING
Prepare the basic recipe, omitting the olives. Add 1 tablespoon fajita seasoning to the bowl with the flour, and sprinkle on more just before baking.

WITH POPPY & PUMPKIN SEEDS
Prepare the basic recipe, omitting the sundried tomatoes and olives. Add ¼ cup (30 g) poppy seeds and ½ cup (60 g) pumpkin seeds to the bowl with the flour. Just before baking, gently brush each breadstick with a little butter and sprinkle generously with more poppy seeds.

Pizzette

Literally translating from the Italian as "mini pizzas," these are smaller than a regular pizza and are often served as a canapé. They're also perfect for children's parties.

Makes about 15 very small pizzas

1 oz. (25 g) fresh yeast
scant 1 cup (250 ml) warm water
pinch sugar
3 cups (350 g) white bread flour, plus extra as required
¼ tsp. sea salt
2 tbsp. olive oil, plus extra to grease

coarse semolina, for dusting
1½ cups (400 g) tomato sauce or puréed canned tomatoes
8 oz. (225 g) mozzarella, chopped finely
bunch of fresh basil leaves
extra olive oil, for drizzling

1 Mix yeast and water with sugar, then add about 2 tablespoons flour. Put yeast mixture in lightly floured bowl and place it somewhere warm to rise for about 30 minutes. Put rest of flour on the counter and add salt. Knead yeast mixture thoroughly, then knead it into rest of flour, adding more water as required. Add the olive oil and knead energetically for about 10 minutes. Transfer mixture to large floured bowl and return to warm place to rise again for about 1 hour or until doubled.

2 Preheat oven to 400°F (200°C). Take little pieces of the dough (half a palm size) in your hands and flatten onto an oiled cookie sheet, sprinkled lightly with coarse semolina. When spreading out dough, dip your fingers in cold water to bring as much moisture as possible into the dough as it bakes and to help flatten it.

3 Top each little base with a little tomato sauce, some chopped mozzarella, and a basil leaf; drizzle with a tiny amount of olive oil; and bake for about 5 minutes or until crisp around the edges. Serve warm.

WITH MUSHROOMS
Prepare the basic recipe, replacing the fresh basil with 2 or 3 thin slices of cooked mushrooms per base.

WITH OLIVES
Prepare the basic recipe, replacing the fresh basil with half a green or black olive and a sprinkling of a little dried oregano.

WITH SALAMI
Prepare the basic recipe, adding a thin slice of salami to the topping on each base.

WITH ANCHOVIES
Prepare the basic recipe, omitting the fresh basil and adding 1 caper, a very small piece of anchovy fillet, and a sprinkling of dried oregano to the topping ingredients.

WITH MARINARA SAUCE
Prepare the basic recipe, replacing the fresh basil leaf and the mozzarella with a little finely chopped garlic and a sprinkling of dried oregano on each pizza base.

Calzone

A calzone, meaning a "pair of trousers," is made of pizza dough with a variety of fillings inside, folded in half and sealed before baking. Sometimes, the filled and folded calzone are deep-fried instead of baked. This recipe starts with half the quantity of pizza dough from the recipe on page 91, and is easily expanded to serve more people. If you want to make 2 large calzoni, simply double the quantity of basic dough.

Makes 1

½ portion pizza dough
  (see page 91)
2 tbsp. fresh ricotta
3 slices salami, chopped
  coarsely
2 sun-dried tomatoes in
  olive oil, drained and
  chopped

1 tsp. chopped fresh flat-
  leaf parsley
extra-virgin olive oil for
  greasing and brushing
sea salt and freshly
  ground black pepper

1 Preheat the oven to 400°F (200°C). Place the circle of pizza dough on an oiled baking sheet. Spread ricotta onto half the circle, keeping to the center so you can fold it in half and seal it easily.

2 Sprinkle salami, sun-dried tomato, and parsley on top of the ricotta. Drizzle with a little olive oil and season lightly with salt and pepper.

3 Fold the calzone in half and seal the edge well with the back of a fork. Bake for about 15 minutes, then serve with a bowl of tomato sauce on the side.

WITH RAGÚ
Instead of salami filling, use a ragú sauce with a few slices of mozzarella and a little freshly grated Parmesan.

WITH GRILLED VEGETABLES
Instead of salami filling, use cooked vegetables such as zucchini, eggplant, peppers, and tomatoes with a few cubes of mozzarella.

WITH MOZZARELLA
Instead of salami filling, fill the calzone with cubes of buffalo mozzarella, a drizzle of olive oil, a sprinkling of dried oregano, and salt and pepper.

WITH PROSCIUTTO & PEAS
Instead of salami filling, fill the calzone with peas cooked in olive oil, chopped onions, and cubes of ham.

WITH ITALIAN SAUSAGE
Instead of salami filling, fill the calzone with chopped mortadella, ricotta, salt, pepper, and a sprinkling of chopped fresh flat-leaf parsley.

Marinara Pizza

This is the recipe for one of the first pizzas, long before the introduction of the myriad of other ingredients that are now common on pizzas the world over. Interestingly, it does not include mozzarella. Though its name translates as "sailor's pizza," it does not contain any seafood — it was made in Naples for sailors when they returned from the sea.

Makes 2 medium pizzas

for the pizza dough
1¼ oz. (30 g) fresh yeast
1 scant cup (250 ml) warm water
pinch sugar
¼ tsp. sea salt
4 cups (400 g) white bread flour
2–3 tsp. olive oil

for the topping
¾ cup (12 tbsp) canned tomatoes, puréed
4 cloves garlic, finely chopped
1 heaped tsp. dried oregano
12 tbsp. olive oil
about 16 leaves fresh basil
salt and freshly ground black pepper
extra olive oil for greasing

1 Mix the yeast, water, sugar and salt, then add 2 tablespoons flour. Put the yeast mixture in a lightly floured bowl and leave in a warm place to rise for 30 minutes. Put the rest of the flour on a work surface. Knead the yeast mixture thoroughly, then knead it into the rest of the flour, adding a little more water as required. Add half the oil and knead for 10 minutes.

2 Transfer the mixture to a floured bowl, cover with oiled plastic wrap, and return to the warm place for about 1 hour or until doubled in size.

3 Preheat the oven to 425°F (220°F). Divide the pizza dough in half, roll each piece into a circle about ¼ in. (6 mm) thick and arrange on oiled baking sheets. Cover thinly with puréed canned tomatoes, sprinkle with garlic, oregano, the remaining olive oil, basil, and a little salt and pepper. Bake until the border is crisp and the pizza dough is dry on the bottom. Serve warm.

PIZZA MARGHERITA
Omit garlic and oregano and add mozzarella slices.

WITH MUSHROOM
Prepare basic recipe, omitting garlic, oregano, and basil, and adding some cooked mushrooms and sliced mozzarella.

WITH ARUGULA
Omit garlic and oregano and add mozzarella slices. When the pizza is cooked, add 2 handfuls of fresh arugula leaves before serving.

WITH PARMA HAM
Prepare basic recipe, omitting garlic and oregano and adding mozzarella slices. Bake the pizza for half the required time. Remove from the oven, lay 4 paper-thin slices of Parma ham over the pizza, drizzle again with olive oil, and return to the oven to finish baking.

WITH SALAMI
Prepare basic recipe, omitting garlic and basil and adding mozzarella slices, then slices of your favorite salami.

Gluten-Free Spinach, Basil & Mozzarella Pizza

This gluten-free base can be used for any of the pizzas in this chapter. Simply switch out the regular dough for the crust recipe below.

Makes 2 large pizzas

for the crust
2 cups (175 g) rice flour
1 cup (115 g) tapioca flour
½ cup (85 g) potato starch
2 tsp. xanthan gum
1 tsp. sugar
1 tsp. agar or unflavored gelatin powder
1 tsp. sugar

1 tsp. salt
2 tsp. instant dry yeast
1½ cups (355 ml) warm water
1 tbsp. extra virgin olive oil
1½ tsp. rice wine vinegar

for the topping
2 cups (60 g) fresh baby spinach leaves
salt and freshly ground black pepper to taste
8 tbsp. pizza sauce, divided (see page 83)
2 cups (240 g) mozzarella cheese
1 cup (30 g) fresh basil leaves
2 tbsp. fine cornmeal

1 Line 2 large cookie sheets with parchment paper and sprinkle with cornmeal. In the bowl of a stand mixer with a dough hook attachment, mix all the dry ingredients for the crust together. Make a well in the center, and add the warm water, olive oil, and rice vinegar. Mix until a dough forms. Knead on a low speed for 5 minutes, and turn out onto a work surface dusted with fine cornmeal.

2 Divide the dough in half. Sprinkle cornmeal over half of the dough, and roll it out to about a 12-in. (30-cm) circle. Transfer to a cookie sheet, dust with cornmeal, cover with plastic wrap, and put in a warm place for 1 hour. Repeat this process with the other half.

3 Preheat the oven to 400°F (200°C). Bake the pizza crusts for 5 minutes. In a large skillet, heat 2 teaspoons olive oil, and fry the spinach in batches for a few seconds until just wilted. Remove from the heat and season with a little salt and freshly ground black pepper. Spread 4 tablespoons pizza sauce on each pizza crust. Break off pieces of mozzarella and lay them on the pizzas. Scatter with the wilted spinach leaves and the basil leaves, and bake for 10–12 minutes. Serve immediately.

WITH ZUCCHINI, CHERRY TOMATO & BRIE
Prepare the basic crust. Spread each pizza base with 4 tablespoons pizza sauce, 6 thin slices zucchini, 6 cherry tomatoes, and 3 oz. (75 g) Brie, sliced. Garnish with 6 basil leaves.

WITH KING PRAWNS
Prepare the basic crust. Spread each pizza with ½ cup (60 g) king prawns, 1 cup (30 g) wilted spinach leaves, and 3 oz. (75 g) mozzarella, sliced.

MEAT FEAST PIZZA
Prepare the basic crust. Spread each pizza base with 4 tablespoons pizza sauce, and add 3 oz. (75 g) Cajun-seasoned cooked chicken, 6 slices pepperoni, and 3 slices bacon, cooked until crispy. Top with a deseeded and finely chopped red chili and 3 oz. (75 g) mixed shredded mozzarella and cheddar cheese.

DAIRY- & GLUTEN-FREE MARGHERITA PIZZA
Prepare the basic crust. Spread each pizza base with 4 tablespoons pizza sauce, and add ½ cup (60 g) caramelized red onion slices, a few halved cherry tomatoes, and 2 tablespoons freshly chopped basil to each one.

Salami, Tomato & Basil Pizza

Making your own pizza is not only easy, but fun, healthy, and cheap!

Makes 2 large pizzas

1 tsp. sugar dissolved in 1½ cups (355 ml) warm water
2 tsp. active dry yeast
4 cups (510 g) white bread flour
2 tsp. salt
10 tbsp. pizza sauce (see page 83)

20 fresh basil leaves
8 slices salami
2 cups mozzarella cheese, sliced
olive oil for greasing and drizzling
fine cornmeal

1   Add the yeast to the sugar–water mix, and leave for 10–15 minutes until frothy. Mix the flour and salt together. Make a well in the center, pour in the yeast liquid, and mix together until a soft dough forms. Turn the dough out onto a floured work surface and knead for 10 minutes until smooth and elastic.

2   Dust the top of the dough with flour, cover with plastic wrap, and leave to rest for 15–20 minutes at room temperature. This makes it easier to roll the dough. Divide the dough in half.

3   Preheat the oven to 500°F (260°F), and put a large roasting pan or pizza stone on the middle rack. Dust your work surface with a little fine cornmeal, take each piece of dough, and roll out to circles about ¼ in. (6 mm) thick. Cut 2 pieces of aluminum foil slightly bigger than the pizza bases, brush them with a little olive oil, dust with fine cornmeal, and place the pizza bases on top.

4   Spread each base evenly with 5 tablespoons pizza sauce, add the basil leaves, lay the salami on top, and place small slices of mozzarella in the gaps. Bake 1 at a time in the middle of a very hot oven for 8–10 minutes only, until golden and crisp. Serve immediately.

PUTTANESCA PIZZA
Prepare the basic crust. Spread each pizza base with 4 tablespoons pizza sauce, and add 1 chopped clove of garlic, 6 anchovies, 1 tablespoon capers, ¼ cup (30 g) olives, 4 oz. (125 g) shredded mozzarella, and 1 tablespoon chopped parsley.

WITH BACON & BLACK OLIVES
Prepare the basic crust. Spread each pizza base with 4 tablespoons pizza sauce, and add 6 slices bacon, cooked until crispy and then broken, 4 oz. (125 g) sliced mozzarella, and a few pitted black olives.

WITH CHERRY TOMATOES & CHEDDAR
Prepare the basic crust. Spread each pizza base with 4 tablespoons pizza sauce, and add 4 oz. (125 g) shredded cheddar cheese and a few cherry tomatoes.

WITH RED ONION, ZUCCHINI & ROSEMARY
Prepare the basic crust. Spread each pizza base with 4 tablespoons pizza sauce, add 3 tablespoons sautéed red onion slices, 6 slices zucchini, 2 teaspoons chopped rosemary. Add 3 oz. (75 g) shredded cheddar cheese.

Olive & Red Bell Pepper Loaf

A wonderful aroma will fill your kitchen while this bread is baking, and you will think of summer and the warm blue Mediterranean.

Makes 1 loaf

1 tbsp. fine cornmeal
3½ cups (450 g) white
    bread flour
2 tsp. active dry yeast
1 tsp. sugar
1 tsp. salt
1¼ cups (300 ml) warm
    water

3 tbsp. olive oil + extra
    for greasing
½ cup (85 g) chopped
    pitted black olives
¼ cup (60 g) chopped red
    bell peppers
¼ cup (15 g) freshly
    chopped basil leaves

1 Line a large cookie sheet with parchment paper and sprinkle it with 1 tablespoon fine cornmeal. In a large bowl, mix the flour, yeast, sugar, and salt together, adding the yeast on one side and the salt on the other. Make a well in the center and add the warm water and olive oil. Mix together to form a soft dough.

2 Turn out onto a lightly floured work surface and knead for 10 minutes until soft, smooth, and elastic. Put the dough in a large lightly oiled bowl and turn to coat it all over. Cover and put in a warm place until doubled in size, about an hour.

3 Turn out onto a lightly floured work surface and punch down. Add the olives, bell peppers, and basil, and knead again until they are evenly distributed through the dough. Mold into a ball, press down firmly, and sprinkle the top with white flour. Mark a deep cross in the top. Place on the lined cookie sheet, cover, and leave for an hour in a warm place, until almost doubled in size.

4 Preheat the oven to 425°F (220°C). Remove the cover and bake for 30 minutes, until golden brown and the bottom of the loaf sounds hollow when tapped. Cool on a wire rack.

WITH ZUCCHINI
Prepare the basic recipe, adding ½ a zucchini, chopped and sautéed in a little olive oil and cooled, with the olives.

WITH EGGPLANT
Prepare the basic recipe, adding ½ small eggplant, chopped, oven-roasted, and cooled, with the olives.

WITH BACON
Prepare the basic recipe, adding ¼ cup (40 g) chopped sundried tomatoes and 4 slices bacon, cooked until crispy and crumbled, with the olives.

WITH CHEESE & SUNDRIED TOMATO
Prepare the basic recipe, adding ½ cup (60 g) shredded cheddar cheese and ¼ cup (40 g) chopped sundried tomatoes with the olives.

Polenta Pan Pizza with Roasted Vegetables

Here instant polenta is cooked in a large skillet and covered with delicious oven-roasted Mediterranean vegetables.

Makes 1 medium pizza

4 ripe tomatoes
1 large eggplant, cut into large chunks
2 red bell peppers, deseeded and cut into chunks
1 red onion, cut into wedges
2 cloves garlic, finely chopped
2 tbsp. fresh rosemary leaves
salt and freshly ground black pepper to taste
3 tbsp. extra virgin olive oil
8 oz. (225 g) quick-cooking polenta
3 tbsp. freshly shredded Parmesan cheese

1 Preheat the oven to 450°F (230°C). Put the vegetables in a large roasting pan, sprinkle the garlic and rosemary leaves on top, and season with salt and freshly ground black pepper. Drizzle with olive oil, toss together, and roast for 40 minutes.

2 While the vegetables are roasting, cook the polenta according to the package instructions. Pour it into a medium-size skillet and leave to set for about 10 minutes.

3 Sprinkle with Parmesan cheese and place under the broiler for 3–4 minutes, until golden and bubbling. Top with the roasted vegetables and serve immediately.

WITH SAUSAGE, MUSHROOM & BACON
Prepare the basic recipe. Top with 4 oz. (125 g) cooked and crumbled Italian sausage, 3 oz. (75 g) sautéed mushrooms, and 3 slices bacon, cooked until crispy and halved. Put back under the broiler for 3–4 minutes and garnish with 6 basil leaves.

WITH SPINACH, GOAT CHEESE & CHERRY TOMATO
Prepare the basic recipe. Spread the crust with 2 tablespoons pizza sauce (see page 83), 1 cup (30 g) fresh spinach leaves, 3 oz. (75 g) goat cheese, sliced, and 6 cherry tomatoes. Put back under the broiler for 3-4 minutes and garnish with 6 basil leaves.

WITH MOZZARELLA, ANCHOVIES, CAPER & PARSLEY
Prepare the basic recipe. Spread the crust with 2 tablespoons pizza sauce (see page 83) 6 anchovies, 1 deseeded and chopped red chili, 1 tablespoon drained capers, and 4 oz. (125 g) shredded mozzarella. Place back under the broiler for 3–4 minutes, and garnish with 2 tablespoons freshly chopped parsley.

Yeast-Free Seafood Chili Pizza

This pizza is loaded with seafood and mozzarella, and with garlic and tomatoes, it is a pizza fit for a king. Swap the crabmeat for calamari, if you prefer.

Makes 1 medium pizza

for the topping
4 cloves garlic, minced
2 tbsp. extra virgin olive oil
1 cup canned crabmeat
1½ cups (175 g) peeled, cooked shrimp
1 tbsp. fresh parsley, chopped
5 tbsp. pizza sauce (see page 83)
1½ cups (175 g) shredded mozzarella cheese, divided

¼ cup (30 g) shredded Romano cheese
1 small red chili, deseeded and finely chopped

for the crust
1½ cups (190 g) all-purpose flour
1 tbsp. baking powder
½ tsp. salt
1 tsp. Italian mixed herbs
½ cup (120 ml) water
2 tbsp. extra virgin olive oil

1 In a large skillet over a medium-low heat, sauté the garlic in the olive oil for 5 minutes, remove from the heat, and set aside to cool. Transfer to a medium bowl and add the crabmeat, shrimp, and parsley, mixing well with the olive oil and garlic. Set aside.

2 Preheat the oven to 400°F (200°C). To make the crust, sift the flour, baking powder, and salt together. Stir in the herbs. Make a well in the center, and add the water and 2 tablespoons olive oil. Mix together by gradually incorporating the flour into the liquid, until a dough comes together. Turn out onto a lightly floured work surface and knead gently for 5 minutes, until the dough is smooth and elastic.

3 Roll out into a circle about 10 in. (25 cm) in diameter. Transfer to the cookie sheet. Spread the pizza crust with the pizza sauce, add the crabmeat and shrimp mixture, sprinkle with chili, and top with the cheeses. Bake for 15–20 minutes, until the crust is golden brown, and the cheese has melted. Serve immediately.

WITH ITALIAN SAUSAGE, MUSHROOM & BASIL
Prepare the basic crust. Spread with 4 tablespoons pizza sauce, add 4 oz. (125 g) shredded cheddar cheese, 4 oz. (125 g) cooked and crumbled Italian sausage, and 2 tablespoons sautéed mushroom slices. Garnish with fresh basil.

WITH HAM & PINEAPPLE
Prepare the basic crust. Spread with 4 tablespoons pizza sauce, and add 4 oz. (125 g) shredded cheddar cheese, 4 oz. (125 g) thinly sliced ham, and ½ cup (60 g) chopped pineapple.

WITH ONION, PEPPERONI, MUSHROOM & PEPPER
Prepare the basic crust. Spread with 4 tablespoons pizza sauce, and add 2 oz. (50 g) shredded cheddar cheese, 3 tablespoons sautéed onion slices, 10 slices pepperoni, 2 tablespoons sautéed mushroom slices, and 2 tablespoons roasted bell pepper slices. Top with 3 oz. (75 g) shredded mozzarella.

WITH SLICED TOMATO & OLIVE
Prepare the basic crust. Spread each pizza base with 3 sliced tomatoes, scatter over a handful of pitted black olives, and top with 4 oz. (125 g) mozzarella, sliced.

Express Stuffed-Crust Pepperoni Pizza

This is a quick pizza dough to mix together and, if available, string cheese is the secret to the stuffed crust. Children especially will love extra pizza sauce for dipping.

Makes 1 large pizza

2 cups (255 g) white bread flour
1 tsp. sugar
1 tsp. instant dry yeast
1 tsp. salt
¾ cup (180 ml) warm water
1 tsp. olive oil

7 mozzarella cheese sticks or 1½ cups
   (175 g) finely shredded mozzarella
8 tbsp. pizza sauce (see page 83)
1 cup (120 g) shredded cheddar cheese
½ cup (60 g) sliced mushrooms, lightly
   sautéed, drained

24 slices pepperoni
1 cup (120 g) shredded mozzarella cheese
2 tbsp. cornmeal for sprinkling

1 Sprinkle a large pizza stone or cookie sheet with fine cornmeal. In the bowl of a stand mixer fitted with a dough hook, add the flour, sugar, yeast and salt. Make a well in the center and add the warm water and olive oil. Mix until a dough begins to form. Knead on a slow speed for 5 minutes.

2 Roll out the pizza dough to a circle about 14 in. (35 cm) in diameter and transfer it to the cookie sheet. Sprinkle with fine cornmeal and cover with plastic wrap. Leave at room temperature for 30 minutes.

3 Preheat the oven to 450°F (230°C). Cut the mozzarella sticks into 1-in. (2.5-cm) lengths, and arrange around the outside of the pizza crust, about 1 in. (2.5 cm) from the edge. Or place the shredded mozzarella around the outside. Bring the edge of the dough up and over the cheese to form the stuffed rim, and pinch it to seal it well.

4 Spread the pizza crust with pizza sauce, cheddar cheese, mushrooms, pepperoni, and mozzarella cheese. Bake in the oven for 15–20 minutes, until the crust is golden brown and the cheese has melted. Serve immediately.

WITH HOT DOGS
Prepare the basic crust. Spread each pizza base with 4 tablespoons pizza sauce, and add 2 oz. (50 g) shredded cheddar cheese, 3 tablespoons sautéed mushroom slices, 4 mini hot dogs, halved, and another 2 oz. (50 g) shredded cheddar cheese.

WITH CAJUN CHICKEN & CHILI
Prepare the basic crust. Spread each pizza base with 4 tablespoons pizza sauce, and add 4 oz. (125 g) Cajun-seasoned cooked chicken, 4 oz. (125 g) shredded mozzarella, and a sprinkling of crushed red pepper flakes.

WITH PARMA HAM & TOMATO
Prepare the basic crust. Spread each pizza base with 4 tablespoons pizza sauce, add 4 slices Parma ham and 2 sliced tomatoes, and cover with 3 oz. (75 g) shredded cheddar cheese.

WITH MEXICAN BEAN & MONTEREY JACK
Prepare the basic crust. Mix 5 tablespoons pizza sauce with 4 oz. (125 g) canned red kidney beans, drained, and 1 crushed clove garlic, ½ teaspoon chili powder, and 2 tablespoons chopped cilantro. Spread it over 1 pizza base, cover with 3 oz. (75 g) shredded Monterey Jack cheese, and garnish with fresh arugula.

CHAPTER 4

Vegetables
& Vegetarian

The fresh, seasonal Mediterranean way of eating naturally lends itself to cooking with vegetables. Here you will find dishes perfect for vegetarians and carnivores trying to cut down their meat consumption. Swapping out meat and fish for plant-based ingredients is also an easy way to increase your vitamin intake.

INGREDIENTS

Cooking vegetable-based Mediterranean food doesn't usually require specialist ingredients and you may find that many of the recipes here call for items you already have in your refrigerator, freezer or store cupboard. Many of the recipes can be adapted to suit those following a vegan diet by substituting ingredients.

Vegetables

Choose the best-looking, freshest produce, which generally means buying seasonal foods. Frozen vegetables can be used as substitute for fresh when the vegetable is out of season. Vegetables used in these recipes are of average size, unless stated otherwise. It is also assumed that they are cleaned and peeled, when necessary.

Grains

Grains are carbohydrates that help to fuel the body. Whole grains release energy slowly, keeping you sustained and energized all day. Whole grains can also be an important source of fiber, and protein—which is particularly relevant to vegetarians and vegans—as well as immune system-boosting antioxidants. Other nutritional components of whole grains are calcium, iron, magnesium, phosphorus, potassium, sodium, zinc, copper, manganese, selenium, and vitamins, which are present in varying amounts in different grains.

If you follow a gluten-free diet it's important to remember that grains such as barley, faro, bulgur wheat, freekeh, kamut, rye, wheat berries, oats, and spelt contain gluten. Gluten-free grains include corn, amaranth, quinoa, teff, rice, millet, buckwheat, and sorghum.

Legumes

Legumes, such as lentils, peas, and beans are a good source of low-fat protein and fiber. The protein is particularly important for people who do not obtain any protein from meat, fish, or dairy sources. Lentils contain about twice as much iron as beans and are also higher in most B vitamins and folate. However, beans contain iron, protein, fiber, and nutrients including potassium, zinc, and many B vitamins, as well as some calcium. Remember to rinse canned beans well before using them as they can be salty.

Nuts

A useful source of protein, different nuts also provide you with different nutrients. Walnuts, peanuts, almonds, cashew nuts, pecans, macadamias, and Brazil nuts are rich in zinc, vitamin E, and omega-3 fatty acids. Almonds contain a reasonable amount of calcium and about four times as much fiber as cashew nuts. Cashew nuts, however, contain about twice as much iron and zinc as almost any other nut. Add nutty goodness to your diet by sprinkling chopped nuts onto salads, or snacking on a bag of mixed nuts.

Eggs

Large eggs should be used unless stated otherwise. It is best to buy free-range eggs, preferably organic. For frying or poaching, indulge in one that tastes good. Make sure your eggs are fresh: they have a thicker white near the yolk that will better hold a round shape as it cooks. Generally speaking, eggs cook better from a cool room temperature rather than refrigerated. Runny eggs are not recommended for people who are immune-suppressed.

Cheese

Traditionally, most cheeses contained animal rennet (an enzyme that helps milk to separate into curds and whey). Today a wide number are made with vegetarians in mind, so always check the label. Cheeses such as Parmesan are strictly controlled and can only be made in a limited geographical location using traditional techniques, so are not suitable for vegetarians. However, substitutes are available, usually called "Italian hard cheese" or "Parmesan-style cheese." The quality of vegan cheeses varies, so try them to find the ones that taste best.

Oils

Olive oil is central to the Mediterranean diet, both for cooking and for dipping and drizzling. A reasonable quality olive oil is the oil of preference for shallow frying, although sunflower or rapeseed oil can be substituted if that is what you usually use. Only splash out on expensive extra-virgin olive oils where it is exposed, such as in salads—then it is worth buying the best you can afford. Butter is used where its flavor is central to the dish.

Easter Pie

This pie is traditionally served on Easter Monday in various parts of Italy, especially in regions such as Liguria and Le Marche, as well as in parts of the south.

Serves 6

2¾ cups (275 g) all-purpose flour, plus extra for dusting
pinch of sea salt
generous ½ cup (125 ml) warm water
4 tbsp. extra-virgin olive oil
1 large onion, chopped
6 artichokes preserved in oil

14 oz. (400 g) fresh spinach leaves, washed
large handful of fresh flat-leaf parsley, chopped
1 lb. (450 g) ricotta
2½ oz. (60 g) Parmesan, freshly grated
6 eggs
freshly ground black pepper

1   To make the pastry, mix the flour and salt in a bowl. Add the water and half the oil and mix to a smooth dough. Knead for 5 minutes on a floured surface, until soft and stretchy. Cover with plastic wrap and set aside for 15 minutes.

2   To make the filling, heat the remaining oil in a large pan over medium heat. Fry the onion for 8 minutes, stirring occasionally. Stir in the artichokes and toss for a few minutes. Pile spinach on top, cover the pan, and wilt over a gentle heat. Set aside to cool slightly. Put the filling mixture in a food processor with the parsley, cheeses, and 3 eggs. Season well with salt and pepper, pulse, and set aside.

3   Preheat the oven to 425°F (220°C). Roll out two-thirds of the pastry on a floured surface to a large circle. Use to line base and sides of a deep, 11-in. (28-cm), loose-bottomed cake pan. Spoon in the filling. Smooth, make 2 deep indents, and crack in 2 eggs. Roll out remaining pastry to a circle and lay on top. Twist edges to seal. Beat remaining egg, brush over pastry, and sprinkle with sea salt. Bake for 30–35 minutes, until golden. Slice and serve.

WITH POTATO & MUSHROOM
Prepare basic recipe, but instead of the basic filling, fill the pastry-lined pan with cooked potatoes and mushrooms, flavored with a little chopped garlic and fresh parsley. Sprinkle with a layer of freshly grated Parmesan and some grated Gruyère cheese before finally adding the pastry top and eggs and baking as normal.

WITH SPINACH & RICOTTA
Prepare basic recipe, but instead of basic filling, fill the pastry-lined pan with chopped cooked spinach mixed with ricotta, bound with a beaten egg, and flavored with freshly grated nutmeg, Parmesan, and salt and pepper. Cover with the pastry top and eggs and bake as normal.

Zucchini Flowers Stuffed with Goat Cheese & Lavender Honey

When small zucchini flower in summer, they are a treat to behold. They are perfect for stuffing and require little time to cook. Honey might seem a surprising ingredient in this dish, but lavender honey has a savory flavor that beautifully complements the salty goat cheese.

Serves 4

vegetable oil for deep-
   frying
4 small zucchini with
   flowers attached
½ cup (100 g) soft goat
   cheese
zest of 1 lemon

4 tbsp. all-purpose flour
2 tbsp. cornstarch
sea salt and freshly
   ground black pepper
ice-cold sparkling water
1 tbsp. lavender honey

1   Heat the oil in a deep-fat fryer or wok to 350°F (180°C). Wipe the zucchini clean with a damp towel and then gently pry open the flower petals. Whip together the goat cheese and lemon zest and split it between the flowers. Seal the petals around the filling to encase it.

2   Gently mix together the flour and cornstarch with the salt and pepper. Whisk in just enough sparkling water to make a medium-thick batter (a bit thinner than a pancake batter). Plunge the zucchini and flowers into the batter to entirely coat them and then, one by one, place them into the hot oil to cook for 4–6 minutes or until the batter is crisp and golden.

3   Scoop out and drain on paper towels. Lay on a serving plate and drizzle with the honey and more sea salt and black pepper.

WITH GOAT CHEESE THYME HONEY
Prepare the basic recipe, replacing the lavender honey with thyme honey for a savory finish.

WITH ASPARAGUS
Prepare the basic recipe, replacing the zucchini with some thick asparagus sliced lengthwise in half. Stuff the asparagus with the cheese filling before sandwiching the halves together and coating with the batter.

WITH PEPPERED CREAM CHEESE
Prepare the basic recipe, replacing the goat cheese with ½ cup (60 g) cream cheese beaten with ½ teaspoon of freshly ground black pepper.

Grilled Vegetables

Serves 6

3 zucchini, sliced thinly lengthwise
4 red peppers, sliced lengthwise and seeded
1 large eggplant, sliced lengthwise (sprinkled with salt, left to stand in a colander under a weighted plate for an hour, rinsed, and dried)

1 large red onion, sliced across center into 8 flat, thick slices (keep root stub intact so onion slices remain whole)
4 large, beefsteak tomatoes, sliced very thick
2 bulbs fennel, sliced very thick

6 tbsp. extra-virgin olive oil, plus more for serving
2 tbsp. chopped fresh flat-leaf parsley
sea salt and freshly ground black pepper

1 Heat the grill to medium. Grill each vegetable separately, brushed with olive oil, until just tender. As soon as they are cooked, arrange them in a shallow, warmed wide bowl or platter and sprinkle with chopped parsley, drizzle with olive oil, and season with salt and pepper, with the different vegetables overlapping each other. Serve at room temperature.

WITH PESTO
Omit parsley. Drizzle dish with 3 tablespoons pesto, thinned with extra olive oil, and a handful of Parmesan shavings.

WITH SMOKED CHEESE
Slice 3 scamorza (smoked mozzarella) in half and fry in a very hot pan in a little oil until just melting. Lay on the grilled vegetables and serve.

WITH BRUSCHETTA
Before grilling the vegetables, toast 6 large slices of crusty Italian bread. Rub each slice with a peeled garlic clove and drizzle with olive oil. Arrange in a serving dish, then proceed with basic recipe.

WITH CAPERS & ANCHOVIES
Chop 2 handfuls pitted green olives and 1 handful capers with 4 anchovy fillets. Scatter olives, capers, anchovies, and croutons over grilled vegetables. Omit parsley but drizzle with olive oil to serve.

Italian Vegetable Stew

Serves 6

1 lb. (450 g) yellow or red sweet peppers
1 lb. (450 g) unpeeled eggplant
4 tbsp. extra-virgin olive oil

generous ½ lb. (225 g) small onions, halved
generous ½ lb. (225 g) small tomatoes, halved
1 cup (250 ml) dry white wine

sea salt and freshly ground black pepper

1 Remove the seeds and inner membranes from the peppers, then cut into even-sized chunks. Cut the eggplant into even-sized cubes. Put the cubes into a colander and sprinkle with salt. Cover with a plate, weigh the plate down with something heavy like a can of tomatoes, and let drain over sink or large bowl for about 1 hour. Rinse and dry the cubes.

2 In a large pot, heat the oil, then add the onions. Cook the onions until just soft, then add eggplant, peppers, and tomatoes. Sprinkle with wine and add salt and pepper to taste. Cover and simmer gently for about 1 hour, keeping the heat low and stirring frequently. Serve hot or cold.

WITH PEPPERS & POTATO
Prepare basic recipe, doubling amount of peppers, omitting eggplant, and adding 3 cubed, peeled potatoes. Sprinkle finished dish with a little white wine vinegar.

WITH MUSHROOMS
Prepare basic recipe, replacing eggplant with about 12 medium mushrooms, halved.

WITH HOT PEPPER
Prepare basic recipe, adding 2 cloves garlic, chopped, and 1 dried red chili pepper, chopped, to onions.

WITH ARTICHOKE HEARTS
Prepare basic recipe, replacing eggplant with 6 raw artichoke hearts.

WITH MOZZARELLA
Prepare basic recipe, then transfer to an ovenproof dish, and dot with cubes of mozzarella. Slide under a hot broiler and allow the cheese to just melt before serving.

Phyllo Pastry with Feta & Spinach

The combination of ingredients for this delicious savory pastry is very classic. The great news is that it works brilliantly with a whole variety of other options. You can freeze what you don't eat, or just eat the leftovers as snacks. You can also make this several hours in advance and bake it just before serving.

Serves 4

½ lb. (225 g) feta cheese
1 lb. (450 g) ricotta
10 oz. (275 g) baby
    spinach, cooked and
    chopped
1 bunch scallions, finely
    sliced
1 green chili, finely
    chopped

⅓ cup (75 g) freshly
    grated Parmesan
1 egg
a good grating nutmeg
½ cup (25 g) fresh white
    bread crumbs
2 tbsp. olive oil
6 sheets phyllo pastry,
    trimmed to snugly fit
    baking pan

1   Heat oven to 350°F (180°C). Mash the feta in a large mixing bowl, add the ricotta, and mash again to thoroughly mix. Stir in the spinach, scallions, chili, Parmesan, egg, nutmeg, and plenty of salt and pepper with half the bread crumbs.

2   Brush an 8 x 12–inch (20 x 30–cm) baking pan with a little olive oil. Layer half the phyllo sheets into the pan, brushing each with oil before adding the next. Scatter with the remaining bread crumbs.

3   Spoon in the ricotta filling and gently spread over the phyllo, so as not to move around the bread crumbs. Cover with the remaining phyllo, brushing with oil as you go, and finishing with a good coating of oil on top. Score into small triangular portions. Bake for 35–40 minutes until golden and crisp.

WITH LEMON
Prepare the basic recipe, adding the zest and juice of 1 lemon to the filling.

WITHOUT SPINACH
Prepare the basic recipe, omitting the spinach and adding the zest and juice of 1 lemon to the cheese mixture.

WITHB PUFF PASTRY
Prepare the basic recipe, but instead of sandwiching between sheets of phyllo pastry, make small turnovers, like Cornish pasties, using pieces of thinly rolled puff pastry.

Baked Mushrooms

Choose the biggest mushrooms you can find for these baked stuffed mushrooms. Fall in Italy heralds the start of the porcini season and you can find huge fresh ones for sale at every vegetable stall, but any mushroom with a dense texture will work very well, such as Portabella mushrooms. You can, of course, vary the type of cheese according to your own preferences.

Serves 6

6 very large mushrooms
6 tbsp. ricotta
4 tbsp. very soft
    Gorgonzola
4 tbsp. freshly grated
    Parmesan
4 tbsp. soft white bread
    crumbs

2 tbsp. chopped fresh
    flat-leaf parsley
5 tbsp. extra-virgin olive
    oil
sea salt and freshly
    ground black pepper

1 Preheat the oven to 350°F (175°C). Wipe the mushrooms clean and remove their stems. Chop the stems up very small and put into a bowl. Add ricotta, Gorgonzola, half the Parmesan, bread crumbs, and parsley. Season with salt and pepper. Use the resulting mixture to fill the mushrooms generously.

2 With 1 tablespoon olive oil, brush an ovenproof dish large enough for all the mushrooms to sit in flat. Place the filled mushrooms in the dish. Sprinkle the remaining Parmesan on top of the mushrooms. Drizzle the remaining oil around and over the mushrooms. Bake for about 25 minutes, or until soft and golden brown on top. Serve at once.

WITH SMOKED CHEESE
Prepare basic recipe, replacing ricotta with grated smoked scamorza (air-dried, smoked mozzarella).

WITH TOMATO SAUCE
Prepare basic recipe, but finish by topping each mushroom with a spoonful of pomodoro sauce (see page 151) before finally sprinkling with Parmesan.

WITH PINE NUTS
Prepare basic recipe, adding a handful of lightly toasted pine nuts to the filling.

WITH WALNUTS
Prepare basic recipe, adding a handful of finely chopped walnuts to the filling.

PANCETTA-FILLED BAKED MUSHROOMS
Prepare basic recipe, adding a handful of crisply fried pancetta cubes to the filling.

Zucchini Cake

This savory zucchini cake is a delicious starter or a dish substantial enough for a light lunch.

Serves 6

12 medium-sized zucchini, topped and tailed
2 small onions
6 tbsp. butter
5 tbsp. extra-virgin olive oil
2 tbsp. chopped fresh flat-leaf parsley
1 tsp. fresh marjoram leaves

sea salt and freshly ground black pepper
5 tbsp. light cream, sour cream, or whole milk
6 eggs, beaten
8 tbsp. freshly grated Parmesan
6 tbsp. Italian dry bread crumbs (Pangrattato preferred)

1 Preheat oven to 375°F (190°C). Slice the zucchini into rounds and place in a colander to drain for half an hour or so. Rinse and dry.

2 Meanwhile, slice the onions finely and fry gently without browning in butter and half the oil. Use half the remaining oil to grease a ring mold or ovenproof dish. Add the sliced zucchini to the onions and continue to cook gently, stirring frequently. When zucchini are soft and onions are cooked, set aside to cool, then add the parsley, marjoram, salt, and pepper.

3 In a separate bowl, beat the cream, sour cream, or milk with eggs and Parmesan, then add seasoning to taste. When the zucchini are cool, stir into the egg mixture. Sprinkle oiled mold or dish thoroughly with half the bread crumbs, making sure they stick to the sides and bottom thickly. Pour or spoon zucchini and egg mixture into the dish and bang it down lightly to allow it to settle.

4 Sprinkle with remaining bread crumbs and drizzle with remaining oil. Bake for about 30 minutes, until firm. Remove from the oven and let cool slightly before turning out onto a serving dish. It can be enjoyed hot or cold.

WITH POTATO
Prepare basic recipe, halving the quantity of zucchini and adding the same quantity of boiled, cubed potatoes.

WITH FENNEL
Prepare basic recipe, replacing the zucchini with 8 fennel bulbs, boiled and chopped coarsely.

WITH CAULIFLOWER & PECORINO
Prepare basic recipe, replacing the zucchini with 1 head of cauliflower, boiled and roughly chopped, and replacing the Parmesan with freshly grated pecorino.

WITH GREEN BEAN, GORGONZOLA & ALMOND
Prepare basic recipe, replacing the zucchini with 6 handfuls cooked green beans chopped into 1-in. (2.5-cm) sections. Add cubed Gorgonzola and 2 tablespoons toasted sliced almonds.

WITH CARROT
Prepare basic recipe, using 12 medium-sized boiled carrots instead of zucchini and flavoring the mixture with the grated zest of 1 orange.

Piperade

This scrambled egg dish is one of those dishes that defines the cuisine of southern France, especially that of the Basque region, where it is a local specialty. In its original version, piperade relies on the wonderful tomatoes and peppers of the region.

Serves 2 generously

3 tbsp. olive oil
1 onion, finely sliced
3–4 red and green bell peppers (at least 1 of each), chopped into quite large pieces
3–4 large ripe tomatoes, peeled, seeded, and chopped

2 cloves garlic, chopped
fresh chili pepper, according to taste and heat wanted
pinch fresh thyme leaves (or 1 bay leaf)
4 eggs, beaten

1 Heat the olive oil in a large skillet. Gently cook the onion until it is soft. Add the peppers and cook gently for 10 minutes. Then add the tomatoes, garlic, chili, and herbs, and continue to cook until everything is soft.

2 Add the beaten eggs to the mixture and cook as with scrambled eggs. Remove from the heat when the eggs start to thicken, and serve immediately.

WITH ZUCCHINI
Prepare the basic recipe, replacing the bell peppers with sliced fresh zucchini.

WITH MUSHROOMS
Prepare the basic recipe, replacing the bell peppers with 5 large mushrooms, cut into chunks.

WITH EXTRA BELL PEPPERS
Prepare the basic recipe, omitting the tomatoes and adding 2 extra bell peppers.

WITH ONIONS
Prepare the basic recipe, omitting the onion, bell peppers, tomatoes, garlic, and chili, and using 3 large red onions, thinly sliced.

WITH PEAS
Prepare the basic recipe, omitting the bell peppers, tomatoes, garlic, and chili. Instead, add 2 cups (450 g) of fresh or frozen peas, cooked slowly, before adding the eggs.

Saganaki

Saganaki dishes take their name from the pan in which they are made. A *sagani* is a two-handled pan made in many different materials. Serve this recipe as an appetizer, an hors d'oeuvre, or as part of a meal made up of a varied selection of small plates. The key to success with this dish is to get the oil really hot—just up to the smoking point before frying.

Serves 6

1 lb. (450 g) kefalotyri or kasseri cheese (or pecorino romano)
⅔ cup (75 g) flour

½ cup (120 ml) olive oil
2–3 lemons, quartered

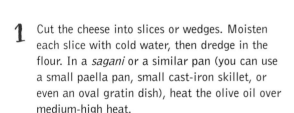

1 Cut the cheese into slices or wedges. Moisten each slice with cold water, then dredge in the flour. In a *sagani* or a similar pan (you can use a small paella pan, small cast-iron skillet, or even an oval gratin dish), heat the olive oil over medium-high heat.

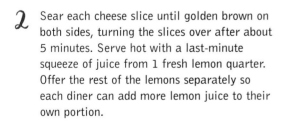

2 Sear each cheese slice until golden brown on both sides, turning the slices over after about 5 minutes. Serve hot with a last-minute squeeze of juice from 1 fresh lemon quarter. Offer the rest of the lemons separately so each diner can add more lemon juice to their own portion.

WITH FRIED EGG
Prepare the basic recipe, but omit the lemon juice and lemon garnish. Top each slice of fried cheese with a fried egg.

WITH FRIED TOMATOES
Prepare the basic recipe, omitting the lemon juice and lemon garnish. Serve topped with 8 cooked tomatoes slices.

WITH SALAD
Prepare the basic recipe. Serve with a salad of fresh lettuce leaves, chopped scallions, and chopped cucumber.

WITH MUSHROOMS
Prepare the basic recipe. Serve topped with 20 small mushrooms fried with a chopped garlic clove.

WITH GARLIC
Prepare the basic recipe, adding a couple of minced garlic cloves to the oil before frying the cheese.

Classic Spanish Tortilla

This mixture makes one very large Spanish tortilla, which is a bit like a frittata, or a flat omelet. You can divide the mixture in half and make two smaller tortillas.

Serves 8

2 lbs. (900 g) potatoes, thinly sliced
sea salt

3 tbsp. olive oil
½ onion, chopped finely
8 extra-large eggs

1 Put the potato slices in a bowl and sprinkle plenty of salt over them, working it down to the bottom of the bowl. In a large skillet, heat the olive oil. When it's very hot, add the potatoes and start to fry them. Be sure to keep stirring them so they don't stick or start to brown. After about 5 minutes, add the chopped onion. Stir the contents of the skillet, then cover it. Keep checking the pan to be sure the potatoes aren't turning brown. Turn down the heat if necessary. Stir frequently. Once the potatoes break easily under the touch of the stirring spoon, they are ready.

2 Meanwhile, break the eggs into a bowl, add a pinch of salt, and beat them until well combined. Add the potato and onion mixture to the bowl of eggs. Drain away any excess oil that's left in the skillet at this point.

3 Mix the potato and egg mixture well while the skillet gets very hot with no extra oil in it. Pour the mixture into the skillet. Flatten it down in the pan and keep the heat at medium for a few minutes. Put a plate over the mix and turn over the tortilla gently. When you return it to the pan, press down the sides to create the classic flat shape of *tortilla de patatas*.

4 Turn the tortilla several times. It is ready when you put a knife into it and the knife comes out clean.

WITH EXTRA ONIONS
Prepare the basic recipe, adding 2 large onions, thinly sliced and fried separately until softened, to the potato and eggs before continuing as above.

WITH FRESH BASIL
Prepare the basic recipe, adding about 20 leaves of fresh basil, torn into pieces, to the potato and egg mixture before frying.

WITH PARSLEY
Prepare the basic recipe, adding a large bunch of freshly chopped flat-leaf parsley to the potato and egg mixture before frying.

WITH TOMATOES
Prepare the basic recipe, adding 3 small tomatoes, sliced, to the potato and egg mixture before frying.

WITH CHEESE
Prepare the basic recipe, adding 3 tablespoons of grated strong-flavored cheese, such as Manchego, Parmesan, or strong Cheddar, to the potato and egg mixture before frying.

Zucchini Frittata

When making a frittata, the ratio of vegetable to egg varies enormously, depending upon the vegetable you are using. The basic rule of thumb is that there has to be enough egg to hold the whole thing together, but there must be enough vegetable to form the main part of the finished frittata. It's best to use about ⅔ vegetable and ⅓ eggs. Be very careful not to add too much cheese, as it will make the frittata stick and thus make it impossible to turn successfully.

Serves 4–6

8 small zucchini, sliced
 into thin discs
2 onions, thinly sliced
6 tbsp. olive oil
sea salt and freshly
 ground black pepper

6 eggs, beaten
2 oz. (50 g) Parmesan,
 freshly grated

1 Put the sliced zucchini and onions into a pan with half the oil, and fry until the onion is softened. Add a little water, salt, and pepper, and continue to cook until the zucchini are softened. You can add the hot cooked zucchini directly into the beaten eggs or wait until they cool before adding. Once the zucchini are mixed with the eggs, add the Parmesan, salt, and pepper.

2 Heat the remaining oil in a wide, shallow pan over medium heat. When very hot, but before it smokes, pour in the egg mixture. Shake the pan to flatten and even out the mixture, pulling liquid egg into the center as you work. Cook until the underside is browned and firm.

3 Turn the frittata over by covering the pan with a lid or plate and inverting the pan. Put the pan down on the heat, right-side up, and carefully slide the frittata (uncooked side down) back into the hot pan. Then cook again, for a shorter time, until golden brown and firm on the underside. Slide the frittata onto a clean, flat platter and serve hot or cold.

WITH ZUCCHINI FLOWERS
Replace zucchini with about 30 zucchini flowers, washed, dried, and roughly chopped. Mix into eggs along with fried onions and proceed with basic recipe.

WITH PEAS
Replace zucchini with about 4 cups cooked peas. Mix into the eggs with the fried onions and proceed with basic recipe.

WITH SPINACH
Replace zucchini with 3 handfuls fresh spinach, cooked, drained, squeezed dry, and roughly chopped. Mix into the eggs along with fried onions and proceed with basic recipe.

WITH POTATO & CHEESE
Replace zucchini, onion, and Parmesan with 1 thinly sliced large leek, cooked in a little olive oil; 3 boiled potatoes, thinly sliced; and 1 chunk taleggio, cubed. Add to beaten eggs and proceed with basic recipe.

Griddled Halloumi with Lemon Vinaigrette

The salty flavor of griddled halloumi cheese is perfect against the backdrop of a lovely fresh, crisp salad with a very garlicky salad dressing that gives the whole dish real zing.

Serves 6

8 ripe plum tomatoes
2 cloves garlic, finely sliced
1 tbsp. chopped fresh thyme
sea salt and freshly ground black pepper
sugar to taste
2 tbsp. balsamic vinegar

2 tbsp. olive oil
1 lb. (450 g) halloumi cheese, cut into bite-sized cubes
4 Little Gem or any crisp lettuce, separated into leaves, enough for 4–6

For the vinaigrette
4 cloves garlic, unpeeled
juice of 1 lemon
½ cup (120 ml) grapeseed oil
sea salt and freshly ground black pepper

1 Preheat the oven to 350°F (175°C). Lay the tomato slices on a cookie sheet. Sprinkle with the garlic, thyme, salt, pepper, a touch of sugar, balsamic vinegar, and olive oil. Roast for 1 hour or until their size has reduced by half. Keep warm.

2 Meanwhile, make the vinaigrette. Bring a small pan of water to a boil, add the unpeeled garlic cloves, and poach for 20 minutes. Drain and peel. In a blender or food processor, place the poached garlic, lemon juice, and grapeseed oil. Pulse-blend until smooth and emulsified. Add water to achieve a pouring yet coating consistency and season to taste with salt and pepper.

3 Heat a griddle pan over a high heat. Cook the halloumi on both sides until a good dark crust has formed on the cheese. In a serving bowl, combine the lettuce, roasted tomatoes, and freshly griddled halloumi with 8 tablespoons of the vinaigrette (storing the remainder for future use). Toss together and serve immediately.

WITH BELL PEPPER SALAD
Prepare the basic recipe, omitting the tomatoes (and all the ingredients used in roasting them) and the lettuce. Instead, serve the griddled halloumi on top of a salad of griddled bell peppers, cut into strips and dressed with the basic vinaigrette.

WITH ARUGULA SALAD
Prepare the basic recipe, omitting the tomatoes (and all the ingredients used in roasting them) and the lettuce. Instead, serve the griddled halloumi on top of a salad of fresh arugula, dressed with the basic vinaigrette.

WITH MUSHROOMS
Prepare the basic recipe, adding pan-fried mushrooms on top of the finished dish.

WITH AVOCADO SALAD
Prepare the basic recipe, adding sliced avocado to the salad.

WITH GRIDDLED EGGPLANT & MINT
Prepare the basic recipe, adding slices of griddled eggplant. Serve the griddled halloumi on the eggplant, dressed with the basic vinaigrette and surrounded with the lettuce leaves and tomatoes.

Mixed Bean & Sun-Dried Tomato Salad

Serves 10

1 x 8-oz. (225 g) jar oil-packed sun-dried
   tomato halves
1 handful chopped fresh flat-leaf parsley
1 handful chopped fresh basil
1 x 15-oz. (425 g) can red kidney beans,
   rinsed and drained

1 x 15-oz. (425 g) can white kidney beans,
   rinsed and drained
1 x 15-oz. (425 g) can black beans, rinsed
   and drained
1 x 15-oz. (425 g) can black-eyed peas,
   rinsed and drained

½ red onion, thinly sliced
⅓ cup (90 ml) red wine vinegar
1 tbsp. sugar
1 tsp. sea salt
½ tsp. Dijon-style mustard
¼ tsp. freshly ground black pepper

1 Drain sun-dried tomatoes in a strainer over a
bowl. Reserve the oil. Put ½ cup (120 ml) of
the reserved oil in a medium bowl. Discard the
remaining oil. Chop drained tomatoes; place in
a separate large bowl. Add parsley, basil, all the
beans, and the onion to the chopped tomatoes.
Stir gently to combine.

2 Add vinegar, sugar, salt, mustard, and pepper to
the reserved oil, stirring with a whisk. Drizzle over
bean mixture; toss gently to coat. Cover and chill
until you are ready to serve.

WITH OLIVES
Prepare the basic recipe, replacing
the sun-dried tomatoes with
pitted green or black olives, and
increasing the amount of oil by 2
or 3 tablespoons.

WITH CAPERS
Prepare the basic recipe, replacing
the sun-dried tomatoes with the
same quantity of drained, rinsed,
and dried capers and increasing
the amount of oil by 2 or 3
tablespoons.

WITH FETA
Prepare the basic recipe, adding
3 oz. (75 g) crumbled feta to the
salad ingredients before mixing
with the dressing.

WITH ARUGULA
Prepare the basic recipe, mixing
in a large handful of fresh arugula
leaves, just before serving.

Lentils with Lemon Juice

Serves 6

1½ lbs. (700 g) black lentils
2 pints (1¼ liters) water
2 potatoes, peeled and chopped

6 garlic cloves, crushed
4 tbsp. chopped fresh cilantro
6 tbsp. olive oil

sea salt and freshly ground black pepper
¼ cup (60 ml) lemon juice

1 Boil lentils in the water for 15 minutes. Add
the potatoes and continue cooking until lentils
are tender, approximately 15 minutes, stirring
occasionally. In a separate pan, fry garlic and
cilantro with the olive oil until slightly tender and
the garlic is very lightly browned. Add the lentils
and potatoes and cook for 10 minutes more on
medium-low heat, stirring occasionally to prevent
sticking or burning.

2 Remove from heat, season with salt and pepper,
and add lemon juice if serving immediately. If not,
set aside to cool in the refrigerator and add lemon
juice just before serving. Serve hot or cold with
pita bread as an appetizer.

WITH TOMATOES
Prepare the basic recipe, replacing
the potatoes with 2 large, fresh,
firm tomatoes, cut into chunks and
seeded. Stir them into the lentils
once they are cooled.

WITH GREEN BEANS
Prepare the basic recipe, adding 2
handfuls cooked and halved green
beans to the salad, mixing them into
the lentils and potatoes once cooled.

WITH RED ONION
Prepare the basic recipe, adding
1 red onion, peeled and very finely
chopped, to the lentils and potatoes.

WITH BASIL
Prepare the basic recipe, replacing
the cilantro with basil. Add 6
shredded fresh basil leaves at the
very end with the lemon juice.

WITH PINE NUTS
Prepare the basic recipe, adding
2 tablespoons pine nuts to the salad,
stirring them through the lentils
while they are still warm.

Conchiglie with Creamy Spinach

Although you can use any shape of pasta you like for this sauce, the cup shape of this particular type holds the creamy sauce perfectly. A great sauce, with a wonderful color.

Serves 4

2¼ lb. (1 kg) fresh
    spinach leaves
8 tbsp. light or whipping
    cream
6 tbsp. freshly grated
    Parmesan cheese, plus
    extra to serve

¼ tsp. grated nutmeg
Salt and freshly ground
    black pepper
2 cups (400 g) conchiglie
1 tbsp. butter

1   Wash the spinach thoroughly, then cram it into a large saucepan with just the water clinging to the leaves. Put a lid on the saucepan and place over a low heat for about 5 minutes, until all the leaves have wilted. Drain well, squeezing out any excess liquid, then put the cooked spinach in the food processor with the cream and Parmesan cheese. Process to create a smooth texture. Stir in the nutmeg, and season to taste.

2   Bring a large saucepan of salted water to the boil. Put the conchiglie into the water and stir thoroughly. Replace the lid and return to the boil. Remove or adjust the lid once the water is boiling again. Cook according to the packet instructions until al dente. Drain the pasta and return it to the pot. Add the butter and toss together thoroughly. Pour over the sauce and toss again. Serve immediately, spinkled with a little extra Parmesan cheese.

WITH SWISS CHARD & PINE KERNELS
Substitute the spinach leaves with roughly shredded Swiss chard leaves for a stronger tasting sauce. In this case omit the nutmeg and add 2 tablespoons of lightly toasted pine kernels instead, sprinkled over the finished dish.

WITH RICOTTA CHEESE
Add 3 tablespoons ricotta cheese to the dish. Stir it into the pasta when combining with the sauce.

WITH CREAMY WILD GREENS
Use a mixture of different leaves such as young nettles, sorrel, wild garlic, and spinach to make this sauce taste really fresh.

WITH CINNAMON & PECORINO
Substitute the nutmeg for some warming cinnamon, and use freshly grated pecorino instead of Parmesan cheese.

WITH WALNUTS
Stir a handful of lightly toasted walnuts into the dish at the end, when combining the sauce and the pasta

Artichoke with Spicy Lemon Crumbs

A whole globe artichoke becomes a magical treat as you peel off the leaves, dip, and eat as you work your way to the more meaty heart. To serve this, everyone just reaches into the center of the table where you have the single artichoke on a plate and the vinaigrette in a bowl next to it—just dunk away.

Serves 4

1 large globe artichoke
juice and zest of 1 lemon
⅓ cup (40 g) dry bread crumbs
2 tbsp. grated Parmesan cheese
pinch dried red pepper flakes
1 tbsp. assorted chopped fresh herbs

1 tbsp. olive oil
sea salt and freshly ground black pepper

for the vinaigrette
1 tsp. Dijon mustard
1 tbsp. sherry vinegar

squeeze of lemon juice
sea salt and freshly ground black pepper
3 tbsp. good Spanish olive oil

1 Simmer the artichoke in salted water, which has been acidulated with a good squeeze of lemon juice, for 30 minutes, or until the leaves can be removed with a slight tug. Remove the artichoke from the water. While still warm, press the leaves gently back, leaving them attached, so that the artichoke resembles a flower. Pull out the small white and purple center leaves and scrape out the choke (the fuzzy part) with a spoon.

2 Stand the artichoke upright in a small baking dish. Preheat the oven to 350°F (180°C). Combine the bread crumbs, Parmesan, lemon zest, red pepper flakes, herbs, and oil. Season to taste with salt and pepper. Pack the mixture into the artichoke. Bake for 25 minutes or until golden.

3 Meanwhile, make the vinaigrette by whisking together all the ingredients until thick and emulsified.

4 To eat the artichoke, pull the leaves off, dip into the vinaigrette and scrape the soft base of the leaf off with your teeth. When you've finished the leaves, eat the rest of the heart.

WITH PRESERVED LEMON
Prepare the basic recipe, omitting the Parmesan cheese and adding 1 chopped preserved lemon to the stuffing mix.

WITH CAPERS & MINT CRUMBS
Prepare the basic recipe, omitting the red pepper flakes and herbs and adding 1 tablespoon chopped capers and 1 tablespoon chopped fresh mint leaves to the stuffing.

BOILED ARTICHOKE WITH CRAB MEAT SALAD
Prepare the basic recipe, omitting the breadcrumb stuffing and the vinaigrette. After boiling and cooling the artichoke, fill it with a salad of 5 tablespoons white crab meat, ½ finely chopped red chili, the juice and rind of 1 lemon, and 1 tablespoon finely chopped cilantro.

BOILED ARTICHOKE WITH VINAIGRETTE
Prepare the basic recipe, but omit the breadcrumb stuffing. Do not bake. To serve, fill the center with the vinaigrette.

Vegetable Lasagne

This vegetarian lasagne is a great, extra-nutritious alternative to the traditional meaty style and guaranteed to be a crowd pleaser.

Serves 4

1 lb. (450 g) dried pasta
   sheets
1 onion, sliced
4 tbsp. extra-virgin olive
   oil
2 zucchini, sliced
2 medium carrots, cubed
½ cup (100 g) shelled
   peas
1 quantity béchamel sauce
   (see page 150)
2 handfuls fresh
   asparagus, lightly
   steamed

1 cup (100 g) cleaned,
   sliced mushrooms
4 oz. (125 g) tomatoes,
   peeled and chopped
3 handfuls fresh spinach
   leaves, lightly steamed
2 cups (300 g) Parmesan
   cheese, grated
1 cup (250 g) mozzarella,
   cubed or sliced

1 Preheat the oven to 400°F (200°C). Boil the pasta sheets in salted water for 2–3 minutes before removing with tongs and laying out, without overlaps, on a clean, damp cloth, or drop into a basin of cold water until required, to prevent the pieces sticking together.

2 Fry the sliced onion in the oil until soft. Add the zucchini, carrots, and peas. Simmer slowly, uncovered, for ten minutes or until softened. Pour a layer of béchamel sauce into a medium baking dish and cover with a layer of the pasta sheets. Cover with a layer of softened vegetables, half the steamed asparagus, a handful of raw mushrooms, 2 tablespoons of Parmesan cheese, a handful of spinach, and a handful of raw chopped tomatoes, and cover with mozzarella.

3 Repeat until all the ingredients are used up, then add a final layer of mozzarella. Bake in the oven for 25 minutes. Remove from the oven and rest for 10 minutes before serving.

WITH ZUCCHINI & WILD GARLIC
Instead of the asparagus and spinach, use lightly steamed and sliced zucchini and fresh wild garlic leaves.

WITH GREEN BEANS
Instead of the peas, use lightly cooked green beans, cut into small chunks and proceed as above.

WITH NUTMEG BÉCHAMEL
Flavor the béchamel sauce with extra freshly grated nutmeg.

WITH SMOKED SCAMORZA
For a subtle smoky flavor, use smoked scamorza, finely sliced, instead of the mozzarella.

WITH NEW POTATOES
For a more filling lasagne, replace the mushrooms with boiled new potatoes, thinly sliced.

Pasta with Vegetable Ragu

This is a lovely rich vegetable ragu that allows you to use whatever vegetables you like best, and that are in season at the time.

Serves 4

1 onion, finely chopped
2 celery sticks, finely chopped
2 carrots, peeled and chopped
4 tbsp. olive oil
¼ cup (50 ml) water or stock
4 garlic cloves, peeled and minced
1 tbsp. tomato puree
1 tbsp. balsamic vinegar

1 cup (250 g) diced vegetables, e.g. a mix of zucchini, peas, green beans, peppers, and mushrooms
2 oz. (50 g) raw red lentils
2 x 14-oz. (400-g) cans chopped tomatoes
8 oz. (225 g) spaghetti (or your favorite pasta)
2 tbsp. Parmesan cheese shavings

1 Tip the onion, celery, and carrots into a large saucepan with the oil and, once the vegetables are sizzling, add the water or stock. Cook gently, stirring often, until the vegetables are soft. Add the garlic, tomato puree, and balsamic vinegar, cook on a high heat for a minute more, then add the diced vegetables, lentils, and tomatoes, and bring to the boil. Reduce the heat and simmer for about 40 minutes, adding a little water or stock if necessary.

2 Bring a large saucepan of salted water to the boil. Put the pasta into the water and stir thoroughly. Replace the lid and return to the boil. Remove or adjust the lid once the water is boiling again. Cook according to the packet instructions until al dente. Drain the pasta and return it to the pot.

3 Season the vegetable ragu and pour over the pasta, mixing well. Serve immediately, sprinkled with the Parmesan cheese.

WITH CHICKPEAS
Instead of red lentils, use chickpeas to add bulk and protein to this delicious sauce.

WITH CHILI
To give the ragu some heat, add 1 or 2 dried chilis to the sauce with the minced garlic, and discard once the sauce has finished simmering.

WITH HERBS
For extra freshness, add a big handful of freshly chopped mixed herbs to the ragu at the every end, once it has been taken off the heat and before combining with the pasta.

WITH FETA
Crumble 4 oz. (125 g) feta cheese into the hot pasta and sauce when you mix everything together. In this instance, do not add the Parmesan cheese although you could use grated pecorino instead.

French Bean, Pepper & Mozzarella Terrine

This pretty pepper and mozzarella terrine is cooked in just over half an hour. Make sure that there are no gaps between the layers, as this will prevent the terrine from being turned out successfully.

Serves 6

3 leeks, trimmed
2 red peppers
2 yellow peppers

10 oz. (275 g) green beans
14 oz. (400 g) buffalo mozzarella, cubed
4 tbsp. extra-virgin olive oil

5 eggs, beaten
sea salt and freshly ground black pepper
2 tbsp. freshly grated Parmesan

1 Cut the leeks in half lengthwise. Strip off larger leaves to blanch for 1 minute in boiling salted water, then drop into a bowl of cold water. Slice rest of leeks thinly and set aside. Roast peppers in the oven, on the barbecue, or under broiler until blackened, then cool and peel, removing all seeds and membranes.

2 Cut peppers into neat strips. Boil green beans in salted water for about 8 minutes, then drain and refresh in cold water. In a skillet, heat oil, add raw sliced leeks and green beans, and sauté gently for about 5 minutes.

3 Line a loaf pan with waxed paper and heat oven to 350°F (175°C). Season eggs with salt and pepper, then add Parmesan. Line pan with the wide, long leek leaves, allowing them to fall out over the sides. Arrange a layer of pepper stips on bottom of terrine, cover with beaten egg and mozzarella cubes, then add a layer of green beans and leeks; then more egg and mozzarella, more pepper—until pan is full and ingredients have been used up. Wrap leek leaves back over the top of the filled terrine and press down gently.

4 Cover loosely with foil, and bake in preheated oven for 20 minutes. After 20 minutes, uncover and finish baking for about 15 minutes. Cool for at least 20 minutes before slicing.

WITH POTATO, TOMATO & MOZZARELLA
Prepare basic recipe, replacing the peppers and beans with thin slices of parboiled potatoes and tomatoes.

WITH EGGPLANT
Prepare basic recipe, replacing the bottom and top layers of leeks with soft grilled eggplant slices and adding a sprinkling of dried oregano to each layer.

WITH ZUCCHINI
Prepare basic recipe, replacing the bottom and top layers of leeks with parboiled large zucchini, sliced into thin strips.

WITH POTATO & MUSHROOMS
Prepare basic recipe, replacing the peppers and beans with parboiled sliced potatoes and cooked, sliced large mushrooms.

WITH BROWN RICE & CAULIFLOWER
Prepare basic recipe, replacing the peppers and beans with cooked cauliflower florets and cooked brown rice.

Orecchiette with Broccoli & Tomato

This is lovely speciality from the south of Italy, with lots of flavor and wonderful colors. Salted ricotta can be hard to find; you could substitute hard goat cheese.

Serves 4

3½ cups (750 g) broccoli
2⅓ cups (350 g) orecchiette
2 cloves garlic, lightly crused
4 tbsp. extra-virgin olive oil
2 salted anchovies, rinsed, boned and chopped

2 cups (200 g) fresh tomatoes, peeled, seeded and chopped
3 tbsp. salted ricotta cheese, grated
Salt and freshly ground black pepper

1 Divide the broccoli into small florets, removing the hard stalks. Wash and boil in lightly salted water for 5 minutes. Drain and set aside.

2 Bring a large saucepan of salted water to the boil. Put the orecchiette into the water and stir thoroughly. Replace the lid and return to the boil. Remove or adjust the lid once the water is boiling again. Cook according to the packet instructions until al dente.

3 Meanwhile, fry the oil and garlic together until the garlic is golden brown. Discard the garlic and add the anchovies. Stir and melt the anchovies, then add the tomatoes. Season and simmer for about 5 minutes over a medium heat. Drain the orecchiette. Pour over the sauce, add the broccoli and half the cheese, and mix everything together. Serve immediately, sprinkled with the remaining cheese.

WITH CHILI
To make this dish really spicy, which helps to bring out the flavor of the broccoli, add one or two dried red chili peppers to the pan with the garlic and then discard together with the garlic. Drizzle with a touch of chili oil before sprinkling with the cheese.

WITH PECORINO CHEESE
Use freshly grated aged, peppery pecorino cheese instead of the ricotta cheese, and then finish off with a generous grinding of black pepper before sprinkling with the cheese.

WITH SARDINES
For an even fishier flavor, substitute the anchovies for 2 canned, boned, drained sardines canned in olive oil. Omit all the cheese.

WITH TUNA
For a milder fishy taste, avoid the anchovies and substitute for a small can of tuna fillets in oil, drained and flaked. Omit all the cheese.

WITH CAULIFLOWER
Instead of broccoli, use cauliflower florets, and add a tablespoonful of rinsed, drained, and chopped salted capers to add an extra-sour flavor to the dish.

Baked Eggplant with Tomato & Parmesan

Popularly known as eggplant parmigiana, this dish originates from southern Italy.

Serves 6

3 long (Japanese) eggplant, unpeeled, cut into ¼-in (½ cm) thick rounds
sea salt and freshly ground black pepper
6 tbsp. extra-virgin olive oil
1½ cups pomodoro sauce (see page 151)

10 oz. (300 g) fresh mozzarella, sliced
6 oz. (175 g) freshly grated Parmesan
about 15 fresh basil leaves, torn

1   Sprinkle eggplant slices with salt and lay them in a wide colander. Put a plate on top, and a weight on the plate. Leave the colander in the sink for 1 hour to let the bitter juices drain away. Rinse and pat the slices dry, then brush lightly with oil. Use the remaining oil to lightly grease a large ovenproof dish.

2   Turn on the oven broiler. Lay oiled eggplant slices on a broiler pan and place pan under the broiler. (You may also grill eggplant slices, if desired.) Broil them until soft and lightly browned, turning them several times.

3   Spread a layer of tomato sauce over the bottom of the ovenproof dish. Cover with a layer of grilled eggplant slices, a layer of mozzarella, a layer of tomato sauce, a sprinkling of Parmesan, and a few torn basil leaves. Repeat until the ingredients are all used. Finish with a thick layer of tomato sauce, a sprinkling of Parmesan, and a little basil.

4   Bake in a preheated 375°F (190°C) oven for about 20 minutes, then remove and allow to stand for about 5 minutes before serving.

WITH ZUCCHINI
Prepare basic recipe, substituting 6 large zucchini for the eggplant.

WITH ARTICHOKE
Prepare basic recipe, replacing eggplant with 20 boiled artichoke bottoms.

WITH POTATOES
Prepare basic recipe, replacing the eggplant with peeled, thinly sliced, parboiled potatoes.

WITH ASPARAGUS
Prepare basic recipe, replacing the eggplant with griddled asparagus.

WITHOUT MOZZARELLA
Prepare basic recipe, omitting all mozzarella and using plenty of freshly grated Parmesan between the layers.

Tagine of Artichokes with Lemon, Mint & Garlic

This light and refreshing and vegan tagine is perfect as a side dish, or serve it as a main with heaps of couscous.

Serves 4 to 6

4 tbsp. olive oil
1 lb. (450 g) fresh or frozen (defrosted) peas
2 large onions, 1 chopped and 1 sliced into rings
3 cloves garlic, peeled finely chopped
1 small preserved lemon, finely chopped
2 tsp. ground ginger
1 tsp. ground pepper
1 tsp. ground turmeric
large pinch of saffron threads, crumbled
2 tbsp. chopped fresh flat leaf parsley
2 tbsp. chopped fresh cilantro
8 large fresh or frozen artichoke hearts
3 tbsp. fresh chopped mint leaves, to serve

1 Use a metal tagine or soak a ceramic tagine in cold water for 30 minutes and drain and dry before using. Always use a diffuser when heating tagines on the hob.

2 Coat the base of a tagine with a little olive oil. Cover the bottom of the tagine with sliced onion rings. In a separate bowl, mix together the chopped onion, garlic, preserved lemon, spices, chopped parsley, and cilantro, then layer this over the sliced onions. Add the peas, then arrange the artichokes on top. Season with salt.

3 Add enough water to barely cover the peas and artichokes. Cover and place over a medium to low heat. Bring to a simmer and then cook for 1 hour. Check occasionally to make sure the tagine is not drying out and add more liquid if necessary. The tagine is ready when you can break the artichokes apart easily. Serve sprinkled with the mint.

WITH BROAD BEANS
Make this dish with frozen or fresh broad beans instead of peas.

WITH BROTH
Use vegetable stock instead of water to cook the artichokes.

WITH POTATOES
To bulk out the dish, add 8 very small new potatoes to the dish with the peas and artichokes.

WITH DILL
Substitute the cilantro for very finely chopped dill to give the dish quite a different flavor.

WITHOUT LEMON
Omit the preserved lemon to give the dish more overall sweetness.

Chickpea Tagine with Currant Couscous

A tagine is an earthenware dish from North Africa, ingeniously designed with a self-basting conical lid. It's also the name for the stew cooked in this dish. If you do not have a tagine (dish), a large saucepan with a close-fitting lid will work equally well when making this vegan recipe.

Serves 4

¼ cup (50 ml) extra-virgin olive oil
1 medium onion, finely chopped
3 garlic cloves, minced
½ tsp. ground cumin
½ tsp. powdered turmeric
¼ tsp. cayenne pepper
1 tsp. Spanish paprika

2 tsp. tomato paste
1 tsp. apricot jam
2 tbsp. finely chopped Italian parsley
2 tbsp. finely chopped cilantro
1 cup (250 ml) water, plus more if necessary
1 lb. (450 g) cherry tomatoes
1 x 15-oz. (425 g) can chickpeas, drained

1 tsp. salt
pinch of freshly ground black pepper
1 cup (225 g) couscous
1 cup (250 ml) vegetable stock
⅓ cup (75 g) currants
⅓ cup (75 g) pine nuts
¼ cup (25 g) finely chopped mint

1 Heat oil in a tagine or large saucepan over medium-low heat. Sauté onions until soft and translucent, about 5 minutes. Add garlic and cook for 1 minute, then add cumin, turmeric, and cayenne. Stir constantly for 1 minute. Add paprika, tomato paste, apricot jam, and 1 tablespoon each parsley and cilantro. Stir to combine.

2 Add water, tomatoes, and chickpeas. Stir, season with salt and pepper, and cover. Simmer for 15–20 minutes, until heated through and tomatoes have popped and softened. Keep warm until serving time.

3 Five minutes before serving, prepare couscous. Bring vegetable stock to a boil in a small pot with a tight-fitting lid. Remove from heat, add couscous, and stir. Cover and let sit for 5 minutes. Fluff couscous with fork, then add currants, pine nuts, and mint. Fluff again and serve with tagine.

WITH BUTTERNUT SQUASH
Prepare the basic recipe, adding 1 lb. (450 g) butternut squash. Peel, seed, and cube the squash and increase simmering time to 30 minutes, or until squash is tender. Add the tomatoes to the squash after it's been simmering for about 10 minutes.

WITH ZUCCHINI
Prepare the basic recipe, adding 1 small zucchini, ends trimmed and diced, with the tomatoes.

WITH KALE
Prepare the basic recipe, adding 2 cups (225 g) roughly chopped and trimmed kale with the tomatoes.

WITH EGGPLANT
Prepare the basic recipe, adding 1 medium eggplant, ends trimmed and diced, with the tomatoes.

Tagine of Sweet Potato & Pomegranate

Serves 4 to 6

2 tbsp. olive oil
1 onion, thickly sliced
2 garlic cloves, finely chopped
1 tsp. ras al-hanout
½ tsp. ground cinnamon
½ tsp. ground ginger
½ tsp. smoked sweet paprika
½ tsp. ground cumin
¼ tsp. freshly ground black pepper
2¼ lb. (1 kg) sweet potatoes, cubed
2 tbsp. pomegranate molasses

1 x 14-oz. (400-g) tin chopped tomatoes
2 tbsp. runny honey
½ tsp. ground saffron
7 fl. oz. (200 ml) water
1½ oz. (40 g) preserved lemon, finely
    chopped
4½ oz. (140 g) soft dried apricots, halved
4 oz. (125 g) green olives, stoned
1½ oz. (40 g) whole blanched almonds
small handful of fresh cilantro, chopped

for the couscous
7 oz. (200 g) couscous
2 tbsp. extra virgin olive oil
½ oz. (15 g) preserved lemon, rinsed,
    drained, pulp removed, flesh finely
    chopped
½ lemon, juice only
pinch sea salt
handful of fresh cilantro, chopped
3 tbsp. pomegranate seeds

1 Use a metal tagine or soak a ceramic tagine in cold water for 30 minutes and drain and dry before using. Always use a diffuser when heating tagines on the hob.

2 Heat a tagine over a medium heat, add the olive oil and the onions and cook for about 5 minutes. Then add the garlic and spices and mix together. Cook for a further minute, then add the sweet potatoes, pomegranate molasses, tomatoes, honey, saffron, water, preserved lemons, apricots, olives and almonds. Stir and bring to a simmer.

3 Add half the cilantro to the tagine. Reduce the heat to minimum, cover and simmer for about 20 minutes, until the potatoes are tender.

4 Meanwhile, place couscous in a heatproof bowl and cover with water by about ½ in. (1.5 cm). Add the olive oil, preserved lemon, lemon juice, and salt. Stir, cover with a plate and set aside for 3 to 5 minutes, until the liquid has been absorbed. Fluff with a fork. Season to taste and sprinkle with the chopped cilantro and the pomegranate seeds. Sprinkle the remaining cilantro over the tagine and serve with the couscous.

WITH CHILI
Substitute the sweet paprika for hot chili to give the tagine extra spice.

WITHOUT LEMON
Omit the preserved lemons and the lemon juice to keep the flavor of the tagine sweeter.

WITH PUMPKIN
Make this dish using pumpkin instead of sweet potatoes and proceed with the main recipe.

WITH PASSATA
For a smoother sauce, use passata instead of chopped tomatoes.

CHAPTER 5

Pasta
& Rice

Comforting gnocchi, velvety risottos, silky polenta, and hearty pasta dishes make up the recipes in this chapter. Perfect for parties and weeknight meals alike, they are real crowd-pleasers.

FRESH PASTA

All of the recipes in this chapter can be made using store-bought dried pasta, but if you would like to make your own this simple recipe is a good place to start. For each potion you will need 1 extra-large egg, beaten, and ½ cup (125 g) all-purpose flour. Put flour in a pile on work surface and make a well in the center. Pour in eggs. Using your fingers, knead eggs roughly into flour and then bring everything together. Knead until really smooth and pliable. Let rest under a clean cloth for 20 minutes. Roll out as thinly as possible with a long rolling pin or pasta machine. Roll the dough over and over again until really elastic, smooth and shiny. Cut it into the desired shape. Stop it drying out by covering with a damp cloth when not using. You can open-freeze the pasta on trays for a few hours then put in bags and freeze for up to 1 month.

DRIED PASTA

Dried durum wheat pasta, in a classic shape such as spaghetti, requires a specific method of kneading, cutting, and drying. It is made with hard, wheat flour mixed with water, and in Italian is called "pasta di semola di grano duro." The gluten content of hard wheat is so high that is raises the overall protein content of this kind of pasta compared to types made with soft wheat flour which has a lower gluten content. This kind of pasta is eaten all over the Mediterranean and each region has its own specific shapes. These are particularly good with the recipes that belong to those areas and many are part of a regional culinary tradition, so much so that some shapes may only be found in one region.

WHOLE-WHEAT PASTA

Whole-wheat pasta has a strong flavor, which makes it difficult to appreciate the quality of the sauce used to dress the finished dish. Normal durum wheat pasta that is cooked al dente (firm to the bite) usually provides plenty of fiber. Conversely, if the pasta is overcooked it will turn into a solid, glutinous mass that is much harder to digest. It is important to respect the al dente rule because not only will the pasta dish taste so much better, it will also be much more beneficial from a digestive perspective.

GLUTEN-FREE PASTA

Almost all sauces can be successfully used to dress gluten-free pasta, and there are countless brands available in stores. With gluten-free pasta it always seems to me that the sauce becomes more important than the pasta as a carrier, because the pasta on its own is not always delicious.

PERFECT RISOTTO

To make prefect risotto, it is important to have the right kind of rice. A risotto made with the wrong kind of rice will not have the right level of creaminess. It is the starch falling from the grains as the rice cooks, blending with the stock, wine, and other flavors, that gives the risotto its velvety texture. It is never necessary to add cream to a risotto.

Making risotto successfully is all about texture, so it is important to master a simple version before moving on to more complicated recipes. Make sure you have the right kind of chalky rice for making risotto, and that you have a good, tasty stock. Risotto takes 20 minutes to make, from the moment the rice is added to the pot. For a risotto to be perfect, the rice needs to remain slightly chewy, with no trace of chalkiness.

HOME-MADE GNOCCHI

Making potato gnocchi is not the easiest thing to do, but the results are much more delicious than anything you can buy. Make sure the potatoes are as floury (starchy) as possible. Russet and Idaho potatoes have a high starch content, so they're good for gnocchi. The cooked gnocchi can be dressed with a wide variety of sauces, just like pasta.

SILKY POLENTA

Polenta is a staple of the Northern Italian diet. You can buy a quick-cook version, which you mix up in just 5 minutes. Using traditional polenta, you need to stir constantly for about 50 minutes, but the end result is very different from the quick-cook kind. Because it is such a time-consuming operation, it's easier to make a large batch, serve it fresh the first time, and then let it set before slicing to be chilled and then fried or grilled on subsequent days.

Arancini

These delicious little balls of rice, named "little oranges" because of their shape and color, are very much a part of the Sicilian menu. They can be made in any size to suit all occasions.

Serves 4–6

about 2¼ cups (400 g) cooled risotto
about ¼ lb. (125 g) cooked peas
3 oz. (75 g) sautéed mushrooms
3 oz. (75 g) chopped Parma ham
3½ oz. (100 g) diced mozzarella

3 tbsp. all-purpose flour
3 eggs, beaten
6 tbsp. fine, dry, white bread crumbs
4 cups (1 liter) vegetable, canola, or sunflower seed oil for deep-frying or olive oil for brushing prior to baking

1　Mix the cold risotto with the peas, mushrooms, and Parma ham. Roll the mixture into balls about the size of small oranges. Push a piece of mozzarella into the center of each ball, and make sure it is well covered.

2　Roll into flour, then beaten eggs, then bread crumbs. Make sure the balls are firm and well-coated. Deep-fry in oil in a large skillet until golden and crisp all over, remove, and drain on paper towel.

3　Alternatively, arrange the rice balls on an oiled baking sheet, brush gently with olive oil, and bake for about 10 minutes at 400°F (200°C) until crisp and golden brown. Serve hot, with a little tomato sauce for dipping, or salad.

WITH MUSHROOM
Prepare basic recipe, omitting peas, mushrooms, and Parma ham. Soak 1½ oz. (40 g) dried porcini mushrooms in a small bowl of hot water for about 1 hour or until softened. Drain carefully and discard the liquid. Toss the mushrooms in a pan with 1 tablespoon butter until cooked through. Mix cooked mushrooms into cold risotto and continue as in main recipe.

WITH EMMENTHAL
Prepare basic recipe, replacing mozzarella with small cubes of Emmenthal.

WITH SALAMI
Prepare basic recipe, using chopped salami in place of the Parma ham.

WITH BOLOGNESE RAGU
Prepare basic recipe, omitting peas, mushrooms, and Parma ham from the rice balls. Insert a teaspoonful of bolognese ragu (see page 153) as well as the mozzarella into the center of each rice ball before rolling in flour, beaten egg, and bread crumbs. Fry or bake as in main recipe.

Venetian Chicken Risotto

This risotto with chicken is a typically Venetian risotto, wet and runny, but also very rich and filling. Make sure the chicken stock is very flavorsome to ensure that the finished risotto tastes properly rich. Although traditionally the risotto is served without any added color, you could stir a bit of parsley into the finished dish if you feel it needs a touch of green.

Serves 6

½ cup (125 g) butter
½ onion, chopped finely
1 lb. (450 g) skinless
   chicken, diced
7 tbsp. dry white wine
2 cups (425 g) risotto rice
   (Vialone Nano,
   Vialone Gigante,
   or Arborio)

4 cups (1 liter) rich
   chicken stock
3 oz. (75 g) Parmesan,
   freshly grated
sea salt and freshly
   ground black pepper

1 Melt half the butter in a deep saucepan on a low heat. Add the onion and fry until just pale golden, then add diced chicken. Cook chicken very gently until lightly browned, then pour in the wine, raise heat, and cook quickly for about 2 minutes to allow the alcohol to burn off.

2 Add the rice. Stir thoroughly, lower the heat, then add the stock gradually, one ladleful at a time, stirring constantly until it is absorbed. Continue until the rice is tender, and most or all of the stock has been used.

3 Stir in the remaining butter and half the cheese. Remove from the heat and cover. Rest for about 3 minutes, transfer to a warmed platter, sprinkle with remaining cheese, and serve.

WITH LIVER
Prepare the basic recipe, omitting the chicken. Instead, cook 1 cup (225 g) cleaned, roughly chopped chicken livers in butter until just browned. Add a spoonful of brandy and flame the livers, then remove from the heat. Stir the livers into the risotto about 5 minutes before risotto is cooked through.

WITH PANCETTA
Prepare basic recipe, adding some chopped smoked pancetta to the onion and chicken at the beginning of the cooking process.

WITH DUCK
Prepare basic recipe, replacing the chicken with finely chopped, skinless duck. Make sure it is well cooked and tender before adding rice.

WITH RABBIT
Replace chicken with finely chopped, skinless rabbit. Double the amount of onion and add 1½ teaspoons finely chopped fresh sage before cooking rice.

Sausage Risotto

This very filling, rustic risotto uses delicious Italian sausages and is a great family favorite.

Serves 6

4 large Italian sausages, casings removed, crumbled
1 onion, peeled and chopped
1–2 cloves garlic, peeled and chopped

1 small sprig fresh rosemary, chopped
4–5 tbsp. light olive oil
2 cups (425 g) risotto rice such as Arborio

2½ pints (1.4 liters) hot chicken or vegetable stock
sea salt and freshly ground black pepper
freshly grated Parmesan, to serve (optional)

1 Put crumbled sausages, onion, garlic, and rosemary into a large heavy-bottomed saucepan with olive oil. Fry gently until onion is cooked. Add the rice and begin the cooking process, adding a little hot stock at a time and waiting for the rice to absorb it, stirring thoroughly each time you add more liquid. Continue in this way until rice is tender and all the grains are plump and fluffy.

2 Season to taste with salt and pepper. Remove from heat, stir, and cover. Let stand for about 3 minutes before transferring to a platter and serving. Offer Parmesan separately, if desired.

WITH BOLOGNESE RAGU
Omit sausages. Stir in some bolognese ragu (see page 153) before adding stock. Add a couple of tablespoons of freshly grated Parmesan to the risotto just before resting.

WITH MUSHROOM RISOTTO
Add a small handful of dried porcini mushrooms (soaked in warm water until soft, then drained and chopped) to sausages at start of cooking process.

WITH LAMB
Replace sausages with cubed lamb removed from 8 small chops.

WITH VENISON
To give the risotto a rich, gamey flavor, replace sausages with chopped, tender venison or other game meat.

WITH TOMATO & PANCETTA
Prepare basic recipe, replacing the sausages with 8 chopped strips of smoked pancetta and 1 large tablespoon concentrated tomato paste, diluted in a little warm water. Garnish the finished risotto with a handful of chopped fresh mushrooms and a couple of crisply cooked and crumbled pancetta strips.

Arabian-style Rice

Serves 4–6

2 cups (425 g) long-grain rice
2 tbsp. sweet melted butter

about 4 tbsp. chopped greens (e.g., spinach or cabbage or tops of Brussels sprouts)

2½ pints (1½ liters) cold water
½ tsp. salt

1   Wash the rice in cold water repeatedly, then cover with cold water and let soak for about 10 minutes before rinsing and draining.

2   Melt the butter in a large skillet over medium heat, then add the rice. Add the greens and mix, being careful not to let the rice or vegetables catch on the bottom of the pan and start burning. After stirring for about 5 minutes, add the water, and season with salt.

3   Cover tightly with a lid and a sheet of waxed paper under the lid, and let simmer until the grains have become swollen and tender and the rice has absorbed all the liquid (or about 20–30 minutes). Use 2 forks to fluff the rice before serving.

WITH SPICES
Prepare the basic recipe, adding ½ teaspoon ground cinnamon and a pinch of ground cloves to the rice with the butter. Fry together before adding the greens. You can omit the greens if you wish.

WITH LENTILS
Prepare the basic recipe, but replace greens with 4 tablespoons cooked lentils.

WITH FRESH HERBS
Prepare the basic recipe, adding freshly chopped herbs such as cilantro, mint, and flat-leaf parsley at the very end. You can omit the greens if you wish.

WITH CHICKEN OR DUCK
Prepare the basic recipe, but replace the greens with 4 or 5 tablespoons finely shredded, cooked chicken or duck meat (or keep the greens as well).

Rice Salad

Serves 4

½ lb. (225 g) long-grain Italian rice
1 large carrot, cubed
2½ oz. (60 g) string beans, diced
1 medium potato, cubed

1 small zucchini, cubed
2 tbsp. coarsely chopped black or green olives
1 tbsp. chopped fresh flat-leaf parsley
7 tbsp. extra-virgin olive oil

3 tsp. lemon juice
sea salt and freshly ground black pepper

1   Boil the rice in lightly salted water for 18 minutes, or until tender. Meanwhile, cook all the other vegetables separately, also in salted water, until tender. Drain the rice and all the vegetables thoroughly.

2   Mix the warm, drained rice with the olives, parsley, and all the cooked vegetables. Use a very large spoon or your hands to distribute everything evenly.

3   Combine the olive oil and lemon juice thoroughly, then pour over the rice mixture. Mix again and season to taste. Let stand for at least 1 hour, or longer, before serving. If you need to chill the salad, make sure it is at room temperature when you serve it so that the flavors come through.

WITH PESTO
Prepare the basic recipe, halving the amount of lemon juice and adding 2 or 3 tablespoons fresh pesto (see page 81) to the olive oil and lemon juice dressing.

WITH CHICKEN
Prepare the basic recipe, adding 2 cooked, skinless chicken breasts, cut into small cubes, to the rice with the vegetables before mixing with the dressing.

WITH TUNA
Prepare the basic recipe, adding 1 small can tuna, drained and flaked, to the rice with the vegetables before mixing with the dressing.

WITH CAPERS
Prepare the basic recipe, adding about 15 plump capers, rinsed and dried and roughly chopped, to the rice with the olives.

WITH ANCHOVIES
Prepare the basic recipe, adding 1 small can anchovies, drained and chopped, to the rice with the olives.

Parmesan Risotto

Cheese and butter risotto is the basic recipe from which all other risotto variations are created. Making risotto successfully is all about texture, so it is important to master a simple version like this one before moving on to more complicated recipes. Make sure you have the right kind of chalky rice for making risotto, and that you have a good, tasty stock. Risotto takes 20 minutes to make, from the moment the rice is added to the pot. For a risotto to be perfect, the rice needs to remain slightly chewy, with no trace of chalkiness.

Serves 6

6 tbsp. butter
1 medium onion, finely chopped
1 lb. (450 g) risotto rice (Arborio, Vialone Nano, or Carnaroli)
4 cups (1 liter) hot vegetable stock
6 tbsp. freshly grated Parmesan
sea salt and freshly ground black pepper

1 Fry the onion in half the butter for about 10 minutes over a very low heat, or until soft but not colored. Stir in rice and toast the grains thoroughly on all sides for about 5 minutes, over medium heat, so that they become opaque and thoroughly coated in butter. Move the pan off the heat for a few moments if the rice looks like it is browning.

2 Add the first 3 ladlefuls of hot stock and stir. Then, stirring constantly, add the stock one ladle at a time, letting the rice absorb the liquid at its own pace. You will know when to add more stock when a clear wake through the grains opens up behind the spoon as you draw it through the cooking risotto.

3 When the rice is almost completely soft and creamy, stir in the cheese and the rest of the butter. Taste and adjust the seasoning, then cover and rest for about 3 minutes, covered with a lid, before transferring to a platter to serve.

WITH PARSLEY
Prepare basic recipe, adding a large handful of fresh flat-leaf parsley, finely chopped, at the very end of the cooking time.

WITH RED WINE
Prepare basic recipe, substituting half the stock for a really good red wine.

WITH GORGONZOLA
Prepare basic recipe, adding about 5 oz (150 g) cubed Gorgonzola to melt in the risotto just before covering and resting. Give the risotto one final stir just before serving. Offer grated Parmesan separately at the table.

WITH SPINACH & WALNUTS
Prepare basic recipe, but about halfway through the cooking process, add a couple of handfuls of finely chopped fresh spinach to the rice. Just before resting, stir in a handful of roughly chopped walnuts.

WITH MUSHROOM
Prepare basic recipe, adding about ½ lb. (225 g) sliced mushrooms with the onion.

Italian Risotto with Scallops

This exquisite risotto uses a zucchini purée to add a delicate flavor that perfectly complements the scallops.

Serves 4

1 pint (225 g) cherry tomatoes
4 tbsp. extra-virgin olive oil, plus 2 tsp.
salt and freshly ground black pepper to taste
¾ cup (175 g) diced onion
1 garlic clove, minced

2 cups (250 g) diced zucchini
¼ cup (50 ml) fresh lemon juice
1 lb. (450 g) uncooked Arborio rice
2–3 cups (450–700 ml) chicken broth

¼ cup (25 g) grated Parmesan
18 medium scallops
¼ cup (25 g) finely chopped parsley, to garnish

1   Preheat oven to 250°F (130°C). Toss cherry tomatoes in 2 teaspoons oil. Season with salt and pepper, transfer to a lightly greased baking sheet, and roast for 1 hour. Set aside.

2   Heat 1 tablespoon oil in a frying pan over medium heat. Add onion and cook for 4 minutes, stirring frequently. Add garlic and cook for 1 minute. Add zucchini and cook for 5 minutes more. Add lemon juice and 1 tablespoon oil, and purée the mixture, using an immersion blender or food processor. Set aside.

3   To prepare the risotto, heat 1 tablespoon oil in a medium pot over medium heat. Add rice and stir to coat. Stir in 1 cup (250 ml) of broth at a time, stirring almost constantly until all the liquid is absorbed and rice is tender. Add zucchini purée and Parmesan and stir until well incorporated. Keep warm.

4   Heat remaining tablespoon of oil in large frying pan. Add scallops, season with salt and pepper, and add roasted tomatoes. Sauté for 5–6 minutes, until scallops are opaque and beginning to brown. Fold scallops and tomatoes into risotto. Garnish each serving with parsley.

WITH PRAWNS
Prepare the basic recipe, replacing the scallops with 1½ lb. (700 g) shelled and deveined prawns. Sauté prawns until they are pink and opaque.

WITH CLAMS
Prepare the basic recipe, replacing the scallops with 2 cups (450 g) cooked clams. Omit the sautéing step.

WITH SCALLOPS & CAULIFLOWER
Prepare the basic recipe, adding 1 head of cauliflower, cut into florets, to the cherry tomatoes for roasting. Add 1 tablespoon oil for tossing the vegetables before roasting.

WITH SCALLOPS & ST. AGUR
Prepare the basic recipe, replacing the grated Parmesan with 4 oz. (125 g) crumbled St. Agur cheese.

Paella

This traditional Spanish dish, full of delicious fresh ingredients, is especially suited to celebrations. Dercorate with small wedges of lemon and sprigs of aromatic herbs.

Serves 8

1 generous cup (240 ml) olive oil
6 oz. (175 g) chorizo, thinly sliced
¼ lb. (225 g) pancetta, finely diced
2 cloves garlic, finely chopped
1 large Spanish onion, finely diced
1 red bell pepper, diced
1 tsp. fresh thyme leaves
1 tsp. red pepper flakes
2 cups (425 g) Calasparra, bomba or Arborio rice

1 tsp. paprika
½ cup (115 ml) dry white wine
4 cups (1 liter) chicken stock, heated with ¼ tsp. saffron strands
8 boneless chicken thighs, each chopped in half and browned
18 small clams, cleaned
¼ lb. (225 g) fresh or frozen peas
4 large fresh tomatoes, seeded and diced
1 head garlic, cloves separated and peeled

12 raw jumbo shrimp, in shells
1 lb. (450 g) squid, cleaned and chopped into bite-sized pieces
5 tbsp. chopped fresh flat-leaf parsley
saffron strands

1 Heat half the olive oil in a paella dish or heavy-based saucepan. Add chorizo and pancetta and fry until crisp. Add garlic, onion, and red pepper, and heat until softened. Add thyme, red pepper flakes, and rice, and stir until all the grains of rice are coated and glossy.

2 Now add paprika and wine, and when the mixture is bubbling, pour in hot chicken stock. Add chicken thighs and cook for 5–10 minutes. Now add clams to the pan. Add peas and chopped tomatoes and continue to cook gently for another 10 minutes.

3 Meanwhile, heat the remaining oil with the whole garlic cloves in a separate pan and add the shrimp once the garlic is softened. Fry quickly for a minute or two, then add shrimp to the paella.

4 Repeat with the squid, frying them quickly for 2 or 3 minutes with the whole garlic cloves (you may need to add a little extra oil), and then add them to paella. Discard garlic cloves. Scatter the chopped parsley over the paella and serve immediately.

WITH RABBIT
Prepare the basic recipe, replacing the chicken with 1 whole rabbit, jointed (but keep the chicken stock).

WITH MUSSELS
Prepare the basic recipe, replacing the clams with about 20 cleaned fresh mussels.

WITH ARTICHOKES
Prepare the basic recipe, adding 8 fresh artichoke bases to the paella with the chicken thighs.

WITH BELL PEPPERS
Prepare the basic recipe, adding 2 red bell peppers, seeded and cut into chunks, with the peas and tomatoes.

Four Cheese Gnocchi

Making potato gnocchi is not the easiest thing to do, but the results are much more delicious than anything you can buy. Make sure the potatoes are as floury (starchy) as possible. Russet and Idaho potatoes have a high starch content, so they're good for gnocchi. The cooked gnocchi can be dressed with a wide variety of sauces, just like pasta. The following is a very rich cheesy dish.

Serves 6

2 lbs. (900 g) floury potatoes, scrubbed
3 eggs, beaten
½ cup (50 g) all-purpose flour, plus more for dusting
sea salt
¼ lb. (125 g) freshly grated Parmesan

¼ lb. (125 g) fontina, thinly sliced
¼ lb. (125 g) Gorgonzola, cubed
¼ lb. (125 g) groviera, cubed or grated
1¼ cups (300 ml) light cream

1 Boil the potatoes until soft, drain, and peel quickly. Press through a potato ricer twice. Blend in the eggs and flour. Make a soft dough with your hands, then roll it into long rolls the thickness of your thumb on a floured board.

2 Cut into half-inch lengths and form into gnocchi by gently pressing each one onto the floured surface with the tines of a fork to leave ridges in the dough. You will need about 12 gnocchi per person. Spread the gnocchi out on a large floured board until required.

3 Bring a large pot of salted water to a gentle boil, drop in the gnocchi in small batches, and cook until they float on the surface. Scoop out with a slotted spoon and arrange in a well-buttered ovenproof dish. Cover with all the cheeses, then pour cream on top. Bake in a preheated oven at 375°F (190°C) for about 25 minutes, or until well browned. Serve at once.

WITH BASIL
Prepare and cook gnocchi. Instead of four cheeses and cream, dress hot gnocchi with a handful of freshly picked basil leaves, some cubed fresh tomatoes, and a little melted butter. Add a handful of freshly grated Parmesan and serve.

WITH MUSHROOMS & FONTINA
Mix a little finely chopped fresh parsley into dough. Instead of four cheeses and cream, gently toss hot gnocchi with some warm sautéed mushrooms, a little warmed heavy cream, and some grated fontina cheese.

WITH BOLOGNESE RAGU
Prepare and cook gnocchi. Instead of four cheeses and cream, gently toss hot gnocchi with bolognese ragu (see page 153).

WITH TOMATO SAUCE
Prepare and cook gnocchi. Instead of four cheeses and cream, gently toss hot gnocchi with pomodoro sauce (see page 151).

WITH GORGONZOLA & WALNUTS
Prepare and cook gnocchi. Instead of four cheeses and cream, gently toss hot gnocchi with Gorgonzola and toasted walnuts.

Roman-style Semolina Gnocchi

This is the ultimate comfort food, a delicately flavored dish of rounded gnocchi made out of cooked semolina, coated in butter and cheese, and baked until golden brown.

Serves 6

4 cups (1 liter) milk
1 cup (100 g) semolina
2 egg yolks
¼ lb. (125 g) Parmesan,
　freshly grated
½ cup (125 g) butter
pinch of ground nutmeg
sea salt and freshly
　ground black pepper

1　Bring the milk to a boil in a large saucepan. Reduce the heat to low, sprinkle in the semolina, and whisk constantly to prevent lumps forming. Continue until the mixture begins to thicken, then use a wooden spoon to stir constantly for about 10 minutes. You will know the mixture is thick enough when it begins to come away from the sides and bottom of the pan and forms a rounded, soft ball.

2　Remove the pan from the heat. Stir in the egg yolks, half the Parmesan, and half the butter. Season to taste with nutmeg, salt, and pepper. Dampen a work surface lightly with cold water, then tip the semolina mixture onto it. Using a spatula dipped in cold water, spread flat to a thickness of about ½ in. (1 cm). Using a 3-to-4-in. (10 cm) biscuit cutter, cut all the semolina into even-sized circles.

3　Use some of the remaining butter to grease a shallow, ovenproof 10 x 12-in. (25 x 30-cm) dish. Arrange a layer of scraps from the cut-out circles on the bottom of dish. Cover with a little grated Parmesan and a few dots of butter. Cover with a layer of slightly overlapping semolina circles, and cover these with cheese and butter as before.

4　Repeat until all ingredients have been used. Melt any remaining butter and trickle it over the top. Bake in a preheated 425°F (220°C) oven for about 15 minutes before serving.

WITH SAFFRON
Prepare basic recipe, but add a little saffron to the semolina mixture for a lightly spiced and deep golden yellow gnocchi.

WITH SMOKED SALMON
Prepare basic recipe. Scatter a little chopped smoked salmon among the layers of gnocchi before baking.

WITH GORGONZOLA
Prepare basic recipe. Add a few cubes of Gorgonzola among the layers of gnocchi before baking.

WITH SAGE BUTTER
Prepare basic recipe. Instead of layering the gnocchi with cubes of butter, melt the remaining 4 tablespoons of butter with a few fresh sage leaves and drizzle over the gnocchi. Add Parmesan and bake as normal.

Pumpkin Gnocchi with Butter & Sage

These pumpkin gnocchi taste sweet and delicious and look gorgeous with their deep orange color. They are especially delectable when served with sage butter.

Serves 6

1½ lb. (700 g) fresh pumpkin or squash
1 cup (100 g) all-purpose flour, plus more
    for rolling

2 eggs, beaten
2 oz. (50 g) freshly grated Parmesan, plus
    more for serving

7 tbsp. butter
8–9 fresh sage leaves, lightly bruised

1 Peel the pumpkin or squash and remove seeds and all stringy parts. Cut into thick slices and sprinkle with salt. Bake at 325°F (160°C) on a sheet covered with parchment paper, until softened enough to mash with a fork, about 30–35 minutes. Remove from the oven and cool, then mash until completely smooth.

2 Working with small quantities at a time, gradually add the flour, eggs, and Parmesan. Mix gently with your hands, incorporating as much air as possible by not pressing down too hard. Sprinkle a clean surface with flour and roll the dough into a cylinder. With a sharp knife, cut into equal-sized sections, about an inch long. Lay the gnocchi on a floured surface, spaced apart, until required.

3 Bring a large pot of salted water to a rolling boil, then lower the heat slightly to a gentle simmer. Melt the butter with the bruised sage over a low heat. Turn off the heat when butter is slightly browned. Drop the gnocchi gently into simmering water in batches of 6–8 at a time. Remove after they bob up to the surface, and transfer to the pan with sage butter. Spoon butter over them to coat.

4 Continue with the next batch of gnocchi until they are all cooked. Transfer onto a warmed serving platter or individual plates. Sprinkle with freshly grated Parmesan and serve at once.

WITH PINE NUTS & PARMESAN
Prepare basic recipe, omitting the sage butter. Dress the hot gnocchi with melted butter, toasted pine nuts, and freshly grated Parmesan.

WITH BUTTER & GORGONZOLA
Prepare basic recipe, omitting the sage butter. In a double boiler, melt some Gorgonzola in enough cream or milk to cover until smooth. Spoon the sauce over the hot gnocchi and sprinkle with just a little freshly grated Parmesan.

WITH CHERRY TOMATOES & CREAM
Prepare basic recipe, omitting the sage butter. Dress the hot gnocchi with warmed heavy cream and coarsely chopped cherry tomatoes. Add some freshly grated Parmesan and a handful of fresh basil leaves to serve.

WITH CHERRY TOMATOES & MASCARPONE
Prepare basic recipe, omitting the sage butter. Dress the hot gnocchi with pasta al pomodoro with mascarpone (see page 151). Add some freshly grated Parmesan and a handful of fresh basil leaves to serve.

Pasta Salad with Peppers

This combination of flavors is really delicious. Prepared in advance, it makes for a perfect weekday lunch.

Serves 4

4 large ripe tomatoes
1 large red pepper
1 large yellow pepper
Juice of 1 lemon
Salt
7 tbsp. extra-virgin olive oil

1 tsp. Italian mustard
2⅓ cups (340 g) fusilli
1 large handful fresh basil leaves, washed and finely chopped

1 Blanch the tomatoes in boiling water, then skin and seed them. Chop into rough chunks. Broil the peppers until browned. Place them in a bowl, cover with a sheet of plastic wrap to steam until completely cooled, then remove then from the bowl and skin them. Remove the seeds from the peppers and cut the flesh into rough chunks. In a small bowl, mix together the lemon juice with the salt, oil, and mustard until thickened and creamy.

2 Bring a large saucepan of salted water to the boil. Put the pasta into the water and stir thoroughly. Replace the lid and return to the boil. Remove or adjust the lid once the water is boiling again. Cook according to the packet instructions until al dente. Drain, and run under cold water until pasta is cool.

3 Transfer the pasta to a large salad bowl and add the tomatoes, peppers, and dressing. Mix together thoroughly. Add the basil and adjust seasoning. Refrigerate for at least an hour before serving.

QUICK PASTA SALAD
Use canned or bottled roasted peppers instead of roasting your own.

WITH ASPARAGUS
Substitute the peppers for 20 steamed, just-cooked asparagus spears, cut into lengths equal to the penne, and precede as main recipe.

WITH TUNA
Add a large can of tuna, flaked, to the pasta salad at the very end when combining all the ingredients together.

WITH CAPERS
Add 2 tablespoons small pickled capers, drained and rinsed, to the pasta salad at the end.

WITH PESTO
Add a tablespoon of fresh pesto and a handful of toasted pine kernels the salad at the end.

Tabbouleh

Serves 4

1 cup (150 g) bulgur wheat
4 fresh ripe tomatoes, seeded and finely
chopped, with their juice

2 medium-sized bunches fresh flat-leaf
parsley, finely chopped
4 scallions, finely chopped
juice of 2 lemons

¾ tsp. sea salt
¼ cup (50 ml) extra-virgin olive oil
freshly ground black pepper
2 tbsp. finely chopped fresh mint

1   Soak bulgur in cold water for 10 minutes. Drain in
a sieve lined with damp cheesecloth, then squeeze
out all the water. Transfer to a serving bowl and
fluff with a fork.

2   Stir in tomatoes with juice, parsley, and scallions.
Add lemon juice, salt, and olive oil; season with
pepper. Toss to coat. You can make the dish up to
this point up to the day before, then just before
serving, stir in mint.

WITH OLIVES
Prepare the basic recipe, adding
about 20 pitted and roughly chopped
green olives to the salad with the
tomatoes, parsley, and scallions.

WITH CHILI
Prepare the basic recipe, adding
1 fresh chili pepper, seeded and
finely chopped, to the salad with the
tomatoes, parsley, and scallions.

WITH TUNA
Prepare the basic recipe, adding
1 small can drained, flaked tuna to
the salad with the tomatoes, parsley,
and scallions.

WITH CHICKPEAS
Prepare the basic recipe, adding
about 1 cup (225 g) drained, cooked
(or canned) chickpeas to the salad
with the tomatoes, parsley, and
scallions. You might like to increase
the quantity of the dressing slightly
as the chickpeas will soak it up.

Couscous Salad

Serves 4

½ lb. (225 g) couscous
scant 2 cups (450 ml) hot vegetable stock
5 tbsp. olive oil
2 tbsp. freshly squeezed lemon juice
sea salt and freshly ground black pepper

10 sun-dried tomatoes, preserved in oil,
quartered
2 medium avocados, peeled, pitted, and cut
into large chunks
4 oz. (125 g) black olives, such as Kalamata

good handful of nuts, such as pine nuts,
cashews, or almonds
½ lb. (225 g) feta, roughly crumbled
¼ lb. (115 g) salad leaves

1   Put the couscous into a large bowl, stir in the hot
stock, cover, and let soak for 5 minutes.

2   Make a dressing with the olive oil, lemon juice,
salt, and pepper. Stir 2 tablespoons of the dressing
into the couscous, and then gently mix in the
tomatoes, avocados, olives, nuts, and feta. Taste,
adding more salt and freshly ground black pepper
if required.

3   Toss the salad greens with the remaining dressing,
divide between 4 plates, and spoon the couscous
on top.

WITH TOASTED ALMONDS
Prepare the basic recipe, replacing
the mixed nuts with a good handful
of lightly toasted slivered almonds.

WITH APRICOTS
Prepare the basic recipe, replacing
the olives with the same quantity of
dried or fresh apricots, chopped into
olive-sized pieces.

WITH FIGS
Prepare the basic recipe, replacing
the olives with 6 firm fresh figs,
unpeeled (or 6 soft dried figs), cut
into olive-sized pieces.

WITH TUNA
Prepare the basic recipe, replacing
the feta with 1 small can tuna,
drained and flaked.

WITH ROASTED BELL PEPPERS
Prepare the basic recipe, adding 2
roasted and sliced bell peppers to
the couscous with the tomatoes.

Polenta with Mushrooms

Polenta is a staple of the Northern Italian diet. You can buy a quick-cook version, which you mix up in just 5 minutes. Using traditional polenta, you need to stir constantly for about 50 minutes, but the end result is very different from the quick-cook kind. Because it is such a time-consuming operation, it's easier to make a large batch, serve it fresh the first time, and then let it set before slicing to be fried or grilled in subsequent days.

Serves 6

2¾ pints (1.5 liters) cold water
large pinch sea salt
1⅓ cups (225 g) ground cornmeal (polenta)
1 lb. (450 g) fresh porcini, oyster, or other mushrooms of your choice, cleaned, trimmed, washed

4–5 tbsp. olive oil
3–4 cloves garlic, finely chopped
sea salt and freshly ground black pepper
1 large pinch finely chopped fresh rosemary

1 To make polenta, pour cold water into a wide, heavy-bottomed, preferably copper pan and place over high heat. Bring to a boil. Trickle the polenta into boiling water in a fine rain with one hand, and whisk constantly with the other. When all the polenta has been whisked into water, reduce heat to medium-low and begin to stir with a strong, long-handled wooden spoon until polenta comes away from the sides of pan. This will take 40–50 minutes.

2 Turn the polenta out onto a wooden board and smooth it into a mound using 2 spatulas or wooden spoons. Let it stand for about 5 minutes. While the polenta stands, slice mushrooms finely.

3 Heat oil and garlic together in a large saucepan on medium heat for about 1 minute, then add mushrooms. Stir, season, and cover. Allow mushrooms to cook through, stirring occasionally. Stir in rosemary. Cover and let stand for another 2 minutes before serving, piping hot, with slabs of polenta.

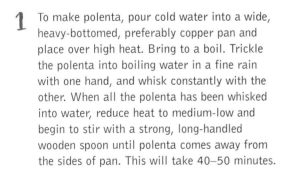

WITH SAUSAGE
Prepare polenta, but omit mushrooms. Fry 12 Italian sausages gently with 1 chopped onion and a little olive oil. Add 2 x 14 oz. (400 g) cans of chopped tomatoes, a sprig of rosemary, and 1 bay leaf. Cover and simmer gently for about 30 minutes, stirring occasionally. Serve on top of hot polenta slices.

WITH BEEF STEW
Prepare polenta, but omit mushrooms. Serve a slice of polenta, covered with a ladleful of beef stew, for each person.

WITH POACHED FISH
Prepare polenta, but omit mushrooms. Poach 6 chunky fillets of haddock or cod in enough milk to cover, with a bay leaf, salt, and pepper. When the fish is cooked through, remove it and allow the milk to reduce, stirring until slightly thickened. Serve each slice of polenta with a fillet and some milk.

WITH GORGONZOLA
Prepare polenta, but omit mushrooms. Slice the set polenta and grill on both sides until browned. Cover each slice with Gorgonzola and return to grill to melt cheese before serving.

Penne Arrabiata

Cheese is not normally served with this recipe, which is called "penne al'arrabiata" in Italian. However if you prefer to serve it with cheese go for an aged, peppery pecorino.

Serves 4

4 cloves garlic, peeled
  and finely chopped
1 to 4 dried red chilis,
  whole
4 tbsp. extra-virgin olive
  oil

2½ cups (500 g) canned
  tomatoes, chopped
sea salt
2⅔ cups (400 g) penne
1 tsp. fresh flat-leaf
  parsley, chopped

1 Fry the garlic and chili in the olive oil until they are slightly blackened. Discard the chili and add the tomatoes to the pan. Season with salt and simmer for about 20 minutes.

2 Bring a large saucepan of salted water to the boil. Put the pasta into the water and stir thoroughly. Replace the lid and return to the boil. Remove or adjust the lid once the water is boiling again. Cook according to the packet instructions until al dente.

3 Drain the pasta, and return to the pot. Pour over the sauce and mix together. Transfer to a warmed serving dish and sprinkle with the parsley before serving.

WITH FRESH CHILI
Use finely chopped fresh chilis instead of dried to give the sauce quite a different taste.

WITH PAPRIKA
Add ½ teaspoon of smoked paprika to the garlic and chili to give the sauce a lovely smoky depth.

WITH PASSATA
Use passata instead of canned, chopped tomatoes to make the sauce really smooth.

WITHOUT GARLIC OR CHILI
Leave the garlic whole and discard it with the chilis for a milder flavor.

WITH EXTRA CHILI
Seed and chop the chilis very finely and leave them in the sauce to make it more fiery.

Pasta al Forno

This is a simple, easy and comforting dish for the whole family. This recipe uses rigatoni but you could also use penne, conchiglie or macaroni. The béchamel sauce is incredibly versatile and can be used to make lasagna and any other dish requiring a white sauce.

Serves 4

2⅔ cups (400 g) rigatoni
6 tbsp. freshly grated
    Parmesan cheese
7 oz. (200 g) cooked ham,
    chopped
3 tbsp. unsalted butter
salt and freshly ground
    black pepper

For the béchamel sauce
2½ oz. (60 g) unsalted
    butter
4 level tbsp. plain flour
1½ pints (700 ml) milk
pinch grated nutmeg

1. Bring a large saucepan of salted water to the boil. Put the pennette into the water and stir thoroughly. Replace the lid and return to the boil. Remove or adjust the lid once the water is boiling again. Cook according to the packet instructions until al dente. Drain, and return to the pot.

2. Meanwhile, make the béchamel sauce. Melt the butter over a low heat, add the flour and mix together to form a paste. Pour in the milk and whisk vigorously to prevent any lumps forming. Add the nutmeg and simmer gently for about 15 minutes, stirring constantly, until thick enough to coat the back of a spoon.

3. Melt two thirds of the Parmesan into the sauce. Add two thirds of the sauce and all of the ham. Mix together. Grease a large ovenproof dish with half the butter. Pour in the dressed pasta and arrange it evenly in a thick layer.

4. Pour over the remaining sauce and dot with the remaining butter. Sprinkle with the remaining Parmesan. Bake in a preheated oven at 375°F (190°C) for about 15 minutes or until golden and bubbling.

WITH PEAS & EMMENTHAL
Add ½ cup (100 g) cooked peas and ½ cup (50 g) cubed Emmenthal to the pasta sauce with the ham.

WITH ZUCCHINI & MOZZARELLA
Add ½ cup (100 g) cubed, sautéed zucchini and ⅔ cup (75 g) shredded mozzarella to the pasta sauce with the ham.

WITH HERBS
To add a herby note, mix 3 tablespoons of finely chopped fresh flat-leaf parsley and 2 tablespoons snipped chives into the béchamel before mixing into the pasta with the ham.

SMOKY PASTA AL FORNO
Add ¼ teaspoon smoked paprika, 1 cup (100 g) cubed smoked scamorza, and use smoked instead of cooked ham to the pasta and sauce.

RICH PASTA AL FORNO
To enrich this dish, mix 2 egg yolks into the béchamel sauce before mixing into the pasta with the ham.

Pasta al Pomodoro

This is the basic tomato sauce from which so many favorites are created. As with all recipes that rely on the quality of a few ingredients for the best results, this sauce needs good olive oil and the sweetest tomatoes for the most perfect flavor. If you wish, you may offer freshly grated Parmesan at the table.

Serves 6

1 medium-sized onion
1 large carrot
1 large stalk celery
4 tbsp. extra-virgin olive oil
1 lb. (450 g) skinned and seeded fresh tomatoes, or 1 x 14 oz. (400 g) can tomatoes

sea salt and freshly ground black pepper
1 lb. (450 g) pasta of your choice

1 Peel and chop the onion very finely. Scrape and wash the carrot, then chop finely. Finally, wash the celery, tear away strings, and chop finely (a few celery leaves would also be welcome). Pour the oil into a heavy-bottomed saucepan and add the chopped vegetables.

2 Fry together very gently and slowly until the vegetables are soft and the onion is transparent. Only at this point, add the tomatoes and stir thoroughly. Cover and simmer for about 30 minutes, stirring regularly. Season with salt and pepper to taste. (If you wish to add herbs, do so at the end once the sauce is cooked through.)

3 Bring a large pot of salted water to a rolling boil, add pasta, and stir. Cook until al dente, then drain and return to the pot. Add the sauce, toss together, and serve in a warmed serving dish or bowl or on individual warmed plates.

WITH GARLIC
Omit onion, carrot, and celery, and replace with 1–2 peeled cloves of garlic (crushed for maximum flavor, or left whole for mildest flavor). Fry garlic slowly in oil until pungent, then continue with basic recipe.

WITH MOZZARELLA
Prepare basic recipe, then add a ball of mozzarella, cubed, and let melt before serving.

WITH MASCARPONE
Prepare basic recipe, then add 2–3 tablespoons of mascarpone and toss together to make a deliciously creamy sauce.

WITH RICOTTA
Prepare basic recipe, then toss with 2–3 tablespoons of ricotta and a handful of Parmesan.

WITH PANCETTA
Prepare basic recipe, then toss with some crisply fried cubes of pancetta and a handful of Parmesan.

Pasta Carbonara

Traditionally served with bucatini (hollow, fat spaghetti), this is the traditional and original recipe for a classic carbonara.

Serves 4

14 oz. (400 g) bucatini or spaghetti
Salt
3 oz. (75 g) pancetta, guanciale, or best quality streaky bacon, cubed

4 eggs, beaten
6 tbsp. grated pecorino cheese
Plenty of freshly ground black pepper

1   Bring a large saucepan of salted water to the boil. Put the pasta into the water and stir thoroughly. Replace the lid and return to the boil. Remove or adjust the lid once the water is boiling again. Cook according to the packet instructions until al dente.

2   While the pasta is cooking, fry the pancetta in a very hot skillet until crisp. Meanwhile, beat the eggs in a bowl with the cheese and plenty of black pepper. When the pasta is cooked, drain and return to the pot.

3   Pour over the eggs and cheese and the pancetta immediately and stir everything together, so that the eggs lightly scramble and pull the dish together. The fat from the pancetta should sizzle and fry as it mingles with the pasta. Serve at once.

WITH PEAS
Give the dish color and sweetness by adding ¾ cup (110 g) fresh or frozen peas to the pancetta once it is half cooked, then continue as before.

WITH SMOKED PANCETTA
Use smoked pancetta, guanciale, or bacon to add another dimension of flavor to this wonderful pasta dish.

WITH PAPRIKA
Add ¼ teaspoon of hot paprika to the beaten eggs.

WITH DUCK EGGS
Use duck eggs in place of hen eggs to make this dish richer.

WITH PECORINO
Substitute Parmesan cheese for the pecorino to make your carbonara taste less piquant.

Bolognese Ragu

This classic pasta sauce is usually used to dress tagliatelle rather than spaghetti. Keep the meat relatively chunky, so that the end result looks like a delicate stew.

Serves 4

4 oz. (125 g) pork loin
4 oz. (125 g) beef steak
4 oz. (125 g) prosciutto crudo
⅓ cup (75 g) unsalted butter
1 carrot, finely chopped
1 stick celery, finely chopped
1 onion, finely chopped
2 oz. (50 g) pancetta or bacon, finely chopped
1 heaped tbsp. tomato puree diluted with 8 fl oz. (240 ml) hot water
salt and freshly ground black pepper
1½ cups (360 ml) hot broth
4 oz. (125 g) chicken livers, washed and trimmed
6 tbsp. heavy cream
14 oz. (400 g) mafaldini pasta (or tagliatelle)

1 Chop the meats together finely with a heavy knife. Melt half the butter and fry together the vegetables and pancetta or bacon for 5 to 6 minutes, stirring. Add the chopped meats and stir together to seal all over. Add the diluted tomato puree, and season to taste. Stir thoroughly, cover and leave to simmer very slowly for about 2 hours. During this time never let it dry out, but stir frequently and keep adding a little broth.

2 After about 4 hours, when all the meat is tender, finely chop the chicken livers and add to the pan. Simmer for just 5 minutes. Then stir in all the cream and remove from the heat.

3 Bring a large saucepan of salted water to the boil. Put the pasta into the water and stir thoroughly. Replace the lid and return to the boil. Remove or adjust the lid once the water is boiling again. Cook according to the packet instructions until al dente. Drain the pasta, and return to the pot. Toss the sauce through the pasta, and serve immediately.

WITH TRUFFLE
For extra luxury, add shaved black or white truffle to the finished sauce just before tossing through the pasta.

WITH CINNAMON
Add a small pinch of ground cinnamon to the meat at the beginning, when browning, to add a mild spice note to the sauce.

WITHOUT TOMATO
Leave out the tomato puree to make a white ragu, finished off with the cream.

WITHOUT CHICKEN LIVERS
Omit the chicken livers altogether for a lighter, less rich sauce.

La Puttanesca

This is a real classic and the flavors need to be really well balanced so you can taste them all. It is traditionally served over freshly cooked spaghetti, tossed together with a little extra olive oil and chopped parsley.

Serves 4

3 cloves garlic, peeled and lightly crushed
8 tbsp. extra-virgin olive oil
8 anchovy fillets (either salted or canned in oil, rinsed and dried)
1 to 4 small dried red chili peppers, chopped finely

1 heaped tbsp. salted capers, rinsed, dried, and chopped
1¼ cup (200 g) passata
Generous pinch dried oregano
Salt and freshly ground black pepper

½ cup (120 ml) dry white wine
Handful stoned black olives, roughly chopped
2⅔ cups (400 g) penne or spaghetti
Handful fresh flat-leaf parsley, chopped

1 Fry the garlic and half the oil together with the anchovy fillets and the dried chili peppers, until the anchovy dissolves. Remove the garlic, add the capers and the passata, and stir together thoroughly. Simmer for a few minutes, and then add the oregano, seasoning, wine, and olives. Stir and leave to simmer gently for at least 15 minutes (cooking it for longer will do no harm).

2 Bring a large saucepan of salted water to the boil. Put the pasta into the water and stir thoroughly. Replace the lid and return to the boil. Remove or adjust the lid once the water is boiling again. Cook according to the packet instructions until al dente.

3 Drain the pasta, and return to the pot. Pour over the sauce and mix well. Serve immediately, with a little extra olive oil and the parsley.

WITH EXTRA GARLIC
Puree the garlic to add a stronger garlic flavor to the sauce.

WITH OLIVE PASTE
Use black olive paste instead of chopped whole olives for a smooth olive taste.

WITH FRESH CHILI
Use chopped fresh chili instead of dried for a different taste.

WITH SARDINES
Use drained and flaked, canned sardines in olive oil instead of anchovies for a more pronounced fishy flavor.

SOUR PUTTANESCA
Add 2 tablespoons of strong white wine vinegar to add a stronger sour note to the sauce.

Vacation Spaghetti

Serves 4

8 large, ripe tomatoes, peeled and seeded
1 clove garlic, crushed or mashed
2 tbsp. finely chopped fresh flat-leaf parsley

9 leaves fresh basil, torn
sea salt and freshly ground black pepper

8 tbsp. extra-virgin olive oil
14 oz. (400 g) spaghetti

1   Chop tomatoes roughly and put them into a bowl with the garlic, parsley, basil, salt, and pepper. Stir in the oil and let stand, covered, for at least an hour, preferably not in the refrigerator.

2   Bring a large pot of salted water to a rolling boil, add the spaghetti, and stir, making sure all the spaghetti is immersed in the boiling water. Cover the pot and return to a boil, then remove the lid and continue to cook the spaghetti until al dente. Drain and return to the pot.

3   Pour in the sauce, toss together, adding more oil if required, and transfer to a dish to serve at once.

WITH MOZZARELLA
Prepare the basic recipe, adding a handful of chopped mozzarella to the sauce.

WITH BLACK OLIVES
Prepare the basic recipe, adding a handful of coarsely chopped pitted black olives to the sauce.

WITH CAPERS
Prepare the basic recipe, replacing the basil with a heaping tablespoonful of capers.

WITH GREEN BELL PEPPER
Prepare the basic recipe, adding a seeded green bell pepper, chopped into small cubes, to the tomato sauce before letting it stand.

WITH RICOTTA
Prepare the basic recipe, adding 3 tablespoons ricotta to the tomato sauce and spaghetti when you toss them together.

Linguine with Pesto

Serves 4

40 large leaves fresh basil
3 cloves garlic (more if desired)
2–3 tbsp. freshly grated Parmesan or pecorino cheese

2–3 tbsp. pine nuts
3 oz. (75 g) best-quality olive oil, plus extra for covering
sea salt and freshly ground black pepper

1 lb. (450 g) linguine
freshly grated Parmesan cheese, to serve

1   Process or pound all the basil leaves with the garlic, cheese, pine nuts, and olive oil using a mortar and pestle or food processor. You should end up with a beautifully green, relatively smooth sauce with a bit of crunch. Season to taste with salt and pepper and set aside at room temperature, making sure the surface of the pesto is completely covered in a layer of olive oil to prevent oxidation.

2   Bring a large saucepan of salted water to a boil. Add the pasta and return to a boil. Cook until tender, then drain thoroughly. Return pasta to the hot saucepan and pour in the pesto, toss together thoroughly, then transfer to a platter. Serve with freshly grated Parmesan.

GNOCCHI WITH PESTO
Pesto is also delicious when used to dress freshly cooked potato gnocchi.

WITH STRING BEANS
Prepare the basic recipe, adding a handful of fresh string beans to the boiling water with the pasta and cooking them together, before draining and dressing with the pesto.

WITH WALNUTS
Prepare the basic recipe, adding 2 or 3 tablespoons lightly toasted walnuts to the pasta and pesto.

WITH EXTRA PINE NUTS
Prepare the basic recipe, adding 2 or 3 extra tablespoons lightly toasted pine nuts to the pasta and pesto when tossing everything together for a little added crunch.

WITH TOMATOES
Prepare the basic recipe, adding 3 ripe tomatoes, seeded, peeled, and chopped into small cubes, to the pasta and pesto when tossing everything together.

Middle Eastern Spaghetti

Koazy al-macarona is a very famous non-vegetarian dish of the Middle Eastern cuisine. This dish, with its rather odd combination of ingredients, is very easy to prepare and the results are really delicious.

Serves 4–6

4 tbsp. canola oil
2 small chickens, quartered, skin left on
½ cup (125 g) plain yogurt
3 sticks cinnamon
1 tbsp. ground cumin
1 tbsp. ground black pepper
6 fresh tomatoes, peeled, seeded, and puréed
2 onions, chopped
sea salt
14 oz. (400 g) spaghetti
3 hard-boiled eggs, shelled and sliced

1   Heat half the oil in a large skillet and fry chicken for about 5 minutes, turning to brown both sides. Add yogurt; half the cinnamon, cumin, and pepper; then the tomatoes. Mix together and cook the chicken, covered, for about 15 minutes.

2   Discard cinnamon sticks. Pour the rest of the oil into another pan and add the onion, salt, and the remaining cinnamon, cumin, and pepper. Mix together and fry gently until onion is cooked. Bring a pot of salted water to a boil, break the spaghetti in half, and boil spaghetti until done.

3   Drain the spaghetti, toss with the onion mixture, and arrange in a serving dish. Discard the cinnamon sticks. Put the cooked chicken on top and pour over the sauce. Decorate with the sliced hard-boiled eggs and serve.

WITH CHILI
Prepare the basic recipe, adding 2 whole dried red chili peppers to the onion and spice mixture. Discard chilis with the cinnamon sticks.

WITH FISH
Prepare the basic recipe, replacing the chicken with thick, skinless fish fillets. Reduce the cooking time by about half so that the fish does not overcook.

WITH LAMB
Prepare the basic recipe, replacing the chicken with 8–12 small lamb chops or cutlets.

157

Ravioli with Spinach & Ricotta Filling

Spinach and ricotta is a classic combination and a traditional filling for ravioli. This dish is definitely worth a little effort for a special occasion.

Serves 4

2 lbs (900 g) fresh spinach
1 cup (110 g) fresh ricotta cheese
Pinch grated nutmeg
Salt and freshly ground black pepper

1½ cups (165 g) freshly grated Parmesan cheese
4 x quantity fresh pasta, rolled out and cut into 3-in.(7.5-cm) circles (see page 131)

For the sage butter
1 stick unsalted butter
5 leaves fresh sage, rubbed gently between your palms to release their flavor

1 Make the filling: Wilt the spinach in a dry skillet, then cool. When it is cool enough to handle, squeeze dry with your hands, then chop it finely. Mix the spinach, ricotta cheese, nutmeg, salt, pepper, and half the Parmesan cheese. Blend together with one egg.

2 Working with one piece of pasta at a time, drop a teaspoon of filling in the center of the circle. Fold the circle in half, encasing the filling. Seal the open edges of each semicircle with the prongs of a fork. If the dough is dry, you may need to run a moistened finger along the inside of the seam first. Continue in this way until all the dough has been used.

3 Bring a large saucepan of salted water to the boil. Put the ravioli in batches into the water and boil until tender and floating on the surface. Drain carefully with a slotted spoon, and arrange in a warmed serving dish. Meanwhile, melt the butter with the sage leaves until warm and golden, not browned. When all the pasta is in the serving dish, pour over the melted butter and mix carefully. Sprinkle with the rest of the cheese and serve immediately.

WITH LEMON
Omit the spinach and use the ricotta cheese on its own, using ½ teaspoon of lemon zest instead of the nutmeg to add flavor.

WITH NUTTY SAGE BUTTER
Dress the cooked ravioli with sage butter that has been allowed to darken slightly to give it a more nutty flavor, and add a handful of pine kernels to the butter while it melts to add crunch.

WITH POMODORO SAUCE
Instead of dressing the pasta with sage butter, mix with pomodoro sauce (see page 151).

WITH CHARD & CINNAMON
Make the filling more robust in flavor by using chard instead of spinach and substituting cinnamon for the nutmeg and proceed as main recipe.

GREEN RAVIOLI
Make the pasta green, by adding pureed spinach to the dough, and use a plain ricotta cheese filling to create a color contrast.

Linguine with Creamy Shrimp Sauce

Linguine—long flat spaghetti—works very well in this delicately flavored dish. Perfect as a starter, or as an entree with a big bowl of salad.

Serves 4

1 small onion, peeled and finely chopped
1 small leek, very finely chopped
3 tbsp. unsalted butter

8 oz. (225 g) raw shrimp, shelled
4 tbsp. dry white wine
Salt and freshly ground black pepper

14 oz. (400 g) linguine
7 tbsp. light (or whipping) cream
2 tbsp. fresh flat-leaf parsley, chopped

1 Gently fry the onion and leek in the butter for a few minutes, or until soft. Add the shrimp and stir together thoroughly. Cook together for 5 minutes, or until the shrimp are nearly cooked, then add the wine and increase the heat for 2 minutes to boil off the alcohol. Season with salt and pepper and remove from the heat.

2 Bring a large saucepan of salted water to the boil. Put the linguine into the water and stir thoroughly. Replace the lid and return to the boil. Remove or adjust the lid once the water is boiling again. Cook according to the packet instructions until al dente. Drain the pasta and return to the pot.

3 Pour the cream over the shrimp mixture, stir, and return to the heat for minute or two, then pour this sauce over the pasta. Add the parsley and mix well. Serve immediately.

WITH PAPRIKA
After adding the wine and boiling off the alcohol, season with salt and ¼ teaspoon of paprika to add a little spice, then continue as above.

WITH SCALLOPS
Substitute the shrimp for scallops, cut in half if they are very large and cook them with the onion and leek for just 3 minutes, then proceed as main recipe.

WITH LEMON
Add some zest to the dish by adding the grated zest of half an unwaxed lemon when you add the parsley.

WITH WHITE FISH
Substitute the shrimp for fillets of white fish, fried gently with the onion and leek, then roughly broken up into large flakes, then proceed as main recipe.

WITH SAFFRON
To add a wonderful color and a touch of spice, add ½ teaspoon powdered saffron to the onion and leek once softened, mix together and fry gently for one minute, then add the shrimp and continue as above.

CHAPTER 6
Meat
& Poultry

Here is a selection of deliciously tasty meat, poultry and game recipes to serve as main courses on their own, or as part of a traditional Mediterranean menu that begins with antipasti, meze or tapas before moving on to the main event. Below you will find handy recipes for stock that can be used throughout this book.

In terms of fresh meat, poultry, and game, try to make sure the meat you buy is of good quality and from a traceable source, preferably organic but certainly chemical-free. It is always better to buy from a butcher, as he or she will not only be able to guide and advise you around the various cuts available, but will also be able to carry out more tricky tasks such as boning or trimming for you. They will know that by utilizing such methods as pot roasting, braising, and stewing you can tenderize less expensive, tougher cuts of meats. Whole joints of meat, known as the silverside, rib, and brisket cuts of beef, shoulder, breast, and shank cuts of lamb, and leg, shoulder, belly, and hock cuts of pork, are boned and rolled, making them ideal for pot roasting. Braising often calls for whole steaks or chops, using shin, leg, or neck cuts of beef; shoulder steak cuts of lamb; and leg or shoulder steak cuts of pork. Stewing calls for cubed meat, using chuck or blade cuts of beef and shoulder or leg cuts of lamb. Ask your butcher for advice as well as assistance with any preparations that need to be done.

MEAT AND THE MEDITERRANEAN DIET

While meat, poultry, and game are enjoyed as part of a Mediterranean diet, meat is generally eaten less frequently in this region than in other parts of the World. The exception to the rule is cured meats. Pancetta, guanciale, bresaola, Parma ham, various kinds of salami, mortadella, and raw Italian sausages like luganega are widely used as an ingredient to flavor and enhance other dishes, and they offer a simple way of preparing an starter or sharing dish. Prosciutto crudo is the generic term for cured, air-dried ham, of which the one from Parma is considered to be the best. Pancetta and guanciale are both a kind of bacon and are interchangeable. Bresaola is one of the few Italian cured meats that is not made out of pork; instead, it is made using beef.

STOCK

Good stocks are at the foundation of good cooking, especially when it comes to sauces, risotto, soups, and stews. Making beef, veal or chicken stock is not difficult; here are basic recipes. Bouquet garni is a simple package of bay leaf, sprigs of sage, rosemary, and thyme all tied together with plain string, or wrapped in cheesecloth.

Beef or veal stock
Makes about 5 pints (2¾ liters)

3¼ lbs. (1.5 kg) beef or veal bones	1 tomato, quartered
1 onion, quartered	1 bouquet garni
2 carrots, quartered	6 peppercorns
1 leek, quartered	1 pinch sea salt
2 celery stalks, quartered	5 pints (2¾ liters) cold water

Place all the ingredients in a large pot. Bring to a boil, then let simmer, skimming off any scum that forms on the surface. Simmer for about 4 hours. Then pour through a sieve into a bowl, pressing down on the pieces in the sieve to extract every bit of flavor. Cool, then skim off any congealed fat. Can be refrigerated for up to 3 days or frozen for 6 months. For a richer, brown stock, roast bones first in a 450°F (230°C) oven for about 45 minutes. Add vegetables to bones about halfway through. Baste with a little water if necessary, then transfer to a stockpot, add the remaining water, and continue as above.

Chicken stock
Makes about 3 pints (1.7 liters)

about 1½ lbs.(700 g) cooked (e.g., carcass from roast chicken) or raw chicken	few sprigs fresh parsley
	6 peppercorns
1 onion, quartered, or 1 leek, halved lengthwise	3 pints (1.7 liters) cold water
2 stalks celery, halved	2 pinches sea salt
2 carrots, halved	

Put all ingredients in a stockpot. Bring to a boil, then cover and simmer for about 2 hours. Skim the surface often to remove any scum. Remove from heat and cool completely, then strain into a bowl, pressing down on pieces in the sieve to extract every last bit of flavor. Once cooled, it will be easy to remove the solidified fat from the surface. Can be refrigerated for up to 3 days or frozen for about 6 months.

Fennel, Salami & Olive Salad

Serves 6

2 fennel heads, cleaned and thinly sliced
large handful pitted black olives
12 slices chili-flavored salami, cut into strips

for the dressing
juice of 2 oranges
grated zest of 1 orange
1 cup (250 ml) extra-virgin olive oil

½ tsp. prepared mustard (preferably Italian Savora)
sea salt and freshly ground black pepper

1 Toss fennel, olives, and salami strips together in a large serving bowl. Combine the dressing ingredients in a jar, screw on the top, and shake until all the ingredients have blended together. Pour over the salad and toss everything together thoroughly. Let stand for about 30 minutes before serving, to allow the flavors to develop.

WITH FIG
Prepare basic recipe, replacing olives with 8 fresh ripe figs. Cut the fennel bulbs into paper-thin strips and mix with quartered figs, peeled only if necessary.

WITH WHITE CABBAGE
Prepare basic recipe, replacing the fennel with half a white cabbage, very finely shredded (as for coleslaw).

WITH ENDIVE
Prepare basic recipe, replacing the fennel with 8 heads of very finely shredded Belgian endive.

WITH GREEN TOMATO
Prepare basic recipe, replacing the fennel with 8 medium-sized, sliced, seeded, barely red tomatoes.

WITH GREEN MELON
Prepare basic recipe, replacing the fennel with 14 oz. (400 g) ripe but firm green melon (such as honeydew), sliced very thinly.

Moroccan Tagine

Serves 4–6

2 tbsp. extra-virgin olive oil
2 lb. (900 g) boneless, skinless chicken breasts, cut into bite-sized pieces
½ onion, finely chopped
3 cloves garlic, minced

2 carrots, chopped
1 x 14-oz. (400-g) can whole tomatoes
1 x 15-oz. (425-g) can chickpeas, drained and rinsed
1½ cups (350 ml) vegetable broth

1 tbsp. lemon juice
1 tbsp. sugar
1 tsp. sea salt
1 tsp. ground coriander
pinch of cayenne pepper

1 Heat oil in a large frying pan over medium heat. Add chicken and onion. Brown all over for 12 minutes, stirring occasionally. Add garlic and continue cooking for 2 minutes.

2 Stir in carrots, tomatoes with liquid, chickpeas, and broth. Add lemon juice, sugar, salt, coriander, and cayenne. Bring to a boil, reduce heat, cover, and simmer for 30 minutes, until chicken is cooked through and vegetables are tender.

3 If using an authentic tagine, transfer mixture to the tagine after it comes to a boil. Bake in a preheated 375°F (190°C) oven for 30–40 minutes.

WITH LAMB
Prepare the basic recipe, replacing the chicken with an equal quantity of cubed boneless lamb.

WITH PORK
Prepare the basic recipe, replacing the chicken with an equal quantity of cubed pork tenderloin.

WITH BEEF
Prepare the basic recipe, replacing the chicken with an equal quantity of cubed stewing beef.

WITH ALMONDS
Prepare the basic recipe, garnishing each serving with 2 tablespoons almond slivers.

Empanadas

These are little pastry envelopes that contain tasty fillings that can vary from meat to fruit. The recipe below is for the classic, rich beef filling. They are excellent served warm with a green salad and a glass of red wine.

Serves 6

For the dough
2 cups (225 g) all-purpose flour
½ tsp. sea salt
⅔ cup (140 g) shortening
6 tbsp. water

For the meat filling
1 yellow onion, roughly chopped
1 green bell pepper, roughly chopped
1 tbsp. olive oil
1 x 8-oz. (225 g) can tomato paste
½ cup (120 ml) water
1 tbsp. distilled white vinegar
1 lb. (450 g) lean steak, cut into 1-in (2½-cm) cubes

1 Preheat oven to 350°F (175°C). To make the dough, combine flour and salt in a medium mixing bowl. Cut in the shortening until pieces are the size of small peas. Add a small amount of water to slightly moisten. Form dough into a ball, then roll out and thin as you can and cut it into 4-in. (10-cm) circles. Lightly flour both sides of circles and set aside.

2 To make the meat filling, sauté the onion and green bell pepper in olive oil in a medium skillet. Add tomato paste, water, and vinegar, and cook for 20 minutes. Add meat and coat thoroughly with the sauce.

3 Place a large spoonful of meat filling in the center of a dough circle. Fold the dough into a half moon and fasten edges together by pressing the edges with a fork. Bake for about 10–15 minutes, or until golden brown.

WITH PORK
Prepare the basic recipe, replacing the beef with pork and proceeding with the basic recipe.

WITH APPLE
Prepare the basic pastry, then make a sweet apple filling. In a small pan, combine 2½ cups (450 g) peeled, cored, and sliced apples; 1 cup (200 g) sugar; 1 teaspoon ground cinnamon; and ½ teaspoon ground nutmeg. Cook gently over low heat until the apples are softened. Let cool, then fill the pastry circles as in the basic recipe.

WITH LAMB
Prepare the basic recipe, replacing the beef with lamb.

WITH TURKEY
Prepare the basic recipe, replacing the beef with turkey.

WITH CHICKEN
Prepare the basic recipe, replacing the beef with chicken.

Warm Chorizo Salad

Crispy fried chorizo with peas and sweetcorn make a wonderfully tasty lunch served with warm crusty bread.

Serves 4

1 tbsp. olive oil
8 oz. (225 g) chorizo, chopped
1 medium red onion, finely chopped
½ red bell pepper, deseeded and chopped
1 tsp. smoked paprika
1¼ lb. (550 g) frozen peas

1¼ lb. (550 g) frozen sweetcorn
8 oz. (225 g) cherry tomatoes, halved
5 tbsp. chopped cilantro
juice of 1 lime
sea salt and freshly ground black pepper
warm crusty bread, to serve

1 Heat the oil in a large frying pan over a medium heat, and add the chorizo. Fry for 2–3 minutes until starting to brown. Add the onion, red pepper and paprika, and cook for 4–5 minutes, until softened.

2 Add the frozen peas and sweetcorn, and cook, stirring continuously, for 5 minutes, until tender and heated through. Remove from the heat and stir in the tomatoes, cilantro, and lime juice. Cook for 3 minutes, season with salt and freshly ground black pepper to taste, and stir to combine. Serve immediately with warm crusty bread.

WITH SWEET POTATO
Prepare the basic recipe. Before adding the chorizo to the pan, fry 1 peeled and diced sweet potato until cooked through and crispy. Proceed as before.

WITH CHICKEN
Prepare the basic recipe. Before adding the chorizo to the pan, fry 1 chopped chicken breast for about 5 minutes, or until cooked through. Proceed as before.

WITH BUTTERNUT SQUASH
Prepare the basic recipe. Before adding the chorizo to the pan, fry 3½ oz. (100 g) peeled, deseeded and chopped butternut squash, until cooked through and crispy. Proceed as before.

WITH WHITE FISH
Prepare the basic recipe. Add 3½ oz. (100 g) chopped white fish to the pan with the onion, and cook until crispy. Proceed as before.

Easy Cassoulet

Serves 4–6

1½ cups (350 g) dried white beans (white haricot beans), soaked in water overnight
10 oz. (275 g) pork belly, rind discarded, thinly sliced
5 oz. (150 g) thick-sliced bacon, cut into ½-in. (1-cm) pieces
2 lb. (900 g) boned lamb shoulder, cut into 1½-in. (3.8 cm) chunks
1 large onion, finely chopped
1 leek, cleaned, white and pale green part julienned
2 cloves garlic, minced
1 x 14-oz. (400 g) can whole tomatoes with liquid
3 sprigs fresh thyme
2 bay leaves
1 cup (250 ml) water
1 cup (250 ml) chicken broth
2 cups (225 g) dry breadcrumbs
⅓ cup (50 g) finely chopped Italian parsley

1 Preheat oven to 375°F (190°C). Drain beans and rinse until water runs clear. Place in a medium saucepan, cover with water, bring to a boil, and cook for 15 minutes, until tender. Drain and set aside. In a large Dutch oven over medium heat, brown pork slices, about 3 minutes. Transfer to plate and set aside. Cook bacon in Dutch oven until crisp, about 7–8 minutes. Transfer to plate with browned pork. Brown lamb in batches in pork and bacon fat, about 4 minutes per side. Transfer to another plate and set aside.

2 Drain fat from Dutch oven, leaving only 2 tablespoons. Cook onion and leek over medium-low heat for 4 minutes, until soft and translucent. Add garlic and continue cooking for 1 minute. Add tomatoes with their liquid, breaking them up into smaller pieces with a wooden spoon. Add thyme, bay leaves, water, and broth. Return meats to Dutch oven, raise heat, and bring to a boil. Cover and transfer to preheated oven. Cook for 45 minutes.

3 In a medium mixing bowl, combine breadcrumbs with chopped parsley. Remove casserole from oven, discard thyme sprigs and bay leaves if desired, sprinkle with breadcrumb mixture, and return to oven, uncovered. Cook for an additional 45 minutes, or until liquid is almost completely absorbed.

WITH CHICKPEAS
Prepare the basic recipe, replacing the haricot beans with dried chickpeas.

WITH PANCETTA
Prepare the basic recipe, replacing the bacon with cubed pancetta.

WITH CLOVES
Prepare the basic recipe, adding another onion, quartered, and studding each quarter with a clove.

WITH MERQUEZ SAUSAGE
Prepare the basic recipe, adding 1 lb. (450 g) Merquez sausage, cut into 1-in. (2.5-cm) chunks. Brown Merquez with the other meats, about 3 minutes per side. Set aside and return to Dutch oven with the other meats.

Lamb Moussaka

Serve this flavorful Greek dish with hunks of crusty bread for soaking up the sauce.

Serves 4–6

1½ lb. (700 g) zucchini
3 tbsp. extra-virgin olive oil
1 large onion, finely chopped
1 lb. (400 g) ground lamb
2 cloves garlic, minced
1 piece of cinnamon
1½ tsp. dried oregano

1 x 10-oz. (275 g) package frozen spinach, thawed and drained
10 oz. (275 g) prepared tomato sauce
1 cube organic chicken bouillon
sea salt and freshly ground black pepper
2 tbsp. unsalted butter

¼ cup (25 g) all-purpose flour
1½ cups (250 ml) milk
pinch of freshly grated nutmeg
2 tsp. lemon zest
⅓ cup (50 g) freshly grated Parmesan

1 Preheat oven to broil. Slice zucchini into ½-in. (1.5-cm) slices. Spread in one layer on large oiled baking sheet. Drizzle with 1 tablespoon olive oil. Broil under the broiler for 5 minutes. Turn zucchini slices over and broil for 5 more minutes. Transfer to paper towel–lined rack to drain. Reduce oven temperature to 350°F (180°C).

2 To prepare the meat sauce, heat remaining 2 tablespoons olive oil over medium-low heat in large frying pan. Add onion to frying pan. Once onion is translucent, add ground lamb and cook until browned. Add garlic, cinnamon, oregano, spinach, tomato sauce, and bouillon cube. Break up bouillon cube until dissolved. Simmer for 10 minutes, stirring occasionally. Remove from heat. Remove and discard piece of cinnamon. Season to taste.

3 To prepare the béchamel sauce, melt butter over low heat in small saucepan. Add the flour and stir until you have a paste that is turning a reddish-brown (roux). Add the milk and whisk continuously until sauce thickens, 5–10 minutes. Whisk in the nutmeg and lemon zest and set aside. To assemble casserole, spread meat sauce over the base of a large, rectangular casserole. Layer zucchini slices over the sauce. Cover with béchamel sauce and sprinkle with Parmesan. Bake for 20–25 minutes until golden.

WITH BEEF
Prepare the basic recipe, replacing the ground lamb with an equal quantity of lean ground beef.

WITH BREADCRUMBS
Prepare the basic recipe, topping the casserole with ½ cup (50 g) breadcrumbs tossed with 2 tablespoons melted unsalted butter and ¼ cup (25 g) grated Parmesan.

WITH EGGPLANT
Prepare the basic recipe, replacing ½ pound (225 g) sliced zucchini with ½ pound (225 g) unpeeled sliced eggplant.

VEGETARIAN MOUSSAKA
Prepare the basic recipe, replacing the ground lamb with an equal quantity of prepared textured vegetable protein.

Pasta with Bacon, Tomato & Chili

Amatrice, where this dish comes from, is a small Italian town near Rome which is famous for its fantastic pork products. This is a real classic, rich and piquant, flavored with deliciously smoky pancetta. One of the few traditional sauces which uses garlic and onion.

Serves 4

8 oz. (225 g) smoked pancetta, cubed
4 tbsp. rich extra-virgin olive oil
1 onion, peeled and finely chopped
3 cloves garlic, peeled and chopped
½ to 2 dried red chili peppers (according to preference), seeded and chopped finely

1½ x 14-oz. (400-g) cans whole tomatoes, drained and coarsely chopped
sea salt
14 oz. (400 g) bucatini or other dried pasta with a chunky shape
3 oz. (75 g) pecorino or Parmesan cheese, grated

1 Fry the cubed pancetta with the oil until the fat is transparent and running freely. Add the onion, garlic, and chili to the pan and fry together gently until the onion is soft and translucent. Add the tomatoes and simmer covered for 20 minutes, stirring frequently, until the sauce is thick and glossy.

2 Bring a large saucepan of salted water to the boil. Put the pasta into the water and stir thoroughly. Replace the lid and return to the boil. Remove or adjust the lid once the water is boiling again. Cook according to the packet instructions until al dente.

3 Drain the pasta thoroughly and return to the pot, then pour in the sauce and mix together thoroughly. Serve immediately, with the cheese offered separately.

WITH PANCETTA
Use unsmoked pancetta to give the sauce a simpler, cleaner flavor.

WITH RED WINE VINEGAR
Add 4 tablespoons red wine vinegar to the onion, garlic, and chili to add a slightly sharp flavor to the sauce.

WITH A SMOOTH SAUCE
For a smoother sauce, use passata instead of chopped canned tomatoes.

WITH A CREAMY SAUCE
Add a heaped tablespoon of mascarpone to the sauce at the end to make it creamy.

Penne with Pork Ragu

This is a perfect winter supper dish—a satisfying baked pasta dish with a lovely cheesy topping, dressed with a tasty pork ragu.

Serves 4

1 clove garlic, peeled and crushed
3 tbsp. extra-virgin olive oil
1 onion, peeled and finely chopped
4 oz. (125 g) coarsely ground pork
1 dried bay leaf
sea salt and freshly ground pepper
2 cups (450 ml) hot meat stock
1 x 14-oz. (400 g) can tomatoes
2⅓ cups (400 g) penne
1 tbsp. finely chopped fresh rosemary leaves
4 tbsp. unsalted butter
3 tbsp. dried breadcrumbs
4 tbsp. freshly grated Parmesan cheese

1 Preheat the oven to 425°F (220°C). Fry the garlic gently in the olive oil until golden, then discard the garlic, and add the onion and cook until softened. Add the meat, cook until browned, and add the bay leaf and seasoning. Add the hot stock and the tomatoes. Stir, cover, and simmer gently for about 50 minutes.

2 Bring a large saucepan of salted water to the boil. Put the penne into the water and stir thoroughly. Replace the lid and return to the boil. Remove or adjust the lid once the water is boiling again. Cook according to the packet instructions until al dente. Drain, and return to the pot. Add the finely chopped rosemary leaves and the sauce. Mix together thoroughly.

3 Butter a large ovenproof dish and transfer the pasta mixture to the dish. Sprinkle the top generously with breadcrumbs and freshly grated Parmesan cheese, and dot with the remaining butter. Bake in the oven for about 10 minutes before serving.

PENNE TOSSED WITH PORK RAGU
Instead of baking the pasta, you could also just toss the sauce, pasta, and Parmesan cheese together, omitting the butter and the breadcrumbs.

WITH BEEF
Use beef instead of pork for a different sauce.

WITH SAGE
Omit the rosemary and use finely chopped fresh sage instead to make the sauce taste quite different.

WITH RED BELL PEPPER
Add a diced red pepper to the meat while you brown it for extra flavor and texture.

WITH SWEET & SOUR SAUCE
Sprinkle 2 teaspoons of balsamic vinegar over the pork while browning it to add a sweet and sour note to the dish.

Circassian Chicken

For the best flavor, begin preparing this dish at least 2 days in advance; the chicken improves with time. Serve warm with a simple bulgur or rice pilaf.

Serves 12–14

2 tbsp. olive oil
6 lbs. (2¾ kg) chicken quarters, trimmed, skinned, and boned, then cut into smaller, even-sized chunks
1 tbsp. garlic, peeled and chopped with salt

sea salt and freshly ground black pepper
2 small onions, sliced
pinch saffron
⅓ cup (40 g) all-purpose flour
1 tsp. white pepper, or more to taste

1 large pinch ground allspice
2¼ cups (225 g) shelled walnuts
1 tbsp. fresh lemon juice
3 tbsp. walnut oil
¼ tsp. paprika

1 Heat oil in a large pot. Add chicken, 2 teaspoons of the chopped garlic, and the onions. Sprinkle with salt, black pepper, and saffron. Cover with water; simmer slowly and gently until chicken is tender. Drain and cool chicken, reserving the liquid. Meanwhile, toast flour in a heavy nonstick skillet, turning it constantly until it becomes light beige. Add white pepper and allspice, and continue stirring over low heat 30 seconds longer. Remove from the heat.

2 Lightly season with salt and black pepper. Use a slotted spoon to skim the grease off the top of the chicken broth and strain. Mix the remaining garlic with a ladleful of broth and pour over the chicken to keep it moist. In a food processor, grind the walnuts and seasoned flour until smooth. Slowly add a ladleful of the broth and process until smooth. Slowly add the remaining broth to make a creamy sauce.

3 Pour sauce into the skillet, set over medium-low heat, and bring to a boil. Cook, stirring occasionally, for 20 minutes. Drain chicken pieces and place in one layer in a ovenproof serving dish. Add 1 cup (240 ml) of the walnut sauce and the lemon juice; mix well. Thin the remaining sauce with water to a thick pouring consistency and add salt to taste. Pour sauce over chicken. Let cool completely, cover with plastic wrap, and refrigerate for at least 2 days before serving.

4 Gently reheat chicken in a 350°F (175°C) oven until warm. Heat walnut oil in a very small saucepan, add paprika, and swirl to combine; heat just to a sizzle. Remove from heat and allow the paprika to settle. Drizzle the red-tinted oil over the dish, making decorative swirls, and serve.

WITH TURKEY
Prepare the basic recipe, replacing the chicken with ¼ of a small turkey, which will need to be stewed to make necessary broth.

WITH DUCK
Prepare the basic recipe, replacing the chicken with duck. The result will be a great deal richer, and still delicious. You will need to make the broth using the duck; degrease with care as it will be a lot fattier.

WITH VEAL
Prepare the basic recipe, replacing the chicken with boneless veal chunks, which will need to be stewed to create a veal broth as in the original recipe.

WITH ALMONDS
To give the dish a nutty flavor, substitute the walnuts for blanched almonds, and use sweet almond oil in place of the walnut oil.

Rigatoni with Meatballs

Meatballs work well served with a short pasta like rigatoni or macaroni, but the more traditional spaghetti can also be used here.

Serves 6

1 onion, peeled and
   chopped
½ cup (120 ml) olive oil
1 lb. (450 g) ground pork
2 eggs, beaten
sea salt and freshly
   ground black pepper
1 clove garlic, peeled and
   chopped finely

Handful of fresh flat-leaf
   parsley, chopped
5 or 6 tbsp. fine, dry
   breadcrumbs
3 cups (750 ml) passata
Handful of mixed fresh
   herbs, chopped finely
3⅓ cups (500 g) large
   macaroni

1   Fry the onion in the olive oil until softened but not browned, then take off the heat until required. Mix the pork with the eggs, seasoning, garlic, parsley, and 2 to 3 tablespoons of the breadcrumbs. With wet hands to prevent sticking, shape the mixture into meatballs about the size of large olives, roll in the remaining breadcrumbs and fry gently in the re-heated onion and oil for about 2 minutes, or until sealed and lightly browned. Drain off any excess oil and add the passata and the chopped mixed herbs. Simmer together for about an hour, stirring frequently and adding a little water if necessary.

2   Bring a large saucepan of salted water to the boil. Put the macaroni into the water and stir thoroughly. Replace the lid and return to the boil. Remove or adjust the lid once the water is boiling again. Cook according to the packet instructions until al dente. Drain, and return to the pot. Pour over the sauce and the meatballs, mix gently to prevent breaking up the meatballs, and serve immediately.

WITH BEEF
Use minced beef instead of minced pork to make the sauce taste different.

WITH PROSCIUTTO
For extra flavor, and 3 or 4 slices of finely chopped prosciutto crudo to the minced pork and then proceed as for main recipe.

WITH LEMON
For a tangy flavor, add 2 teaspoons of finely grated unwaxed lemon zest to the minced pork mixture.

WITH EXTRA GARLIC
If you love garlic, add a finely minced clove or two of garlic to the minced pork mixture then proceed as before.

WITH CHILI
Add 1 teaspoon ground chili to the pork mixture, and then proceed as for main recipe.

Tagliatelle with Chicken Livers

Like all recipes that contain very few ingredients, this recipe relies heavily on the quality and freshness of the chicken livers to make it taste special.

Serves 4

5 oz. (140 g) fresh
   chicken livers
4 tbsp. unsalted butter
6 tbsp. rich chicken stock
12 oz. (350 g) tagliatelle
4 tbsp. freshly grated
   Parmesan cheese

sea salt and freshly
   ground black pepper
2 tbsp. fresh flat-leaf
   parsley, chopped

1 Clean and trim the chicken livers, removing all traces of bile, and chop roughly. In a very large saucepan, quickly fry the butter and chicken livers together. As soon as they are well browned, add the stock and remove from the heat.

2 Bring a large saucepan of salted water to the boil. Put the pennette into the water and stir thoroughly. Replace the lid and return to the boil. Remove or adjust the lid once the water is boiling again. Cook according to the packet instructions until al dente. Drain, and transfer to the pot with the cooked chicken livers and mix thoroughly together.

3 Season, stir the Parmesan cheese through the mixture, and serve sprinkled with the chopped parsley.

WITH SHERRY
Omit the chicken stock and add the same quantity of dry sherry instead.

WITH SAGE
Add 6 leaves of fresh sage, chopped, to the butter and chicken livers to add a deliciously fragrant flavor to this dish.

WITH PANCETTA
For a more substantially meaty taste, add 4 tablespoons cubed pancetta to the butter and fry until crispy before adding the chicken livers.

WITH MASCARPONE
To make this dish really creamy, add 3 tablespoons of mascarpone to the dish when tossing the chicken livers and the pasta together.

WITH BALSAMIC VINEGAR
To add a note of rich sweetness, add a tablespoon of balsamic vinegar to the chicken livers while they are browning.

Succulent Lamb with Harissa & Sweet Potato

Serves 4

1 tbsp. olive oil
1 onion, finely chopped
1½ lb. (675 g) lamb fillet or lamb steaks, cut
   into bite-sized pieces

2 carrots, peeled and diced
8 oz. (225 g) puy lentils
1 tbsp. harissa paste
1 tbsp. tomato purée

600 ml (1 pint) lamb or chicken stock
1 large sweet potato, peeled and diced
sea salt and freshly ground black pepper
5 tbsp. chopped cilantro leaves, to serve

1 Preheat the oven to 325°F (170°C). Heat the oil in
a large flameproof casserole dish over a medium
heat. Add the onion and lamb, and fry together
until lightly browned. Stir in the carrots, lentils,
harissa, tomato purée, stock and sweet potato, and
stir to combine. Cover, and cook in the oven for
1½–2 hours.

2 Remove from the oven, and season to taste with
salt and freshly ground black pepper. Serve
immediately, sprinkled with chopped cilantro.

WITH TAMARIND
Prepare the basic recipe, omit
the harissa and substitute with
tamarind paste.

WITH CELERY & CINNAMON
Prepare the basic recipe. Omit
the lentils and harissa paste. Add
2 chopped celery stalks, 2 tsp.
cinnamon and 4 cloves to the
casserole dish.

WITH BELL PEPPERS
Prepare the basic recipe. Omit the
lentils, harissa paste and 8fl oz.
(240 ml) stock. Add 1 deseeded,
chopped red bell pepper, 2 tbsp.
paprika, 1 x 14 oz. (400 g) tin
of chopped tomatoes, 8fl oz.
(240 ml) red wine and 2 tbsp. red
wine vinegar.

Small Spicy Moorish Kebabs

Serves 6

2 garlic gloves, finely chopped
2 tsp. sea salt
1 tsp. mild curry powder or pinchito spice
   mixture

½ tsp. coriander seeds
1 tsp. Spanish paprika
¼ tsp. dried thyme
freshly ground black pepper

1 lb. (450 g) lean pork, cut into small cubes

1 Crush the garlic with the salt in a mortar (or with
the flat of a knife on a board), then work in the
curry powder or pinchito spice, coriander seeds,
paprika, thyme, and pepper. Skewer the pork, 3–4
cubes to a small stick, and marinate them in a
shallow dish with the marinade of garlic, herbs, and
spices, turning so they are well coated. Let stand
for at least a couple of hours in the refrigerator.

2 Spread out the kebabs on a hot barbecue or on foil
under a broiler. Cook them for about 3 minutes on
each side.

WITH BEEF
Prepare the basic recipe, replacing
the pork with cubes of tender beef
steak.

WITH CHICKEN
Prepare the basic recipe, replacing
the pork with cubes of tender,
skinless chicken breast.

WITH TURKEY
Prepare the basic recipe, replacing
the pork with cubes of tender,
skinless turkey breast.

WITH LAMB
Prepare the basic recipe, replacing
the pork with cubes of tender
boneless lamb.

Traditional Lasagne

This is one of the best-loved and much-imitated of all Italian pasta dishes.

Serves 4

1 onion, peeled and chopped
1 carrot, scraped and chopped
1 stick celery, chopped
Pinch dried marjoram
½ cup (55 g) dried porcini mushrooms, soaked in hot water until soft, drained and chopped
3 tbsp. olive oil
8 oz. (225 g) stewing veal, minced coarsely
2 oz. (50 g) prosciutto crudo, chopped,
1 tbsp. all-purpose flour
1 large glass red wine
¼ tsp. freshly ground nutmeg
1½ cups (350 ml) thick passata
4 oz. (125 g) chicken livers, cleaned and sautéed in butter until just browned, and thinly sliced
4 x quantity fresh pasta (see page 131), cut into 4 x 5-in. (10 x 13-cm) rectangles, and blanched
2¼ cups (500 ml) béchamel sauce (see page 150)
1 cup (110 g) freshly grated Parmesan cheese

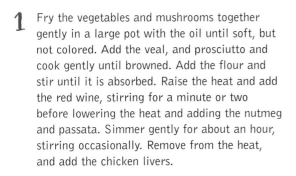

1 Fry the vegetables and mushrooms together gently in a large pot with the oil until soft, but not colored. Add the veal, and prosciutto and cook gently until browned. Add the flour and stir until it is absorbed. Raise the heat and add the red wine, stirring for a minute or two before lowering the heat and adding the nutmeg and passata. Simmer gently for about an hour, stirring occasionally. Remove from the heat, and add the chicken livers.

2 Butter a medium ovenproof dish and cover the bottom with a layer of pasta sheets. Cover with the meat sauce, and then a layer of béchamel sauce. Continue in this way until you have filled the dish and used up all the ingredients, ending with a layer of pasta covered with a generous sprinkling of Parmesan cheese. Bake in a pre-heated oven at 350°F (180°C) until golden brown and bubbling hot. Leave to stand for at least 5 minutes before serving.

WITH TRUFFLE
For added decadence add a small black or white truffle to the lasagne together with the cooked chicken livers.

WITH BEEF
Use stewing beef steak instead of veal and proceed as main recipe.

WITH PORK
Use pork loin instead of veal and proceed as main recipe.

WITH SAGE
Use a pinch of dried sage instead of the dried marjoram for a different herby flavor, and proceed as main recipe.

WITHOUT MUSHROOMS
Omit the dried porcini mushrooms and proceed as main recipe.

Moroccan Chicken

Serves 4–6

2 tsp. paprika
1 tsp. ground cumin
1 tsp. ground ginger
1 tsp. powdered turmeric
½ tsp. ground cinnamon
¼ tsp. freshly ground black pepper
1 x 3–4 lb. (1⅓–1¾ kg) chicken, cut into 8 pieces (or same weight chicken thighs and legs)

2 tbsp. olive oil
sea salt
3 cloves garlic, minced
1 onion, chopped
peel from 1 preserved lemon, rinsed in cold water, pulp discarded, peel cut into thin strips
1 cup (140 g) green olives, pitted
½ cup (75 g) raisins

½ cup (115 ml) water
4 tbsp. chopped fresh flat-leaf parsley
4 tbsp. chopped fresh cilantro

1 Combine spices and pepper in a large bowl. Put chicken pieces in the bowl, coating well with spice mixture. Let the chicken stand for 1 hour in the spices. In a large, heavy-bottomed skillet, heat the olive oil on medium-high heat.

2 Add chicken pieces, sprinkle lightly with salt (go easy on salt; the olives and lemons are salty), and brown, skin-side down, for 5 minutes. (If you are using a clay tagine, skip the browning step; heat only to medium heat and use a heat diffuser on the heating element to prevent the tagine from cracking.)

3 Lower heat to medium-low, add garlic and onion, cover, and cook for 15 minutes. Turn chicken pieces over. Add lemon slices, olives, raisins, and water. Bring to a simmer on medium heat, then turn heat to low, cover, and cook for 30 minutes, until the chicken is cooked through and quite tender. Mix in fresh parsley and cilantro just before serving. Adjust seasoning to taste. Serve with couscous, rice, or rice pilaf.

WITH PORK & CAPERS
Prepare the basic recipe, replacing the chicken with large chunks of lean pork and adding 1 tablespoon capers, rinsed, to the dish with the olives and lemon.

WITH LAMB
Prepare the basic recipe, replacing the chicken with large chunks of boneless lamb.

WITH RABBIT
Prepare the basic recipe, replacing the chicken with jointed rabbit. Before using, soak the rabbit overnight in a bowl of water with a splash of vinegar. Drain and dry the rabbit joints, before proceeding with the recipe.

WITH PHEASANT
Prepare the basic recipe, replacing the chicken with 2 or 3 jointed young pheasants.

WITH GUINEA FOWL
Prepare the basic recipe, replacing the chicken with jointed guinea fowl.

Osso Bucco

This wonderful Italian casserole takes its name from the marrowbone. Ask your butcher for large, meaty, crosscut veal shanks for this dish.

Serves 4

4 large (10-oz./275 g)
   veal shanks
¼–½ cup (25–50 g) all-
   purpose flour
2 tbsp. unsalted butter
1 tbsp. extra-virgin olive
   oil
½ large onion, finely
   chopped
1 celery rib, diced
1 carrot, diced
½ cup (100 ml) white
   wine
1 x 14 oz. (400 g) canned
   whole tomatoes

2 garlic cloves, minced
1 tbsp. finely chopped
   Italian parsley, plus
   ¼ cup (25 g), to
   garnish
¼ tsp. dried summer
   savory
¼ tsp. dried rosemary,
   crushed
1½ cups (250 ml) chicken
   stock
sea salt and freshly
   ground black pepper
zest of ½ lemon, to
   garnish

1 Preheat oven to 325°F (160°C). Lightly coat veal shanks in flour. Heat 1 tablespoon butter and the oil in Dutch oven and brown veal on all sides, about 10–12 minutes. Transfer veal to plate and set aside. Melt remaining butter in Dutch oven. Sauté onions, celery, and carrots until onions are translucent and celery and carrots are tender, about 5 minutes.

2 Add white wine and cook, letting some of the liquid evaporate. Add tomatoes, garlic, 1 tablespoon parsley, summer savory, rosemary, and chicken stock. Raise heat and bring to a boil. Arrange veal shanks in a single layer in the sauce, then reduce to simmer.

3 Cover Dutch oven and transfer to oven. Braise for 2–2½ hours, until meat is very tender and falling off the bone. Check after 1½ hours and, if necessary, add a little more chicken stock. Season to taste. Sprinkle each serving with chopped parsley and lemon zest.

WITH OLIVES
Prepare the basic recipe, adding ½ cup (100 g) pitted and halved kalamata olives with the tomatoes.

WITH CREMINI MUSHROOMS
Prepare the basic recipe, stirring in 1 cup (225 g) sautéed cremini mushrooms before serving. To prepare mushrooms, melt 1 tablespoon unsalted butter in frying pan. Sauté quartered mushrooms, sprinkled with salt, pepper, and a pinch of thyme. Cook until mushrooms begin to give off liquid. Remove from heat.

WITH GREMOLATA
Prepare the basic recipe, omitting lemon–parsley garnish. To make gremolata, combine 2 tablespoons chopped parsley, 2 tablespoons minced garlic, and 1 tablespoon grated lemon zest. Garnish each serving with gremolata.

WITH PEPPERS
Prepare the basic recipe, adding ½ cup (100 g) chopped red bell pepper with the carrot and celery.

Rabbit Braised in White Wine

If you have never prepared rabbit at home before, this uncomplicated recipe with impressive results is the perfect place to start. Have your butcher cut the rabbit for you.

Serves 4

½ cup (50 g) all-purpose
    flour
sea salt and freshly
    ground black pepper
1 x 3 lb. (1.4 kg) rabbit,
    cut into 6 pieces
2 tbsp. extra-virgin olive
    oil

½ lb. (225 g) whole
    shallots, peeled
4 garlic cloves, peeled
1 lb. (450 g) new potatoes
1 bottle dry white wine
2 bay leaves
2 tbsp. chopped fresh
    chives, to garnish

1   In a small bowl, combine flour with ½ teaspoon salt and ¼ teaspoon pepper. Clean rabbit and pat dry with paper towel, then coat pieces evenly with seasoned flour. Set aside.

2   In a large Dutch oven, heat oil over medium-high heat. Brown rabbit pieces for 5 minutes per side. Transfer to plate and set aside. Reduce heat to medium. Add shallots to Dutch oven, sprinkle with salt, and sauté until translucent, about 5 minutes. Add garlic and cook for 3 more minutes.

3   Add potatoes and rabbit pieces to Dutch oven. Pour in wine, stir, and add bay leaves. Bring to a boil, then reduce heat to low. Cover Dutch oven and simmer for up to 3 hours, until rabbit is tender and still moist. Remove bay leaves. Serve garnished with chopped chives.

WITH RED WINE
Prepare the basic recipe, replacing the white wine with an equal quantity of red wine.

WITH CHAMPAGNE
Prepare the basic recipe, replacing the white wine with an equal quantity of champagne or sparkling wine.

WITH DILL
Prepare the basic recipe, replacing the chopped chives with an equal quantity of freshly chopped dill.

WITH CHICKEN
Prepare the basic recipe, replacing the rabbit with 1 x 3 lb. (1.4 kg) chicken, cut into 8 pieces.

WITH PESTO
Prepare the basic recipe, replacing the chopped chives with 1 teaspoon pesto (see page 81) per serving.

Pepperoni, Tomato & Mozzarella Pan Pizza

This is a deep pan pizza, with a thick layer of tomato sauce and a luscious topping of Cheddar and mozzarella cheeses, pepperoni, mushrooms, and scallions, spiced up with chili flakes if you like it hot.

Serves 2–4

6 tbsp. olive oil, for greasing tins and
   brushing dough
1 packet dried yeast (2¼ tsp)
2 tsp. sugar
8 fl oz. (240 ml) warm water
1½ tbsp. olive oil
11 oz. (300 g) all-purpose flour

½ tsp. sea salt
3½ oz. (100 g) grated Cheddar cheese
3½ oz. (100g) sliced mozzarella cheese
3 oz. (75 g) pepperoni slices
1 tsp. crushed chili flakes (optional)
4 mushrooms, sliced
4 scallions, thinly sliced

for the sauce
8 fl oz. (240 ml) tomato passata or pizza
   sauce
1 tsp. dried oregano
½ tsp. dried marjoram
½ tsp. dried basil
½ tsp. garlic powder
½ tsp. sugar

1 Generously brush two 9 in. (23 cm) cake tins with 2 tbsp. oil in each and set aside. In a medium jug, combine all the ingredients for the sauce and set aside.

2 In the bowl of a stand mixer, place the yeast and sugar. Add the warm water and stir. Leave for 2 minutes, add the oil and stir again. Add the flour and salt and stir until the dough starts to come together. If the dough seems too dry, add a little more water, and if it seems too wet, add a little more flour. Knead on medium speed for 5–8 minutes, until the dough is smooth and elastic. Divide the dough into two pieces.

3 On a lightly floured work surface, roll out the dough to small circles and transfer to the cake tins, pressing them out to fit the tins. Brush around the edge of the pizza bases with the remaining olive oil. Cover each tin with a plate and leave somewhere warm for about an hour, until doubled in size.

4 Preheat the oven to 450°F (230°C). Remove the plates from the tins and divide the tomato sauce between the two pizza bases, spreading it out to within ½ in. (1.5 cm) of the edge. Add half the

grated Cheddar and mozzarella cheeses, and divide the pepperoni, crushed chilies, mushrooms and scallions between the two. Finish with the remaining cheese. Bake in the oven for about 15 minutes, or until the base is cooked and golden and the top is bubbling. Serve immediately, with a whole pizza or just half per person, depending on how hungry your guests are.

WITH SPICY BEEF
Prepare the basic recipe, omitting the pepperoni. Fry 8 oz. (225 g) lean minced beef with 1 chopped onion, 2 crushed garlic cloves and 1 tsp. chili powder in 1 tbsp. olive oil over a high heat for 5 minutes until browned. Proceed as before.

WITH ZUCCHINI & FRESH TOMATO
Prepare the basic recipe, omitting the pepperoni and substituting 1 sliced zucchini and 2 sliced tomatoes.

WITH CHORIZO
Prepare the basic recipe, omitting the pepperoni and substituting sliced chorizo. Proceed as before.

WITH HAM & ARUGULA
Prepare the basic recipe, adding a few slices of smoked ham with the pepperoni. Just before serving, add 2¼ oz. (60 g) arugula to the pizza as it comes out of the oven.

Peas with Pancetta

Serves 6

7 oz. (200 g) pancetta, chopped
2 onions, chopped
4 tbsp. olive oil

1 lb. (450 g) frozen or fresh peas
sea salt and freshly ground black pepper

1 Fry pancetta, onions, and oil together until the pancetta is lightly browned and crisp. Add the peas and stir together thoroughly. Keep moist as you braise the peas until tender, adding water when they appear to be drying out. Season to taste with salt and pepper and serve.

WITH MUSHROOMS
Cook the peas as above, replacing the pancetta with same quantity of small button mushrooms, sautéed with the onions and oil until softened.

WITH FAVA BEANS
Prepare basic recipe, replacing the peas with fresh or frozen tender broad (fava) beans. Bear in mind that they may need to be individually peeled before use if they are large and a bit tough.

WITH POTATO & LETTUCE
Prepare basic recipe, adding 6 small cubed parboiled potatoes and 3 lettuce hearts, shredded coarsely, to cook with the peas.

WITH PARMA HAM
Prepare basic recipe, replacing the pancetta with chopped Parma ham.

Veal Parmigiana

Serves 4

2 tbsp. unsalted butter, melted
½ cup (50 g) freshly grated Parmesan, plus 2 tbsp.

¼ cup (25 g) all-purpose flour
½ tsp. sea salt
¼ tsp. freshly ground black pepper

⅔ cup (175 ml) evaporated milk
4 veal cutlets
8 oz. (225 g) plain tomato sauce

1 Preheat oven to 350°F (175°C). Pour melted butter into an 8-in. (20-cm) square casserole. In a small bowl, combine 2 tablespoons grated Parmesan, flour, salt, and pepper. Pour half of the evaporated milk into a shallow dish. Dip each veal cutlet in the milk, coating both sides. Then roll each cutlet in the flour mixture. Place the veal in a single layer in casserole and bake for 30 minutes.

2 In another bowl, combine remaining evaporated milk with the remaining Parmesan. Remove veal from oven. Pour tomato sauce around the cutlets, then spread the milk and Parmesan mixture over each cutlet. Return to oven for another 20–25 minutes until bubbly. Veal should be faintly pink in center when sliced.

WITH CHICKEN
Prepare the basic recipe, replacing the veal with 4 skinless, boneless chicken breasts.

WITH EGGPLANT
Prepare the basic recipe, replacing veal with 2 medium-sized eggplants, sliced into ¼-in. (5-mm) thick slices.

WITH MOZZARELLA
Prepare the basic recipe, reducing quantity of evaporated milk to ⅓ cup (60 ml). Omit evaporated milk and Parmesan topping. Top veal with 8 slices mozzarella cheese.

WITH HERB BREADCRUMBS
Prepare the basic recipe, adding one more step after dredging in flour. Combine 2 large eggs and 1 teaspoon water and whisk in a shallow dish. Combine 1½ cups (175 g) dry breadcrumbs, ½ cup (50 g) grated Parmesan, and 1 tablespoon each freshly chopped basil and Italian parsley in another shallow dish. Working with one at a time, dip the flour-coated veal into the egg mixture, and then into the breadcrumb mixture. Proceed with recipe.

Veal in Milanese Sauce

This veal and tuna dish tastes better with homemade mayonnaise. Whisk 1 egg until pale yellow. Gradually add ½ cup (120 ml) each of sunflower oil and extra-virgin olive oil in a thin, slow, steady stream. Gradually, the oil and egg will emulsify and acquire a thick, smooth texture. Add 1 tablespoon lemon juice and season to taste.

Serves 6

2¼ lbs. (1 kg) veal fillet joint

for the marinade
1 bottle dry white wine (less 1 glass, to be set aside)
1 onion, peeled and sliced
1 carrot, scraped and sliced
4 whole cloves
3 bay leaves, chopped
sea salt and freshly ground black pepper
2⅓ cups (600 ml) veal or chicken stock (see page 163)

for the sauce
1¼ cups (275 ml) thick homemade mayonnaise
8 oz. (225 g) canned tuna in olive oil, drained and flaked
sea salt and freshly ground black pepper
2 handfuls capers, rinsed, dried, and chopped
the reserved glass of wine

for the garnish
black olives
capers
gherkins
lemon slices
chopped fresh parsley

1 Lay the veal in a deep bowl. Mix together the marinade ingredients and pour over the veal. Let stand overnight. Remove the meat from the marinade, wrap it tightly in cheesecloth, tie it up tight, and lay in a deep saucepan. Pour the marinade and stock over the veal. Simmer slowly, covered, for about 1½ hours or until the meat is cooked through.

2 Let the meat cool in its marinade, then remove and unwrap. Slice the veal very thinly onto a large, flat platter. Mix the sauce ingredients together and coat the sliced meat with sauce. Garnish the platter and serve at once, or chill until required.

WITH CHICKEN
Prepare basic recipe, omitting veal and marinade. Use the sauce to cover gently poached skinless chicken breasts.

WITH OLIVES
Prepare basic recipe. Mix two handfuls of coarsely chopped, pitted black and green olives into the sauce before serving.

WITH FISH
Prepare basic recipe, omitting veal and marinade. Poach thick fillets of haddock or cod until cooked through, then serve with a thin coating of sauce. Offer the rest separately in a sauceboat.

WITH POTATOES
Prepare basic recipe, omitting veal and marinade. Use the tonnato sauce to dress freshly boiled and peeled new potatoes or as a filling for baked potatoes.

WITH PORK
Prepare basic recipe, replacing the veal with fillet of pork.

Pot-au-Feu

Serves 6–8

2 lb. (900 g) beef shank, with bone
2 lb. (900 g) stewing beef, in one piece
2 lb. (900 g) beef ribs
2 lb. (900 g) large marrowbones
1 large onion, peeled
4 cloves
2 sprigs fresh thyme
2 bay leaves
2 celery stalks with leaves
6 sprigs fresh Italian parsley

1 tbsp. coarse sea salt
1 tsp. freshly ground black pepper
10 carrots, peeled and roughly chopped
8 leeks, cleaned, tough ends removed, cut in half lengthwise, and then in 1-inch pieces
1½ lb. (700 g) turnips, peeled and roughly chopped
1½ lb. (700 g) new potatoes

1 Using kitchen twine, tie beef shank, stewing beef, and ribs together. Place in large Dutch oven. Wrap marrowbones in cheesecloth, tie with kitchen twine, and add to Dutch oven. Cover ingredients with water and place over medium-high heat. Bring water to a boil, then reduce heat to low, and let simmer. Stud onion with cloves and add to Dutch oven.

2 Wrap thyme, bay leaves, celery stalks, and parsley in cheesecloth to make a bouquet garni. Add to Dutch oven with salt, pepper, carrots, leeks, and turnips. Simmer for 40 minutes. Add potatoes and simmer for another 20 minutes, until they are tender.

3 Untie and unwrap meats and place on a large platter. Place marrow bones on a separate plate and set aside. Arrange cooked vegetables around meats. Cover with aluminum foil.

4 The marrow can be spooned out of bones and spread on toasted baguette slices. Discard onion and strain cooking liquid through cheesecloth into a medium saucepan. Place saucepan over medium-high heat and bring to a boil. Simmer for 15 minutes until slightly reduced. Place in serving dish and serve with meats and vegetables.

WITH GRAINY MUSTARD
Prepare the basic recipe, spreading each baguette toast with ¼ teaspoon grainy mustard before adding the soft marrow.

WITH HORSERADISH
Prepare the basic recipe, spreading each baguette toast with ¼ teaspoon horseradish.

WITH CINNAMON
Prepare the basic recipe, adding 1 cinnamon stick with the other herbs and spices.

WITH PORK RIBS
Prepare the basic recipe, replacing the beef ribs with an equal quantity of pork ribs.

WITH CORNICHONS
Prepare the basic recipe, garnishing each baguette toast with a cornichon.

Polenta Casserole with Italian Sausage

This polenta casserole makes a great lunch offering, served with ratatouille or mixed grilled vegetables.

Serves 8

3 tbsp. unsalted butter
3 oz. (75 g) pancetta, cut into small cubes
10 oz. (275 g) mild Italian sausage, casings removed, crumbled
7 cups (1.8 liters) water

1½ cups (350 g) fine cornmeal
¾ cup (75 g) mozzarella, cut into ½-in. (1-cm) cubes
⅓ cup (50 g) freshly grated Parmesan

1 Preheat oven to 400°F (200°C). Butter a large casserole or earthenware dish. In large, heavy-based frying pan, melt 1 tablespoon butter over medium-high heat. Add pancetta and cook until it begins to get crisp, about 3 minutes. Transfer pancetta with drippings to heatproof bowl and set aside. In same frying pan, brown sausage about 8 minutes. Transfer to plate with paper towel to drain.

2 In large, heavy-based saucepan, bring water to a boil. Add cornmeal, pouring it slowly in a continuous stream, whisking constantly. Reduce heat to low and cook, stirring almost constantly, for 20 minutes or until polenta thickens and pulls away from sides of saucepan. Remove from heat.

3 Stir in pancetta with drippings, cubed mozzarella, and remaining butter. Transfer polenta mixture to buttered casserole or earthenware dish, spread sausage on top, and sprinkle with grated Parmesan. Bake for 25 minutes, or until polenta is set and Parmesan has melted.

WITH OLIVES
Prepare the basic recipe, adding ½ cup (100 g) pitted and chopped kalamata olives when combining the polenta and sausage.

WITH ASIAGO CHEESE
Prepare the basic recipe, replacing the mozzarella with an equal quantity of cubed Asiago cheese.

WITH ROASTED RED PEPPERS
Prepare the basic recipe, adding ½ cup (100 g) drained and chopped roasted red bell peppers when combining the polenta and sausage.

WITH BASIL
Prepare the basic recipe, adding 6–8 torn fresh basil leaves when combining the polenta and sausage.

Scalloped Potatoes with Prosciutto

The bites of salty prosciutto found amidst slices of creamy potato elevate this comforting dish to new heights.

Serves 6

3 tbsp. unsalted butter
¼ cup (50 g) finely
    chopped onion
3 tbsp. all-purpose flour
seaalt and freshly ground
    black pepper
2½ cups (600 ml) whole
    milk

8 oz. (225 g) prosciutto,
    cut into bite-sized
    pieces
2 lb. (900 g) russet
    potatoes, peeled and
    finely sliced

1   Preheat oven to 350°F (175°C). Butter a large rectangular casserole. Set aside.

2   To prepare the sauce, melt 3 tablespoons butter in large saucepan over low heat. Add chopped onions and sauté until translucent, about 5 minutes. Add flour, salt, and pepper. Stir constantly, until mixture is smooth and bubbling. Continue stirring for 1 minute, then remove from heat. Whisk in milk and return to stove. Bring mixture to boil, whisking constantly. Remove from heat when mixture has thickened, about 1–2 minutes after it comes to a boil. Stir in prosciutto.

3   Spread potato slices in casserole. Pour sauce over potatoes, ensuring that all potatoes are covered with sauce. Cover casserole with aluminum foil and bake for 30 minutes. Remove foil and continue cooking for 60–70 minutes, until potatoes are tender and browned at the edges. Allow to cool slightly before serving.

WITHOUT PROSCIUTTO
Prepare the basic recipe, omitting the prosciutto.

WITH HAM
Prepare the basic recipe, replacing the prosciutto with an equal quantity of chopped cooked ham.

WITH PANCETTA
Prepare the basic recipe, replacing the prosciutto with an equal quantity of chopped pancetta.

WITH MUSHROOMS
Prepare the basic recipe, adding 1 cup (100 g) sliced cremini mushrooms to the sliced potatoes in the buttered casserole.

LIGHTER SCALLOPED POTATOES
Prepare the basic recipe, replacing the butter with margarine and the whole milk with skim milk.

Skewered Lamb Kebabs

The key to tender lamb souvlaki is the marinade, so don't skimp on the timing (even though it takes three days!). The longer the kebabs marinate, the better this souvlaki arnisio will taste!

Serves 12

8–10 lbs. (4–4½ kg) leg of lamb, trimmed and boned, cut in 1-in. (2½ cm) cubes

for marinade 1
1 cup (250 ml) olive oil
1 tsp. ground cumin
1 tsp. dried Greek oregano
2 bay leaves, crushed
sea salt and cracked peppercorns

for marinade 2
1 cup (225 g) chopped green bell peppers
2 medium onions, chopped
½ cup (120 ml) tomato paste

for marinade 3
¼ cup (50 ml) port wine
¼ cup (50 ml) red wine vinegar
¼ cup (50 ml) fresh lemon juic

1 Mix the first marinade in a bowl, add lamb, and stir well to coat. Cover and refrigerate overnight. The following day, add the ingredients in marinade 2, stir well, cover, and refrigerate overnight. The next day, add the ingredients in marinade 3, stir well, cover, and refrigerate overnight. Soak small wooden skewers (5–8 in./12–20 cm long) in water for an hour or more.

2 Thread the lamb on the skewers, leaving a little space between pieces. They can be cooked under the broiler, on the barbecue, or even in a hot skillet on the stovetop. Whichever cooking method you use, turn frequently until crispy brown on all sides (about 15 minutes). Serve hot on the skewers with other mezethes accompanied by lemon wedges and crusty bread.

WITH PORK
Prepare the basic recipe, replacing the lamb with cubes of pork.

WITH CHICKEN
Prepare the basic recipe, replacing the lamb with cubes of chicken.

WITH BEEF
Prepare the basic recipe, replacing the lamb with cubes of beef.

WITH MIXED MEAT
Prepare the basic recipe, using a combination of different meats cooked together, making sure they are all cut to the same size so that they can cook evenly.

Neapolitan Frittata

There are countless versions of this classic dish all over Italy, using a huge variety of ingredients. Here's a favorite version from the city of Naples.

Serves 4

2 oz. (50 g) prosciutto or pancetta, cut into strips
1¾ lbs. (800 g) onions, thinly sliced
6 fresh mint leaves, chopped
5 tbsp. olive oil

6 large eggs, beaten
3 tbsp. grated pecorino
2 tbsp. grated Parmesan
1 small handful fresh basil leaves, finely shredded

3 canned tomatoes, drained, seeded, and cut into strips
sea salt and freshly ground black pepper
3–4 tbsp. canola or vegetable oil

1 Fry the prosciutto or pancetta, onions, and mint together in a little of the olive oil, stirring regularly until the onions are soft. This should take about 10 minutes. In a bowl, beat the eggs with the cheese and the basil.

2 Fry the tomato strips in a separate pan with the remaining olive oil for 5 minutes or until softened, and season with salt and pepper. Cool, and then stir into the egg mixture. Then stir in the softened onion mixture.

3 Heat the canola oil in a pan large enough to take all the mixture. When a small piece of bread dropped into the hot oil sizzles instantly, pour in the egg mixture. Flatten it out with a spatula and shake the pan to even out the mixture. Keep the heat under the pan quite high, but lower it if the frittata appears to be catching on the bottom or burning. Move the mixture around, lifting up the edges of the frittata as it sets, for about 6 minutes.

4 Cover the pan with a large lid or flat plate. Turn the frittata over onto the plate, replace the pan on the stove, and slide the frittata back into the pan to cook on the other side. Cook for about another 6 minutes, and then slide it out onto a platter to serve either hot or at room temperature (but never chilled).

WITH ZUCCHINI
Prepare the basic recipe, replacing the prosciutto or pancetta and mint with 4 cooked and thinly sliced zucchini fried with the onions. Omit the tomatoes.

WITH STRING BEAN
Prepare the basic recipe, replacing the prosciutto or pancetta with a large handful of just-cooked string beans, cut into short pieces.

WITH POTATO
Prepare the basic recipe, replacing the prosciutto or pancetta with 2 parboiled and thinly sliced potatoes.

WITH SPINACH
Prepare the basic recipe, replacing the tomatoes with 2 tablespoons steamed, drained, and chopped spinach.

WITH LEEK
Prepare the basic recipe, replacing the onions with the same quantity of sliced leeks.

CHAPTER 7
Fish & Seafood

Fresh fish and seafood is a central part of the Mediterranean diet. Really fresh fish and seafood will never smell fishy, but will have the scent of the salty sea—when shopping for fish or seafood, you should always trust your nose.

Fish and seafood are hugely enjoyed as part of everyday eating in the Mediterranean, not just as an occasional treat. Always cooked very simply and briefly to make the most of their amazing freshness, fish and seafood are either eaten on their own or combined with other ingredients such as vegetables, rice, pasta, or couscous.

HOW TO ENSURE QUALITY

Long ago, the only fish or shellfish available to cooks was the locally caught variety or preserved seafood, such as salted and dried cod in Mediterranean cuisines. The problem was transportation. Fish and shellfish are very perishable and can go from delicate and briny to mushy with the "off" aroma of ammonia in a day or so.

Today, seafood is shipped, iced-down, from coast to coast on the same day it's caught. You can also buy "FAS," fish and shellfish that have been "frozen at sea," the same day they're caught. Freshwater catfish or farmed shrimp can be "IQF" or "individually quick frozen."

So, what is fresh? Freshness is apparent in the smell, texture, and taste, not always in the state in which seafood is offered for sale. To further complicate matters, fish that is offered for sale "fresh" at many grocery stores has actually been thawed from frozen.

Whether the seafood you're buying is fresh or thawed from frozen, the best way to determine freshness is with your eyes and nose, so go to a quality fish market—don't buy fish at a supermarket unless you are absolutely certain they have top-quality fish. Don't be afraid to ask the fishmonger if you can smell or touch the fish before you buy.

Whole fish should have clear eyes and a briny, fresh aroma.

Clams, mussels, and oysters should have tightly closed shells and a briny aroma.

Fish fillets and steaks should be delicate yet firm and have a sweet, briny aroma.

Squid, calamari, and octopus should be firm to the touch and have a sweet, briny aroma.

Sea or bay scallops out of the shell as well as shrimp should be firm to the touch and have a sweet, briny aroma.

Crabs, crayfish, langoustines, and lobsters should be alive and moving, or cooked, with their meat picked out of the shell and chilled, canned, or frozen.

SEAFOOD PREPARATION TIPS

There are a variety of ways to prepare seafood, but there are a few basic guidelines to follow, whatever method you use:

• For food safety reasons, keep fish and shellfish—especially shellfish—chilled until you're ready to cook.

• When in doubt, go for underdone. Fish and shellfish continue to cook for a minute or so more, away from the heat, and that can make a big difference, so pull them off the heat a minute or so before you're sure they're done. Worse case scenario? The seafood is a bit undercooked, and you can put it back in the poacher, in the oven, or on the grill to get it more done if necessary.

• Understand which is the skin side and the flesh side on fish fillets. Even when the skin has been removed from a fish fillet, you can still see darkened areas where it used to be. So when you follow the directions for grilling or planking fish, you'll know which side is which.

EQUIPMENT

Seafood can be prepared with the usual indoor kitchen equipment: blender or food processor, chopping board and knives, measuring cups and spoons, pots and pans, garlic press, grater, wooden spoons, etc. Outdoors, a simple barbecue grill with a lid and barbecue equipment such as grill tongs and spatula are enough to get you started. If you cook seafood regularly, you might want to check out the following kitchen helpers:

Deep-fryer—with a deep-fryer, you can set the temperature, heat the oil, and fry seafood in an exact yet effortless way.

Hardwood planks—planks made from cedar, alder, maple, or oak are used to plank-cook seafood on the grill or in the oven.

Oyster knife—with heavy gloves and a sturdy, sharp, wide-bladed oyster knife, you can learn to open the most uncooperative oyster.

Thermometer—a candy thermometer, clipped to the side of a pan of oil, will let you know the temperature of the oil so seafood fries up crisp and golden.

Tuna & Bean Salad

Serves 6

10 oz. (275 g) canned, fresh, or dried borlotti
  (or cranberry) beans
10 oz. (275 g) canned tuna in olive oil, flaked

1 large red onion, thinly sliced
2 tbsp. chopped fresh flat-leaf parsley
5 tbsp. olive oil

1 tbsp. white or red wine vinegar
sea salt and freshly ground black pepper

1 If using canned beans, drain and rinse in cold water. If using fresh or dried borlotti beans, you need to soak them in cold fresh water. Dried beans need to be soaked overnight; fresh beans do not require as much soaking. Drain the beans, then cook them in fresh water for 5 minutes. Drain and rinse, then cook slowly in fresh water until tender. Do not salt the water until the beans are tender, or the skins will toughen.

2 Mix the cooled beans with the flaked tuna. Add the onion and parsley, and mix together. Dress with olive oil, vinegar, and salt and pepper. Mix together thoroughly. Let the salad stand for about 30 minutes, then serve with plenty of crusty bread to mop up the juices.

WITH SHRIMP
Prepare basic recipe, replacing the tuna with cooked shrimp, red onion with a little chopped scallion, and vinegar with lemon juice.

WITH MUSSELS
Prepare basic recipe, replacing the tuna with about 25 cooked, shelled mussels. Omit the onion. Replace the vinegar with lemon juice.

WITH GARBANZO BEANS
Prepare basic recipe, replacing the beans with drained canned garbanzo beans.

WITH PRAWNS & GARBANZO BEANS
Prepare basic recipe, replacing the beans with garbanzo beans, tuna with cooked shrimp, red onion with chopped scallion, and vinegar with lemon juice.

Tuna & Caper Stuffed Eggs

Serves 6

12 eggs, hard-boiled
1 small can tuna in olive oil
6 tbsp. mayonnaise

4 tsp. lemon juice
about 12 capers, rinsed and chopped
5 dill pickles, chopped

sea salt and freshly ground black pepper
lettuce leaves, to garnish

1 Shell the hard-boiled eggs, slice in half lengthwise, and carefully remove the yolks. In a bowl, mash the yolks with a fork. Drain and flake the tuna, then mash it into the egg yolks with the mayonnaise. Mix in the lemon juice, then stir in the capers and dill pickles. Season with salt and pepper.

2 Pile this mixture back into the halved eggs and arrange them on a large plate. Garnish with lettuce leaves and chill until required.

WITH SHRIMP
Prepare the basic recipe, replacing the tuna with 6 ounces of cooked peeled shrimp and omitting the capers and dill pickles.

WITH HAM
Prepare the basic recipe, replacing the tuna with 5 oz. (150 g) of chopped cooked ham and omitting the capers.

WITH TUNA
Prepare the basic recipe, but omit the capers and dill pickles.

WITH POACHED FISH
Prepare the basic recipe, replacing the tuna with 5 oz. (150 g) of cooled poached white fish (such as cod), carefully checked for bones.

Huevos Revueltos

This is a variation of a popular tapas dish from Seville, the southern Spanish city acknowledged as the birthplace of the tapas tradition. If you want to be faithful to the original Sevillian recipe, remove the pan from the heat while the eggs are still a little runny.

Serves 6

14 oz. (400 g) baby
    spinach leaves
4 tbsp. olive oil
sea salt and freshly
    ground black pepper
6 large eggs or 5 extra-
    large eggs
1 tbsp. roughly chopped
    fresh flat-leaf parsley

½ tsp. Spanish paprika
½ tsp. dried oregano
1 onion, finely chopped
3 garlic cloves, crushed
scant ½ lbs. (225 g)
    cooked shrimp, peeled
warm crusty rolls, to
    serve

1 Wash the baby spinach leaves, then steam them in the water that's still on the leaves, for about 1 minute, or until the leaves just begin to wilt. Drain the spinach leaves well, lightly squeeze dry, then toss in a bowl with half the olive oil and sea salt and freshly ground pepper to taste. Set aside.

2 Break the eggs into a separate bowl, then add the parsley, paprika, oregano, and sea salt and freshly ground pepper to taste. Lightly whisk together.

3 Heat the remaining oil in a nonstick pan. Sauté the finely chopped onion and crushed garlic until they begin to soften but not brown. Add the shrimp and mix with the onion and garlic for 1–2 minutes. Add the spinach, and continue to toss the ingredients in the pan.

4 Pour the seasoned eggs into the pan, and stir gently over medium heat, pausing for several moments at a time to allow the mixture to begin to set. Serve immediately with warm crusty rolls.

WITH MUSHROOMS
Prepare the basic recipe, adding thinly sliced pan-fried mushrooms to the eggs before cooking. Omit the spinach, shrimp, and oregano, and halve the quantity of olive oil.

WITH ONIONS
Prepare the basic recipe, omitting the spinach and shrimp and adding 2 more chopped onions.

WITH BELL PEPPERS
Prepare the basic recipe, omitting the spinach and shrimp, and add 4 sliced and seeded bell peppers, lightly fried in a little oil in a separate pan.

WITH TOMATOES
Prepare the basic recipe, omitting the spinach and shrimp and using 6 large, ripe tomatoes, quartered and seeded, instead.

WITH SPINACH
Prepare the basic recipe, omitting the shrimp.

Provençal Fish Soup

Known as bouillabaisse in Marseilles, this seafood soup has many different versions. Most contain certain ingredients—the freshest fish and shellfish, saffron, aromatic orange peel and fennel, and garlic.

Serves 6–8

¼ cup (50 ml) olive oil
6 cloves garlic, minced
2 cups (225 g) chopped onion
1 cup (100 g) chopped bulb fennel
2 cups (450 g) canned tomatoes with their liquid
½ tsp. saffron threads
1 tsp. grated orange zest or dried orange peel
1 tsp. dried thyme
1 lb. small, bony fish (rascasse, red mullet, drum, and/or bream), heads removed, cut into 3-inch pieces, rinsed, and patted dry
1 lb. (450 g) meaty fish (John Dory, monkfish, Pacific cod, or halibut), cleaned, heads removed, cut into 3-inch pieces, rinsed, and patted dry
1 lb. (450 g) shellfish, such as shell-on shrimp, clams, bay scallops, and/or langoustines
rouille (optional)
buttered and oven-toasted slices of French bread

1 Heat the olive oil in a large pot over medium-high heat. Sauté the garlic, onion, and fennel until the onion is transparent, about 5 minutes. Stir in the tomatoes, saffron, orange zest, thyme, and bony and meaty fish pieces. Add enough water to cover. When the water comes to a boil again, cover and simmer for 10 minutes.

2 Add the shellfish, bring to a simmer again, cover, and simmer for an additional 10 minutes. To serve, ladle the soup into large bowls and serve with toasted bread and rouille, if liked.

HOMEMADE ROUILLE
In a food processor, combine 4 large egg yolks, 4 cloves garlic, a few saffron threads and salt and pepper. With the motor running, slowly add 325 ml (12 fl oz) extra-virgin olive oil in a thin stream, creating a mayonnaise-like consistency. Keep refrigerated for 3–4 days.

WITH POTATOES & EXTRA FENNEL
Prepare basic recipe, adding 1 extra cup (100 g) chopped bulb fennel and 1 lb. (450 g) small new potatoes to vegetables.

WITHOUT SHELLFISH
Prepare basic recipe, omitting shellfish and adding 1 extra pound fish and 1 bay leaf. When fish and vegetables are cooked, pass soup, in batches, through a food mill. Discard solids. Return brothy puree to the pot, bring to a boil, then strain through a sieve. Serve with toasted bread and rouille.

WITH RED SNAPPER & SHRIMP
Prepare basic recipe, adding 1 cup (100 g) chopped celery to onions and garlic. Use red snapper for the fish and shrimp for the shellfish. Add 1 bay leaf and 1 cup (250 ml) dry white wine to the water.

Crisp Shrimp Fritters

Known as *tortillitas de camarones* in Spain, these delicious fritters are wonderful served as an appetizer with a glass or two of dry white wine or chilled dry sherry.

Serves 6

½ lb. (225 g) small
  shrimp, peeled
1½ cups (200 g) chickpea
  flour or all-purpose
  flour
1 tbsp. chopped fresh flat-
  leaf parsley

3 scallions, finely chopped
½ tsp. sweet cayenne or
  paprika
sea salt
olive oil, for deep-frying

1 Cover the shrimp with water and bring to a boil over high heat. As soon as water starts to boil, quickly lift out shrimp with a slotted spoon and set aside. Scoop out 1 cup (250 ml) cooking water and let cool. Discard remaining water. When the shrimp are cool, cover and refrigerate.

2 To make batter, combine flour, parsley, scallions, and paprika in a bowl. Add pinch of salt and the cooled cooking water, and mix well. Cover and refrigerate for 1 hour. Mince shrimp very fine, and add to chilled batter; mix well again.

3 Pour olive oil into heavy sauté pan to about 1 in. (2½ cm) deep, then heat until almost smoking. Add 1 tablespoon batter to the oil for each fritter and, using the back of a spoon, flatten into a 3½-in. (10-cm) round. Do not crowd pan. Fry, turning once, for about 1 minute on each side, or until the fritters are golden and very crisp.

4 Using a slotted spoon, lift out the fritters, holding them briefly over pan to allow excess oil to drain, and transfer to ovenproof platter lined with paper towels. Keep warm in low oven while frying the rest of the fritters, always making sure oil is very hot before adding the mixture. When all the fritters are cooked, arrange on a platter and serve immediately.

WITH SQUID
Prepare basic recipe, replacing shrimp with small squid, boiled until tender, drained, and well dried before chopping. Replace the cup (250 ml) of shrimp cooking water with 1 cup (250 ml) of squid cooking water.

WITH MUSSELS
Prepare basic recipe, replacing shrimp with very large, steamed mussels, shelled and well drained before chopping. Replace the cup (250 ml) of shrimp cooking water with 1 cup (250 ml) of mussel cooking liquid.

WITH COD
Prepare basic recipe, replacing shrimp with cubes of cod, lightly poached and well drained before chopping. Replace the cup (250 ml) of shrimp cooking water with 1 cup (250 ml) of cod poaching water.

WITH SCALLOPS
Prepare basic recipe, replacing shrimp with clean, medium-sized scallops, lightly seared in a little oil before chopping, chilling, and coating with the batter. In this case, because the scallops are not poached, use tap water for thinning the batter.

Serrano Ham & Shrimp Tostadas

Serves 4

4 slices crusty bread
1 x 14-oz. (400 g) jar tomato sauce or the
    same amount of homemade tomato sauce

3 thin slices Serrano ham, cut into strips
8 jumbo shrimp (peeled and deveined,
    tails left on)

4 heaping tbsp. grated Manchego cheese
10 fresh basil leaves

1 Preheat the broiler. Place bread slices on counter and spread a generous amount of tomato sauce over each piece. Place the Serrano ham strips on top of the sauce. Place 2 shrimp on top of the Serrano ham. Sprinkle the Manchego cheese over the top, and then add the basil. Slide under the broiler and cook until done, then transfer onto plates and serve at once.

WITH MOZZARELLA
Prepare the basic recipe, replacing the Manchego cheese with 5 oz. (150 g) mozzarella, finely chopped.

WITH TOMATOES
Prepare the basic recipe, replacing the tomato sauce with 8 cubed and seeded tomatoes, divided evenly between the 4 slices of bread.

WITH AVOCADO
Prepare the basic recipe, then scatter 2 peeled and cubed avocados over the top just before serving.

WITH SCALLOPS & MOZZARELLA
Replace the shrimp with 8 large scallops, cleaned and halved.

Tuna & Cherry Tomato Kebabs

Serves 4–6

14 oz. (400 g) fresh tuna, cut into cubes
    about the same size as the cherry tomatoes
20 cherry tomatoes

For the marinade
4 tbsp. extra-virgin olive oil
2 tbsp. fresh lemon juice
2 tbsp. finely chopped fresh flat-leaf parsley

2 cloves garlic, minced or crushed
1 tsp. sea salt
½ tsp. freshly ground black pepper
lemon wedges, for serving

1 Thread the tuna and cherry tomatoes alternately onto each skewer, using about 6 to 8 skewers, depending how many cubes of tuna you have cut. Lay the skewers in a shallow pan. Mix together the marinade ingredients in a small bowl until well combined, then pour over the tuna and tomato skewers. Marinate, covered, in the refrigerator for 1 hour or longer, turning the skewers halfway through.

2 Cook the skewers under a hot broiler for 8 minutes, turning and brushing regularly with the marinade. Serve the skewers with lemon wedges for squeezing.

WITH SWORDFISH
Prepare the basic recipe, replacing the tuna cubes with cubed swordfish.

WITH CHILI
Prepare the basic recipe, adding 2 fresh chili peppers, seeded and finely chopped, to the marinade to give the kebabs extra fire.

WITH CILANTRO
Prepare the basic recipe, replacing the parsley in the marinade with chopped fresh cilantro.

WITH MUSHROOMS
Prepare the basic recipe, replacing half the cherry tomatoes with small button mushrooms. Alternate fish, cherry tomatoes, and mushrooms on the skewers.

Seafood Brochettes

Cooking fish or seafood on skewers can be done on the barbecue, in the oven, or under the broiler. These brochettes look good and taste wonderful.

Serves 4–6

½ lb. (225 g) cod fillets, halved
½ lb. (225 g) scallops (halved, if large)
1 lb. (450 g) large shrimp, shelled and deveined
2 green or red bell peppers, seeded and cut into chunks
1 bunch large scallions, cut into chunks, or 2 red onions, cut into segments

For the marinade
5 tbsp. fresh lemon juice
¼ cup (50 ml) white wine
8 tbsp. finely chopped fresh flat-leaf parsley
½ cup (120 ml) extra-virgin olive oil
3 cloves garlic, finely chopped
1 small ripe tomato, finely chopped
1 tbsp. mild chili powder
¾ tsp. sea salt
¾ tsp. dried oregano

1 Soak 8 or 10 small wooden skewers in water for an hour or more. Thread an alternating combination of cod, scallops, shrimp, bell peppers, and scallions or onion pieces on each of the skewers. Place brochettes in a large, shallow dish or baking pan.

2 Make the marinade by mixing the ingredients in a jar with a tight-fitting lid. Shake well and pour over the brochettes. Marinate in the refrigerator at least 4 hours, turning occasionally. Preheat broiler. Remove brochettes from pan, reserving marinade.

3 Broil brochettes 5 in. (12 cm) from heat for 5–7 minutes on each side, or until seafood is opaque and firm to the touch. Do not overcook. Place brochettes on a warmed serving platter. Bring reserved marinade to a boil and pour over brochettes to serve.

WITH SHRIMP
Prepare the basic recipe, replacing all the seafood with 2 lb. (900 g) of shelled and deveined large shrimp.

WITH BABY SQUID & SHRIMP
Prepare the basic recipe, replacing the cod and scallops with 1 lb. (450 g) cleaned baby squid.

WITH SCALLOP & MUSHROOM
Prepare the basic recipe, using 1 lb. (450 g) cleaned whole scallops (medium-sized) and 1 lb. (450 g) firm mushrooms of a similar size (omitting the cod, shrimp, and bell peppers).

WITH CHILI
Prepare the basic recipe, adding 1 or 2 finely chopped fresh chili peppers to the other marinade ingredients.

Sea Bass in Salt Crust

This dramatic dish is a very special way to serve fresh fish. The crust is very thick, and it must be cracked open like a shell to reveal the perfectly cooked white fish within. It is important to protect the fish from becoming too salty—the skin of the fish will protect it all over, but use foil or waxed or parchment paper along the belly slit to prevent the salt from seeping inside the fish.

Serves 6

1 fresh sea bass,
    approximately 3⅓ lbs.
    (1½ kg)
2 egg whites, beaten until
    foaming and thickened
about 3⅓ lbs. (1½ kg) sea
    salt

1   Preheat the oven to 400°F (200°C). Clean and gut the fish carefully. Wash thoroughly and pat dry. Protect the slit in the fish's belly with a sheet of foil or waxed paper tucked inside the fish. Mix the egg whites and salt together thoroughly to make a wet cementlike texture.

2   Find a large ovenproof dish that is larger than the fish itself to allow space for the salt crust. Line the bottom with about half the salt mixture. Lay the fish on top, then cover completely with more of the mixture. Bake in the oven until the surface of the salt crust is dark brown. This should take about 45 minutes.

3   Take the dish out of the oven and crack the salt crust. Carefully remove the fish and brush off any excess salt before serving.

WITH SEA BREAM
Prepare the basic recipe, replacing the sea bass with sea bream.

WITH SALMON
Prepare the basic recipe, replacing the sea bass with salmon.

WITH HERBS
Prepare the basic recipe, adding a large handful of chopped fresh mixed herbs to the salt and egg white mixture before spreading it over the fish.

WITH LEMON ZEST
Prepare the basic recipe, adding the grated zest of 2 lemons to the salt and egg white mixture before spreading it over the fish.

Grilled Shrimp with Citrus Aïoli

This is a perfect way to whet appetites before the main part of the meal begins, or you can make it into a light meal by serving it with crusty French bread and a green salad.

Serves 4

12 oz. (350 g) raw jumbo shrimp, peeled and deveined
2 tsp. extra-virgin olive oil
¼ tsp. ground cumin
pinch cayenne pepper
pinch sea salt
pinch freshly ground black pepper

For the citrus aïoli
⅓ cup (70 g) mayonnaise
½ tsp. grated lemon zest
½ tsp. grated lime zest
½ tsp. grated orange zest
1 small clove garlic, minced
pinch freshly ground black pepper

1 Preheat broiler to medium-high heat. In a bowl, combine shrimp, oil, cumin, cayenne pepper, salt, and black pepper. Toss until shrimp are well coated in seasonings. Place shrimp under broiler and cook, turning once, until shrimp are pink and opaque, about 4 minutes. Transfer shrimp to plate and refrigerate until cold.

2 To make the citrus aïoli, in a small bowl, whisk together all the ingredients. If you wish, you can make the aïoli ahead and refrigerate it in an airtight container for up to 2 days. Serve the shrimp on a platter, with the sauce offered separately in a small bowl.

WITH CLASSIC AÏOLI
Prepare the basic recipe, replacing all the citrus zest in the aïoli with 2 extra cloves minced garlic and 1 heaped tablespoon of finely chopped fresh flat-leaf parsley.

WITH PESTO MAYONNAISE
Prepare the basic recipe, replacing all the citrus zest and garlic in the aïoli with 1 heaping tablespoon pesto.

WITH HERBED MAYONNAISE
Prepare the basic recipe, replacing all the citrus zest in the aïoli with 3 tablespoons finely chopped fresh mixed herbs, stirred into the mayonnaise with the minced garlic.

WITH SQUID
Prepare the basic recipe, replacing half the shrimp with cleaned baby squid.

Steamed Mussels with Pesto

This is a great way to serve mussels. Make sure there is plenty of good crusty bread with which to soak up all the lovely juices left in the bowl once the mussels have been eaten, and offer your guests finger bowls and plenty of napkins because this can get decadently messy!

Serves 6–8

2 cups (60 g) fresh basil leaves
¼ cup (25 g) coarsely chopped walnuts
5 garlic cloves (1 whole, 4 thinly sliced)
¼ cup (45 g) freshly grated Parmesan cheese
1¼ cups (300 ml) extra-virgin olive oil

1 cup (120 g) halved cherry or grape tomatoes
sea salt and freshly ground black pepper
3 large shallots, thinly sliced
1 cup (250 ml) dry white wine

5 lbs. (2⅓ kg) mussels, scrubbed and debearded
crusty bread, for serving

1 To make the pesto, combine the basil, walnuts, and whole garlic cloves in a food processor and pulse until fine. Add the Parmesan and roughly one-third of the olive oil, and process until smooth. Transfer the pesto to a medium bowl and add another 2 tablespoons of the oil with the tomatoes and season with salt and pepper. Use a final drizzling of the oil to cover the surface and set aside.

2 In a very large, deep skillet or large soup pot, heat the remaining olive oil until simmering. Add the shallots and 4 sliced garlic cloves. Cook over high heat, stirring, until lightly golden, about 4 minutes. Add the white wine and a generous pinch each of salt and pepper, then bring to a boil. Add the mussels and stir for 1 minute. Cover and cook, stirring occasionally, until all of the mussels have opened, about 6–8 minutes. Discard any mussels that do not open.

3 Add the pesto-tomato mixture and stir until the mussels are evenly coated. Transfer the mussels and broth to bowls and serve with crusty bread.

WITH WHITE WINE, SHALLOTS & GARLIC
Steam the mussels according to the basic recipe, and omit the pesto. Simply serve the steamed mussels with crusty bread.

WITH CHILI
Prepare the basic recipe, omitting the pesto. Add 1 teaspoon crushed red chili pepper to the steaming liquid to add fire to the whole dish.

WITH COUSCOUS
Prepare the basic recipe. Strain the liquid from the mussels before mixing with the pesto, and use the liquid to pour over a scant 8 oz. (225 g) couscous. Cover and steam until cooked, fluff with a fork, and use as the base for the mussels, mixed with the pesto, instead of crusty bread.

WITH BUTTER BEANS
Prepare the basic recipe, replacing the tomatoes with 1 x 14-oz. (400 g) can of butter beans, drained, then stirred into the pesto.

Lobster Florentine

This easy casserole will be met with "oohs" and "aahs." Serve as an elegant side dish, or as an appetizer with thin slices of toasted baguette.

Serves 4–6 as a side dish

1 lb. (450 g) cooked lobster meat, cut into bite-sized pieces
3 tbsp. unsalted butter
2 tbsp. all-purpose flour
1 cup (250 ml) heavy cream
½ cup (100 g) freshly grated Parmesan

¼ cup (50 g) dry breadcrumbs
10-oz (275-g) packet frozen spinach, thawed and drained
8 oz. (225 g) chopped mozzarella

1   Preheat oven to 350°F (175°C). Butter a 9-in. (23 cm) pie plate, then arrange lobster meat in a layer on the bottom. In medium saucepan, melt butter over medium heat. Add flour and stir constantly, until mixture is smooth and bubbling. Continue stirring for 1 minute, then remove from heat.

2   Whisk in cream and return to stove. Bring mixture to boil, whisking constantly. When mixture has thickened, about 1–2 minutes after it comes to a boil, add half the parmesan. Stir until blended and remove from heat.

3   In small bowl, combine breadcrumbs with salt and pepper. Set aside. Place paper towel in a fine sieve and press spinach lightly to remove any remaining liquid. Spread spinach over lobster in pie plate. Pour cream sauce over spinach. Sprinkle with remaining Parmesan, mozzarella and the breadcrumb mixture. Bake for 20 minutes, or until heated through and bubbly.

WITH CRAB
Prepare the basic recipe, replacing the lobster meat with crabmeat.

WITH SCALLOPS
Prepare the basic recipe, replacing the lobster meat with 1 lb. (450 g) sea scallops. To prepare the scallops, simply bring a large pot of water to a boil. Immerse scallops and boil for 2 minutes. Remove scallops with a slotted spoon and pat dry with paper towel.

WITH FRESH BASIL
Prepare the basic recipe, adding 2 tablespoons freshly chopped basil to the breadcrumbs before sprinkling over the sauce.

WITH PARSLEY
Prepare the basic recipe, adding 2 tablespoons freshly chopped parsley to the breadcrumbs before sprinkling over cheese sauce.

Linguine with Fish Sauce

Use a fish that can withstand a fairly long cooking time without losing all its flavor and texture, such as swordfish steak, chopped into small cubes, and some white fish, which will flake better. In this way, there are two completely separate textures within the same dish. However, you can use any combination of fish of your choice, or even squid if you prefer. Cheese is never served with fish pasta dishes, or at least, extremely rarely.

Serves 6

3 tbsp. olive oil
2 cloves garlic, thinly
   sliced
2 or 3 tbsp. chopped fresh
   flat-leaf parsley
¼ dried red chili pepper
1 swordfish steak, cubed
2 cod fillets, cubed
2 or 3 tbsp. dry white
   wine

1¼ cups (200 g) puréed
   canned tomatoes
sea salt and freshly
   ground black pepper
1 lb. pasta of your choice
2 tbsp. chopped fresh
   mint

1 Pour the olive oil into a large skillet, add the garlic, parsley, and chili, and cook very gently for about 5 minutes. Discard the chili. Add all the fish and fry together for about 3 minutes before adding the wine. Stir for about 2 minutes, boiling off the alcohol, then add the tomato purée. Stir together thoroughly, season, and cover. Simmer for about 15 minutes or until the sauce is thick and glossy.

2 Meanwhile, bring a large pot of salted water to a boil, then add the pasta. Return to a boil and cook until tender, then drain and return to the saucepan. Pour in the sauce, sprinkle with the mint, and toss everything together very thoroughly. Transfer onto a platter and serve immediately.

WITH SCALLOPS
Prepare the basic recipe, replacing the swordfish and cod with 8 large scallops, cut into quarters. Simmer the scallops in the tomato sauce for just 5 minutes to prevent them from becoming rubbery.

WITH EXTRA CHILI
Prepare the basic recipe, increasing the amount of chili pepper by as much as 1 whole dried red chili pepper or equivalent chili powder to give the finished sauce extra fire. Be careful not to add so much chili that the flavor of the fish is overwhelmed.

WITH MUSSELS
Prepare the basic recipe, adding about 12 cooked and shelled mussels to the sauce about halfway through the simmering stage.

Spaghetti with Clams

As with all recipes using clams do make sure they are as clean as possible before you cook them to avoid an unpleasant muddy taste or a gritty sensation under your teeth.

Serves 4

3½ lbs. (1½ kg) fresh, live clams
6 tbsp. extra-virgin olive oil
¾ cup (175 ml) dry white wine

3 cloves garlic, chopped finely
14 oz. (400 g) spaghetti or vermicelli

3 tbsp. chopped fresh flat-leaf parsley
sea salt and freshly ground black pepper

1 Clean clams really thoroughly in several changes of fresh water to make sure you have removed all traces of sand or mud. When the water the clams are covered with is completely clear, the clams are clean. Drain clean clams and put them in a wide, fairly deep skillet with about 2 tablespoons of the oil and all the wine. Cover and heat. When the pan is very hot, shake it regularly over the heat to help the clams open up.

2 After about 6 or 7 minutes, any clams that are going to open should have opened. Discard any closed clams. Drain the rest, reserving the liquid. Strain liquid through a fine sieve. Heat remaining oil with the garlic for a few minutes, then add clams and reserved liquid. Mix everything together and bring to a boil, then cover and remove from heat.

3 Meanwhile, bring a large pot of salted water to a boil. Add pasta and stir. Cover and return to a boil. Uncover and boil until tender, then drain and return to pot. Pour in clams and toss to combine. Add parsley and plenty of freshly ground black pepper, toss again, and transfer to a warmed platter or bowl. Serve at once.

WITH TOMATO
Prepare the basic recipe, adding 3 fresh and very ripe, chopped, and seeded tomatoes to the pan with the garlic before adding the clams.

WITH CHILI PEPPER
Prepare the basic recipe, adding 1 or 2 dried red chili peppers, finely chopped, to the garlic before adding the clams.

WITH MUSSELS
Prepare the basic recipe, substituting mussels for half of the clams. Bear in mind that the mussels might take a minute or two longer to steam open depending on their size.

Baked Stuffed Baby Squid on a Bed of Fennel

Sweet and tender baby squid come into their own when paired with spicy chorizo and salty feta. Served on a fragrant bed of cooked fennel, they are really wonderful.

Serves 4

½ lb. (225 g) uncooked chorizo
generous ½ cup (125 ml) dry white wine
scant ½ lb. (225 g) feta or other hard white
   goat's cheese

20 baby squid, cleaned, tubes and tentacles
   only
vegetable oil, for greasing and frying
2 fennel bulbs, thinly sliced

1 tbsp. good quality extra-virgin olive oil,
   plus extra to serve
sea salt and freshly ground black pepper

1 Put the chorizo in a saucepan with the white wine (the wine should cover the chorizo). Bring to a boil, then lower heat and simmer for 15 minutes. Remove from heat and let the chorizo cool in the pan. When cool, peel off chorizo skins and chop meat into small cubes. Put in a bowl. Chop the feta into similar-sized cubes as the chorizo, and mix with the chorizo. Carefully spoon the mixture into the squid tubes, filling tubes to three-quarters full. Fasten the opening closed with a toothpick.

2 Lightly oil a baking dish large enough to take all the filled squid. Preheat oven to 375°F (190°C). Heat vegetable oil in a very large skillet over high heat. When very hot, add the squid bodies and cook in batches, searing them for 1 minute on each side. As each batch of squid is seared, transfer to the prepared baking dish after draining on paper towels. When all the squid are seared, place the dish in the oven to finish cooking for 3–4 minutes. Add the squid tentacles to the skillet and fry for 1–2 minutes, or until just cooked through, then drain on paper towels.

3 Bring a pan of salted water to a boil. Add the fennel and boil for 1 minute. Drain the fennel and place in a bowl. Drizzle with 1 tablespoon olive oil and season, to taste, with salt and pepper. To serve, place equal portions of the fennel into the center of each plate. Top each with 5 stuffed squid tubes and a few tentacles. Drizzle with a little olive oil and serve.

WITH OLIVE FILLING
Prepare the basic recipe, replacing the chorizo and feta filling with a filling made from soft bread crumbs mixed with chopped garlic, chopped mint, chopped green pitted olives, a little olive oil, salt, and pepper.

WITH POTATO FILLING
Prepare the basic recipe, replacing the filling with a mixture of mashed potatoes, 2 tablespoons crumbled feta or goat's cheese, oregano, minced garlic, salt, pepper, and olive oil.

WITH POTATOES
Prepare the basic recipe, replacing the boiled fennel with a bed of boiled new potatoes, thickly sliced and dressed with a little olive oil and freshly ground black pepper.

WITH CHILI
Prepare the basic recipe, adding 1 teaspoon chili powder to the feta and chorizo filling mixture.

Pesce al Forno

Whole fish that are too small to grill, but too big to fry, work well with this traditional Italian oven method. They bake to a luscious, aromatic, crusty finish, so be sure to have lots of Italian bread to mop it all up.

Serves 8–10

1½ lbs. (700 g) whole, small fish, such as sardines, lake perch, smallmouth bass, or mackerel, with head and tail intact
5 tbsp. olive oil
2 bay leaves

4 tbsp. panko or other dried breadcrumbs
¼ cup (25 g) finely chopped fresh parsley
1 tsp. dried oregano
1 tsp. grated lemon zest
½ cup (120 ml) dry white wine

1 Preheat the oven to 425°F (220°C). Cut the heads off the fish. Place each fish, cut-side down, on a flat surface and press down on fish with both hands to open like a book and flatten. With your fingers, remove the backbone, then cut off the tail.

2 Drizzle 2 tablespoons of the olive oil in a baking dish and arrange the bay leaves on the bottom. Arrange the fish in dish, skin-side down, so that they fit snugly. In a bowl, combine remaining 3 tablespoons olive oil, breadcrumbs, parsley, oregano, and lemon zest. Sprinkle this mixture over the fish and pour in the wine.

3 Roast for 18–20 minutes or until the fish flake when tested with a fork in the thickest part.

WITH FISH FILLETS
Prepare the basic recipe, using 1½ lb. (700 g) fish fillets in place of small whole fish. Roast for 10–12 minutes or until the fish begins to flake when tested with a fork in the thickest part.

WITH SHRIMP
Prepare the basic recipe, using 1½ lb. (700 g) whole, large shrimp, peeled and deveined, in place of fish. Roast for 8–10 minutes or until the shrimp are pink and opaque.

WITH LOBSTER
Prepare the basic recipe, using 4 rock lobster tails. Have your fishmonger dispatch live lobster and cut the lobster tails for you; do not butterfly. Arrange them in the dish with the other ingredients. Roast for 10–12 minutes, or until the lobster meat is white and opaque, and the shells are red.

WITH WHOLE LARGE FISH
Prepare the basic recipe, using 1 large whole fish in place of the small fish. Roast for 20–22 minutes or until the fish begins to flake when tested with a fork in the thickest part.

Roasted Monkfish Romesco

Serve this dish with crusty bread to mop up all the delicious juices. Colorful Romesco, a classic sauce from Catalonia, also functions as a vegetable in this dish.

Serves 4

for the romesco
½ cup (100 g) almonds, toasted
1 slice white bread, toasted and crumbled
2 red bell peppers, roasted, seeded, and peeled
1 tbsp. chopped fresh Italian parsley
2 cloves garlic, minced
½ tsp. red pepper flakes
¼ tsp. each sea salt freshly ground black pepper

⅓ cup (75 ml) red wine vinegar
⅔ cup (150 ml) extra-virgin olive oil
1 medium zucchini, thinly sliced into rounds
1 red onion, thinly sliced into rounds
olive oil for drizzling
fine kosher or sea salt and freshly ground black pepper to taste
4 skinless monkfish fillets

1 To make the sauce, finely grind the almonds in a food processor. Add the toasted bread, peppers, parsley, garlic, pepper flakes, salt, and pepper. Puree to form a smooth paste. Add the vinegar and blend. While the motor is running, slowly add the olive oil in a thin stream until all the ingredients are incorporated.

2 Preheat the oven to 425°F (220°C). Arrange the zucchini and onion slices on a cookie sheet, drizzle with olive oil, and season to taste. Place the fish fillets on the vegetables, drizzle with olive oil, and season to taste. Roast for 10–12 minutes or until the monkfish begins to flake when tested with a fork in the thickest part. Serve with Romesco.

WITH SHRIMP
Prepare the basic recipe, using peeled and deveined large shrimp in place of monkfish. Roast for 8–10 minutes or until the shrimp are pink and opaque.

WITH HALIBUT
Prepare the basic recipe, using halibut in place of monkfish.

WITH ROUILLE
Prepare the basic recipe, using Rouille (see page 196) in place of Romesco. Serve the roasted vegetables and fish in shallow bowls, topped with hot prepared fish stock. Dollop with the Rouille.

WITH SHRIMP & ROUILLE
Prepare the basic recipe, using half monkfish and half peeled and deveined large shrimp and Rouille (see page 196) in place of Romesco. Roast for 8–10 minutes or until the shrimp are pink and opaque. Serve the roasted vegetables and seafood in shallow bowls, topped with hot fish stock. Dollop with the Rouille.

Basque-style Roast Fish

Serves 4

¼ cup (50 ml) olive oil
2 medium onions, chopped
2 cloves garlic, minced
1 x 4-oz. (100 g) can sliced pimentos

1 cup (225 g) chopped fresh or canned
  tomatoes, drained
1 tsp. smoked or Hungarian paprika
½ cup (50 g) chopped fresh parsley

4 whole, small rainbow trout, cleaned, heads
  and tails removed
½ cup (120 ml) dry white wine

1. Preheat the oven to 425°F (220°C). In a bowl, mix the olive oil, onions, garlic, pimentos, tomatoes, paprika, and parsley together. Stuff each fish with the mixture, place the fish in a large, oiled baking dish, pour in the wine, and cover with foil. Roast for 30–35 minutes or until the fish begins to flake when tested with a fork in the thickest part.

WITH BACON
Prepare the basic recipe, wrapping each trout with a slice of bacon, before cooking. Remove the foil during the last 10 minutes of cooking to crisp the bacon.

WITH SALSA
Prepare the basic recipe, stuffing the fish with 2 cups (450 ml) tomato salsa in place of the olive oil, onions, garlic, tomatoes, pimentos, and parsley.

WITH BLACK BEANS
Prepare the basic recipe, using a mixture of ½ cup (100 g) chopped green onion, ½ cup (100 g) fermented black beans, and 2 tablespoons grated fresh gingerroot to stuff the fish in place of the olive oil, onions, garlic, tomatoes, pimentos, and parsley.

Flash-fried Calamari

Serves 4

vegetable oil for frying
1 lb. (450 g) small squid, heads removed, cut
  into thin rings, tentacles left whole

1 cup (100 g) all-purpose flour
2 large eggs, beaten
1 cup (100 g) fine dry breadcrumbs

coarse kosher or sea salt to taste
dipping sauces of your choice

1. Heat oil in a large skillet over medium-high heat. Rinse the calamari under cold, running water and gently pat dry. Put the flour in one bowl, the beaten eggs in a second bowl, and the breadcrumbs in a third bowl.

2. Toss the calamari with the flour first, then dip the calamari in the eggs, and finally in the breadcrumbs. When the oil is hot (test it with a small piece of bread or a thermometer; it should be 375°F/190°C), fry the calamari, in batches, until golden brown. Drain on paper towels and season to taste. Serve hot with dipping sauces.

WITH CLAMS
Prepare the basic recipe, using fresh clams cut into thin strips in place of calamari.

FRIED CLAM ROLL
Prepare the flash-fried clam strips variation above, serving the clam strips in a hot dog bun. Serve with tartar sauce.

MARINATED CALAMARI
Instead of the basic recipe, marinate sliced calamari in a mixture of 2 beaten large eggs, 2 minced cloves garlic, 1 tablespoon soy sauce, and 1 teaspoon freshly grated gingerroot for 1 hour. Keep covered in the refrigerator. Heat oil in a large skillet. Remove calamari from marinade and dust with 2 cups (225 g) all-purpose flour. Fry in batches, turning once, until golden brown. Drain on paper towels and season to taste. Serve with sliced cucumber and sweet chili sauce.

Fritto Misto

Italian seafood fritto misto, usually served with the green sauce known as salsa verde, often features small whole fish known as whitebait or smelts, shrimp, calamari, and small sole. The batter is light and eggy, so serve with a fresh squeeze of lemon as well.

Serves 6–8

olive oil for frying
1 cup (100 g) all-purpose flour
1 tsp. salt
1 tsp. ground white pepper
4 large eggs, beaten
8 oz. (225 g) fresh whole whitebait or smelts
1 lb. (450 g) raw large shrimp, peeled and deveined, tails on, rinsed, and patted dry
1 lb. (450 g) small squid, heads removed, rinsed, and patted dry, body cut into rings, and tentacles
6 very small sole, cleaned and heads removed, rinsed, and patted dry
Salsa verde and lemon wedges, to serve (optional)

1 Heat ½ in. (1 cm) of olive oil to 375°F (190°C) in a large skillet set over medium-high heat. Combine the flour and seasonings in a shallow bowl. Put the beaten eggs in a second bowl. Dredge the seafood in the flour mixture, then in the beaten eggs. When the oil is hot, fry the seafood, in batches, turning once, until golden brown. Drain on paper towels. Serve with the salsa and wedges of lemon.

WITH SHELLFISH
Prepare the basic recipe, using 1 lb. (450 g) large shrimp, 1 lb. (450 g) shucked oysters, and 1 lb. (450 g) bay scallops in place of the variety of fish and shellfish.

WITH VEGETABLES
Prepare the basic recipe, using 6 trimmed baby artichokes in place of the small sole and 1 lb. (450 g) trimmed asparagus in place of the whitebait. Fry the vegetables first, then the seafood.

WITH AÏOLI
Prepare the basic recipe and serve with aïoli in place of the salsa verde.

WITH FISH FILLETS
Prepare the basic recipe, using 1 lb. (450 g) each of four different varieties of freshwater or ocean fish fillets cut into chunks in place of the variety of fish and shellfish.

Roasted Baby Octopus in Sherry Marinade

Serve with a glass of chilled fino sherry to echo the marinade. Octopus needs high heat to cook quickly so it doesn't get rubbery, so it's best roasted or grilled.

Serves 8 as an appetizer

for the sherry marinade
¼ cup (50 ml) olive oil
¼ cup (50 ml) dry sherry
6 garlic cloves, minced
1 tsp. paprika

½ tsp. fine kosher or sea salt
2 lbs. (900 g) baby octopus, cleaned
8 fresh plum tomatoes, cut in half
1 cup (200 g) pitted Kalamata or niçoise olives, halved

½ cup (100 g) pimento-stuffed green olives, drained and diced
¼ cup (25 g) finely chopped fresh parsley, to garnish

1 For the marinade, combine all the ingredients in a sealable plastic bag. Pour half the marinade into another container to reserve. Add the octopus to the marinade in the bag, seal, and marinate in the refrigerator for up to 12 hours.

2 Preheat the oven to 500°F (230°C). Arrange the tomatoes in a roasting pan and drizzle with a fourth of the reserved marinade. Roast the tomatoes for 10 minutes or until beginning to soften and brown.

3 Remove the octopus from the marinade, do not pat dry, and place them with the tomatoes in the roasting pan. Return pan to the oven and roast for 3–5 minutes or until the octopus is white and opaque. Combine the octopus and tomatoes with the remaining reserved marinade and the olives. Portion onto plates and garnish with parsley.

WITH CUTTLEFISH
Prepare the basic recipe, using baby cuttlefish in place of octopus.

WITH BABY SQUID
Prepare the basic recipe, using baby squid, heads removed, in place of octopus.

WITH SHRIMP
Prepare the basic recipe, using peeled and deveined large shrimp in place of octopus. Roast for 5–7 minutes or until the shrimp turn pink and opaque.

WITH SCALLOPS
Prepare the basic recipe, using medium sea scallops in place of octopus. Add 1 cup (225 g) chopped zucchini and 1 coarsely chopped red onion, drizzled with olive oil and seasoned to taste, to the tomatoes before roasting them.

Crab Cakes

Serves 4

8 oz. (225 g) fresh lump crabmeat
⅔ cup (75 g) fresh breadcrumbs
¼ cup (50 g) sliced green onion

1 tbsp. Dijon mustard
½ tsp. dried tarragon
¼ tsp. dried red pepper flakes

1 large egg, beaten
vegetable oil for frying

1 Combine the crabmeat, breadcrumbs, onion, mustard, tarragon, red pepper flakes, and egg. Shape into eight ½-in. (1-cm) thick patties. Chill in the refrigerator for about 2 hour to firm up.

2 Heat ½ in. (1 cm) of oil in a large skillet over medium-high heat. When the oil is hot (test it with a small piece of bread or a thermometer; it should be 375°F/190°C), fry the crab cakes, in batches, until golden brown, turning once. Drain on paper towels and salt to taste. Serve hot.

WITH WHITEFISH
Prepare the basic recipe, using 1 cup (225 g) chopped whitefish or pollock fillets in place of crabmeat.

WITH SALMON
Prepare the basic recipe, using 1 cup (225 g) chopped fresh salmon fillets in place of crabmeat.

WITH SMOKED SALMON
Prepare the basic recipe, using 1 cup (225 g) chopped smoked salmon in place of crabmeat.

WITH LOBSTER
Prepare the basic recipe, using 1 cup (225 g) chopped steamed lobster in place of crabmeat.

Mediterranean-Style Grilled Swordfish

Serves 4

¼ cup (50 ml) olive oil
1 tsp. dried rosemary
1 clove garlic, minced

4 swordfish steaks, rinsed, and patted dry
sea salt and freshly ground black pepper

1 Combine the olive oil, rosemary, garlic, and seasonings in a bowl. Brush all over the swordfish and let rest for 30 minutes. Prepare a hot fire in your grill. Grill the swordfish for 4–5 minutes per side, turning once, or until you have good grill marks and the swordfish is firm to the touch.

WITH FRESH ROSEMARY
Prepare basic recipe, omitting the dried rosemary. Add 2 branches of fresh rosemary to the olive oil, garlic, and seasonings in microwave-safe bowl and cook on high heat for 1 minute. Let steep and cool for 15 minutes. Pour the infused oil over the swordfish steaks and let them infuse at room temperature for 30 minutes before grilling.

MARINATED GRILLED SWORDFISH
Instead of the rosemary vinaigrette, whisk together 2 tablespoons fresh lemon juice, 2 minced cloves garlic, 1 teaspoon sea salt, and ¼ cup (50 ml) olive oil to make a marinade. Pour the marinade over the swordfish steaks and marinate at room temperature for 30 minutes. Remove steaks from marinade and grill as in basic recipe.

Moroccan Baked Fish

A spice caravan of flavor infuses this dish as it bakes. Serve it with a flatbread, such as pita or naan, warmed in the oven, or couscous to soak up all the juices.

Serves 4

1 large onion, thinly
   sliced
1 large tomato, thinly
   sliced
1 lemon, ends trimmed
   and thinly sliced
4 medium fish fillets, such
   as red snapper, ocean
   perch, haddock, or
   John Dory, rinsed and
   patted dry

1 tbsp. ground cumin
1 tbsp. sweet paprika
1 tbsp. ground coriander
1 tsp. ground caraway
   seeds
2 tbsp. olive oil
sea salt and freshly
   ground black pepper

1 Preheat the oven to 375°F (190°C). Oil a large baking dish. Place a layer of onion, then tomato, then lemon in the baking dish. Place the fish fillets on the lemon slices. Combine the cumin, paprika, coriander, caraway, red pepper, and salt in a bowl. Sprinkle the spice mixture over the fish, then drizzle with olive oil. Cover and bake for 35 minutes or until the fish begins to flake when tested with a fork.

WITH SUMAC & CUMIN
Prepare the basic recipe, using 1 tablespoon ground sumac, 1 tablespoon ground cumin, and 1 teaspoon salt in place of spice mixture. Mix 2 cloves minced garlic with the olive oil and drizzle over fish before baking.

WITH ITALIAN SEASONING
Prepare the basic recipe, using ¼ cup (25 g) dried Italian seasoning in place of seasoning mixture.

FISH GRATIN
Instead of the basic recipe, arrange 4 fish fillets, such as turbot, haddock, or halibut, in one layer in an oiled baking dish. Pour ½ cup (120 ml) dry white wine and 1 tablespoon fresh lemon juice over fish. Cover and bake at 400°F (200°C) for 20 minutes. Pour ½ cup (120 ml) heavy cream over the fish, sprinkle with ¾ cup (75 g) grated Gruyère, and bake, uncovered, until browned and bubbling, about 15 more minutes.

SCALLOP GRATIN
Prepare Fish Gratin (above), using 1 lb. (450 g) bay scallops in place of fish.

Brandade de Morue with Cherry Tomatoes

This traditional comfort food dish from the Mediterranean uses dried salt cod, usually available at Italian grocery stores. Allow 48 hours to soak the salt cod. Serve with French bread.

Serves 6–8

2 lbs. (900 g) boneless salt cod
2 cups (450 ml) heavy cream
10 garlic cloves, peeled

1 lb. (450 g) baking potatoes, diced
sea salt and freshly ground pepper to taste
1 pint (450 g) cherry tomatoes

¼ cup (50 ml) extra-virgin olive oil
2 tsp. chopped fresh thyme
2 tsp. chopped fresh rosemary

1 Soak the salt cod in cold water for 48 hours and change the water at least 4 times. Then, cut the salt cod into 8 pieces.

2 Preheat the oven to 400°F (200°C). In a saucepan, heat the cream, garlic, and salt cod pieces over medium-high heat until the fish is tender, about 8 minutes. Set aside. Place the potatoes in a large pot, cover with water, and bring to a boil. Cook until tender, about 15 minutes. Drain and mash the potatoes.

3 Transfer the fish and cream mixture and mashed potatoes to a food processor and pulse to blend. Season. Spoon the mixture into the center of an oiled 8-in. (20-cm) square baking pan. Surround the brandade with the cherry tomatoes. Drizzle with olive oil, sprinkle with fresh herbs, and bake until bubbling, about 15 minutes.

WITH FRENCH BREAD
Prepare basic recipe. Cut a French roll in half. Brush cut sides generously with olive oil. Place a lettuce leaf on the bottom, then top with ¼ cup (50 g) brandade, ¼ cup (50 g) baked cherry tomatoes, and the other half of the roll.

WITH CHERRY TOMATOES
Prepare basic brandade, drizzle with olive oil, and bake until bubbling. Scoop out a little of the flesh of each cherry tomato and cut a small slice off the bottom so it sits firmly. Stuff each tomato with 1 rounded teaspoon brandade, sprinkle with the herbs, and arrange on a platter.

WITH MUSHROOMS
Prepare basic brandade, omitting cherry tomatoes. Stuff 16 mushroom caps with the mixture, drizzle with olive oil, scatter with the herbs, and bake until bubbling.

WITH CROSTINI
Prepare basic brandade, omitting tomatoes. Slice Italian or French bread, brush with olive oil, and toast at 350°F (175°C) for 15 minutes. Spoon 1 tablespoon brandade on each slice. Drizzle with olive oil, sprinkle with herbs, and bake until warmed through.

Sicilian Stuffed Swordfish Rolls

This Sicilian dish, known as *involtini di pesce spada*, is a really wonderful way to enjoy this very typical local fish. These swordfish rolls are equally delicious served at room temperature or piping hot.

Serves 6

2½ lbs. (1⅓ kg) swordfish steak
1 large red onion
12–15 bay leaves
2 tbsp. olive oil
6 tbsp. dried bread crumbs

For the filling
4 tbsp. pitted green olives
3 tbsp. capers
2 tbsp. chopped fresh flat-leaf parsley
6 tbsp. dried bread crumbs

4 tbsp. grated Parmesan or pecorino cheese
5 tbsp. olive oil

1 Bone and skin the swordfish steak (or ask your fishmonger to do it for you), cut it into quarters, and slice each quarter across into 6 very thin slices. What you are aiming for is 24 very thin slices roughly 3 by 4 in. (10 by 13 cm). But given the price of swordfish, it is wise to tolerate considerable irregularity rather than to trim lavishly—it won't show in the end anyway. Peel the onion, cut it into quarters or sixths, depending on its size, and then separate these wedges so that you have slices of onion that are wide enough to thread on a skewer.

2 To make filling, chop olives, capers, and parsley together until quite fine. Stir in bread crumbs and cheese, moisten with oil, and blend thoroughly. Place a teaspoon of filling on one end of each slice of fish, roll up as neatly as possible, and spear it on a skewer onto which you have already threaded a piece of onion. Follow with a bay leaf, then another roll of fish, then a slice of onion, and so on until you have 6 skewers, each with 4 rolls of fish interspersed with onion slices and bay leaves. Run a second skewer through each roll, parallel to the first and about an inch distant, so that the fish rolls don't spin about and break as you turn them over while they cook.

3 Preheat broiler. When all 6 servings are ready, moisten them with oil and then dip them in the bread crumbs (they should be just lightly coated). Broil them gently for about 8–10 minutes. They can also be baked, which might be simpler if the shapes of the rolls are very irregular.

WITH RAISINS & PINE NUTS
Instead of the basic filling, combine 4 tablespoons raisins, 5 tablespoons bread crumbs, 3 tablespoons pine nuts, and 2 tablespoons chopped parsley. Moisten with water and season with salt and pepper, then proceed with the basic recipe.

WITH CHILI
Prepare the basic recipe, adding 2 seeded and finely chopped fresh chili peppers to the filling.

WITH TUNA
Prepare the basic recipe, replacing the swordfish with thin slices of tuna.

WITH PLAICE
Prepare the basic recipe, replacing the swordfish with evenly trimmed plaice (flounder) fillets. Bear in mind that the plaice will be more delicate than the swordfish and will cook more quickly.

CHAPTER 8

Desserts
& Fruit

In hot weather imaginative and refreshing fruit dishes and desserts are an absolute must. This chapter contains many the classic desserts, as well as some more unusual ones, prepared in many of the Mediterranean countries during the hot summer, when fresh produce is at its very best.

EQUIPMENT

Most desserts in this chapter can be made using basic kitchen equipment, although if you're a keen and adventurous cook you might want to invest in a few extra items.

The basics

Mixing bowls of different sizes; measuring spoons, measuring cup, and scales (which are invaluable if you're doing a lot of baking); rolling pin; grater; wooden spoons; hand whisk; wire-mesh sieve; cutting board; small and large chopping knives and serrated knife. Also, large and small saucepans; baking sheets; wire cooling rack; spatula; and finally, waxed paper, aluminum foil, plastic wrap, and baking parchment.

Electric mixer

An electric hand whisk or freestanding food mixer makes light work of all sorts of time-consuming tasks, such as making meringues, whipping cream, whisking custard mixtures, creaming cake batters, and beating choux pastry.

Food processor & blender

Food processors are useful for grinding dry ingredients such as nuts, cookies, and spices to a powder and also for puréeing fruits. Blenders work in a similar way, grinding and puréeing ingredients, but they require at least some liquid to be added to the mixture for them to work efficiently.

Baking pans & ovenproof dishes

Loaf pans, round, and square cake pans, as well as springform pans, muffin pans, and pie or tart pans are essential for a baker. Additionally, a few ramekins or other small ovenproof cups are useful.

Serving plates & dishes

A selection of attractive serving plates, bowls, dishes, and especially small glass dishes of varying sizes will show off your culinary creations to maximum advantage. These needn't be made from the best china or cut glass — pretty side plates, plain wine glasses, inexpensive glass bowls will all work well. Remember that any dish that needs to go into the oven or under the broiler must be heatproof to a high temperature.

TECHNIQUES

Mastering a few simple basic techniques is the key to producing perfect desserts every time.

Melting chocolate

Break or chop the bar into small pieces, place in a heatproof bowl and stand the bowl over a pan of gently simmering—not boiling—water, making sure the bottom of the bowl is not in contact with the water. Leave until the chocolate has completely melted, stirring occasionally until smooth, ensuring the water doesn't come into contact with the chocolate. Alternatively, chocolate can be melted in the microwave on defrost setting in 30 second bursts, again stirring until smooth.

Whisking egg whites

The secret to perfect meringues and other dishes containing whisked egg whites is to whisk the whites to soft peaks first before starting to add the sugar. To begin with, slowly add the sugar 1 teaspoonful at a time until the whites start to thicken and become shiny. The remaining sugar can then be added in a steady stream. If sugar is added too quickly, the egg whites will be unable to incorporate it quickly enough, resulting in the whites not whipping up to sufficient bulk and the sugar leaking out as syrup when the meringues dry out in the oven.

Folding in egg whites

When folding in egg whites, it's important to do it gently so all the air you've whisked into the whites isn't beaten out. However, as the mixture you're folding the whites into is likely to be quite heavy, soften it first by stirring in a tablespoonful of the whites. Once incorporated, fold in the remainder of the whites using a large metal spoon and a figure-eight motion.

Toasting nuts

Nuts can be toasted under a conventional broiler, in a dry frying pan over a low heat, or spread out on a baking sheet in a low oven. Whichever method you choose, watch the nuts carefully and turn them over from time to time, as they quickly go from golden brown to black and burned.

Lemon Granita

This is like a very simple lemon sorbet, only much more gritty and granular. It is very refreshing and can help you feel a lot less full after a very big, heavy meal. In Italy this would be eaten either as a light dessert, or just to help you cool off. It's also delicious with a mixed citrus fruit salad.

Serves 8–10

1½ pints (1 liter) cold
    water
1 generous cup (180 g)
    sugar

1 cup (240 ml) freshly
    squeezed lemon juice

1 In a saucepan, heat 2 fl oz. (60 ml) fl oz. of the water with all the sugar. Bring it to a boil and cook long enough to dissolve all the sugar. Allow sugar syrup to cool, then add the remaining water and lemon juice. Stir well and pour into a shallow aluminum pan (a cake pan is perfect). Place pan in the freezer.

2 Remove from the freezer after half an hour and scrape down the sides and bottom of the pan, breaking up the part that has solidified, and blending it into the part that is still liquid. Repeat this every half hour, until the granita has become a fairly firm, flaky slush. At this point, remove it from the pan and ideally serve at once. If you are not eating it immediately, transfer it to a sealable plastic container and return to the freezer. If you leave it too long in the metal container, it will "burn" (the water will separate and form ice crystals).

WITH COFFEE
Prepare the basic recipe, replacing the lemon juice with 1 cup (240 ml) of very strong espresso. The classic coffee granita is perfect served with a topping of whipped cream.

WITH WATERMELON
Prepare the basic recipe, replacing the lemon juice with the thick, pulpy juice of watermelon. Adjust the sugar content accordingly by tasting the mixture before freezing.

WITH ORANGE
Prepare the basic recipe, replacing the lemon juice with orange juice and adjusting the sugar content accordingly (the orange juice is not so sour).

WITH LIME
Prepare the basic recipe, replacing the lemon juice with fresh lime juice.

Orange Salad with Almonds

Serves 6

10 large oranges
4 tbsp. slivered almonds
vanilla ice cream or crème fraîche, to serve

amaretti cookies or toasted slivered almonds, to serve

1 Peel 9 of the oranges carefully, removing all the pith. Slice them into neat segments or rounds, removing any seeds. Put them in a large bowl. Toast the almonds briefly in a hot skillet until just golden and scented. Add the almonds to the oranges and mix. Serve now or refrigerate until ready to serve.

2 Slice the remaining orange into thin segments. Serve the salad with vanilla ice cream or crème fraîche, orange segments, and a few crumbled or whole amaretti cookies or toasted, slivered almonds on top.

WITH PISTACHIOS
Prepare the basic recipe, replacing the almonds with coarsely chopped pistachios.

WITH WALNUTS
Prepare the basic recipe, replacing the almonds with chopped walnuts.

WITH PINK GRAPEFRUIT
Prepare the basic recipe, replacing 4 of the oranges with 3 pink grapefruit.

WITH POMEGRANATE SEEDS
Prepare the basic recipe, adding a handful of pomegranate seeds to the oranges before adding the almonds.

WITH GRAND MARNIER
Prepare the basic recipe, adding some Grand Marnier or other orange-flavored liquor over the oranges before mixing in the almonds.

Watermelon & Feta Salad

Serves 4

2 large slices watermelon
¼ lb. (115 g) feta cheese, crumbled
5–6 leaves fresh mint

1 Remove the seeds from the watermelon and cut the flesh into chunks or scoop into balls. Arrange these on a dish or in a bowl and sprinkle the crumbled feta cheese over them. Chop the mint finely and scatter over the dish to serve. If you wish to make the recipe ahead, chill the prepared watermelon until required, then add the feta and mint just before serving.

WITH CANTALOUPE MELON
Prepare the basic recipe, replacing the watermelon with 1 small cantaloupe.

WITH HONEYDEW MELON
Prepare the basic recipe, replacing the watermelon with a combination of watermelon and honeydew melon.

WITH CHILI
Prepare the basic recipe, then sprinkle ½ or ¼ finely chopped chili over the watermelon.

WITH CHERVIL
Prepare the basic recipe, replacing the mint with finely chopped chervil for a more delicate flavor.

WITH PISTACHIO
Prepare the basic recipe, replacing the mint with 2 tablespoons chopped pistachios.

Almond Ice Cream

Cooling ice creams made with nuts such as pistachios, hazelnuts, and almonds are very popular all over the Mediterranean. The whole milk can be replaced with almond milk for an even nuttier taste.

Serves 4

¼ cup (40 g) blanched almonds
2 cups (475 ml) whole milk
¾ cup (180 ml) heavy cream
3 egg yolks
½ cup (100 g) superfine sugar
1 teaspoon kirsch (or liquor of your choice)

1 Pound the almonds into a paste. Add milk and heavy cream and mix thoroughly together. Pour the almond mixture into a saucepan and bring it to a boil. Remove from heat and allow to cool.

2 In a separate bowl, mix egg yolks, sugar, and kirsch for 5 minutes. Slowly pour the cooled almond milk into the yolks and mix well with a wooden spoon. Return the mixture to a low heat for 5 minutes, stirring constantly and without letting it boil. Remove from the heat and allow to cool again. Strain it carefully through a sieve into an ice cream maker and freeze until the ice cream is very firm.

3 If you do not have an ice cream maker, pour the mixture into a plastic container with a lid and place it in the freezer. Mix well with a fork every hour, or when the edges of the ice cream are beginning to solidify, until the ice cream is set and crystal-free.

WITH PISTACHIO
Prepare the basic recipe, then before freezing add a handful of chopped pistachios for a crunchy texture.

WITH PINE NUTS
Prepare the basic recipe, using ⅛ cup (30 g) almonds and ⅛ cup (30 g) pine nuts.

WITH HAZELNUTS
Prepare the basic recipe, using ⅛ cup (30 g) almonds and ⅛ cup (30 g) skinned hazelnuts (toast them briefly in the oven, then wrap in a clean cloth while still warm and rub vigorously to remove the skins).

WITH RAISIN
Prepare the basic recipe, adding 3 tablespoons raisins, soaked in kirsch, to the mixture just before freezing.

WITH AMARETTO
Prepare the basic recipe, replacing the kirsch with 1 tablespoon amaretto liquor and 4 crumbled amaretti cookies. Bear in mind that the extra alcohol in the amaretto will prevent the ice cream from becoming entirely solid.

Cinnamon Frost

Originating from Sicily, this is a very light dessert, perfect to serve at the end of a long and spicy meal. The flavor of cinnamon is incredibly intense and surprisingly refreshing. As the cinnamon sticks need to infuse in the water for a very long time, do start preparing this dessert the day before you need it.

Serves 6

4 cinnamon sticks
3¼ cups (750 ml) water
1½ cups (340 g) sugar
½ cup (50 g) cornstarch
2 squares baking
    chocolate

ground cinnamon and
    grated chocolate,
    to decorate

1 Put the cinnamon sticks and cold water into a saucepan. Set it over medium heat and bring to a boil, then boil gently for about 5 minutes. Remove from the heat and let stand to infuse for 12 hours. Strain the cinnamon liquid carefully and return to the pan. Discard cinnamon sticks. Add the sugar to the cinnamon liquid.

2 Dissolve the cornstarch in 2 tablespoons of the liquid, then add the thickened liquid to the pan. Bring to a boil, stirring constantly, and boil very gently until thickened. Remove from the heat and add the chocolate. Stir until the chocolate has melted. Turn into 1 large or 6 small individual molds and chill until solid. Turn out to serve, decorated with cinnamon and grated chocolate.

CLEAR CINNAMON FROST
If you prefer a clearer finish, replace the cornstarch with unflavored gelatin (follow instructions on the package). In this case, you will add the gelatin to the liquid once you have strained it and returned it to a boil.

WITH LEMON
Prepare the basic recipe, adding 1 teaspoon fresh lemon juice and 1 teaspoon grated lemon zest to the mixture to give the frost a light lemony flavor.

WITH CLOVES
Prepare the basic recipe, adding 2 whole cloves to the water to infuse with the cinnamon.

WITH MELON
Prepare the basic recipe. Serve the cinnamon frost, cut into small cubes once set, over a salad of cubed, chilled fresh melon.

WITH GINGER
Prepare the basic recipe, adding ½ teaspoon ground ginger to the water to infuse with the cinnamon.

White Chocolate & Raspberry Semifreddo

The name of this classic dish means semi-cold, meaning an ice cream that is softer than normal. This is due to the addition of alcohol, which slows down the freezing process. Because you can't make a semifreddo without adding alcohol, this makes it a grown-up dessert.

Serves 6

½ lb. (225 g) raspberries, fresh or frozen
3–4 tbsp. sweet fruit liquor such as cherry brandy
10 oz. (275 g) mascarpone

2 extra-large egg yolks
⅔ cup (85 g) confectioners' sugar, sifted
1 cup (250 ml) heavy cream

4 oz. (125 g) crushed ready-made meringues
7 oz. (200 g) white chocolate, melted
2 oz. (50 g) white chocolate, splintered

1 Mash the berries with a fork to bruise them; then, if you wish, push them through a sieve to remove seeds. Stir in the liquor. In a separate bowl, beat the mascarpone, egg yolks, and confectioners' sugar together until smooth and pale.

2 Whip the cream until it holds a soft peak, then fold in the crushed meringues. Gently fold together with the berries. Pour in the melted chocolate and fold it through. Fold in the splintered chocolate.

3 Line an 8-in. (20 cm) springform cake pan with baking parchment or Teflon paper. Pour the mixture into the pan and freeze for about 6 hours. Remove the pan from the freezer about 30 minutes before you wish to serve. Remove the paper and slide the semifreddo onto a board. (If necessary, dip the pan into hot water for a few seconds to loosen the edges a little.) Slice into 6 wedges, decorate as desired, and serve immediately.

WITH BITTERSWEET CHOCOLATE
Prepare basic recipe, omitting the raspberries and white chocolate and replacing the fruit liquor with chocolate liquor. Add 1 tablespoon powdered chocolate to the mascarpone and egg mixture before adding whipped cream. Before freezing, melt some good-quality bittersweet chocolate and drizzle it into the mixture, stirring gently, to create a marbled effect.

WITH AMARETTO
Prepare basic recipe, replacing the raspberries with 10 crumbled amaretti cookies and replacing the fruit liquor with amaretto.

WITH NOUGAT
Omit raspberries and white chocolate. Add about 7 oz. (200 g) of crushed nougat to the mascarpone and egg mixture before adding the whipped cream. To serve, sprinkle with crushed nougat and melted bittersweet chocolate.

WITH ORANGE & HONEY
Prepare basic recipe, omitting raspberries and white chocolate. Replacing the fruit liquor with orange liquor. Beat the mascarpone and egg yolks with ½ cup (175 g) orange blossom honey instead of confectioners' sugar and add the grated zest of 1 orange and juice of 2 oranges.

Zabaglione

Serves 6

6 extra-large egg yolks
6 tbsp. Marsala
6 tbsp. superfine sugar

1 Mix the ingredients together in a large, rounded, heavy bowl. Place the bowl over a pan of very hot but not boiling water and whisk constantly with an electric whisk until foaming, pale yellow, thick, and shiny. This will take up to 10 minutes, or 20 minutes if using a handheld balloon whisk. Pour into stemmed wine glasses and serve with cookies or a thin slice of panettone.

COLD ZABAGLIONE
Prepare basic recipe. To serve the zabaglione cold, whisk 1 sheet of softened gelatin into the warm zabaglione before pouring into glasses and chilling.

WITH WHITE WINE
Prepare basic recipe, replacing the Marsala with the same amount of medium-dry white wine.

WITH RED WINE
Prepare basic recipe, replacing the Marsala with the same amount of rich red wine and add an extra spoonful of sugar to the egg yolks at the start of the recipe.

WITH CREAM
Prepare basic recipe. Cool the cooked zabaglione slightly, then fold in 6 tablespoons whipped cream before pouring into glasses to serve.

Ricotta Pudding

Serves 6

1 lb. (450 g) ricotta
scant ½ cup (60 g) confectioners' sugar, sifted
3 extra-large egg yolks
4 tbsp. dark rum
1 tbsp. dessert wine such as Marsala or Vinsanto
1 cup (250 ml) whipping cream, whipped until stiff

1 Mix together the ricotta, confectioners' sugar, and egg yolks until you have a thick creamy texture. Stir in the rum and dessert wine, then fold in the whipped cream. Serve in chilled stemmed glasses, with biscotti for dunking.

2 You can make this in advance and keep chilled until required, or whip it together quickly at the last moment.

WITH TOASTED ALMONDS
Prepare basic recipe, adding 3 tablespoons slivered toasted almonds along with the rum and dessert wine. Sprinkle the top of each serving with a few more almonds.

WITH COFFEE
Prepare basic recipe, replacing the dark rum with the same amount of strong espresso coffee. Garnish each serving with a coffee bean.

WITH LIMONCELLO
Prepare basic recipe, adding the grated zest of 1 lemon and replacing the rum and dessert wine with 5 tablespoons limoncello liquor.

WITH AMARETTI
Prepare basic recipe, crumbling 6 amaretti cookies into the mixture before folding in the whipped cream. Serve with amaretti cookies for dunking.

Ice Cream Panettone

Panettone is Italy's answer to fruitcake, a deliciously light yet rich cross between a cake and a sweetened bread, studded with candied fruit and golden raisins. Created in Milan, it is first cousin to the pandoro, which comes from Verona.

Serves 6

1 x 1 lb. (450 g) panettone

1 lb. (450 g) best-quality ice cream (vanilla, chocolate chip, nougat, chocolate, or hazelnut)

1 Cut the top off the panettone and scoop out most of the interior, leaving a relatively thick border around the edges and bottom. (You can use the extra panettone to make another dessert.) Allow the ice cream to soften to a spreading consistency.

2 Fill the hollowed-out panettone with ice cream, then replace the top. Freeze until about 15 minutes before you want to eat. Slice into wedges to serve.

WITH PANDORO
Prepare basic recipe, replacing panettone with 1 lb. (450 g) pandoro.

WITH CHOCOLATE
Prepare basic recipe, replacing ice cream with melted chocolate, poured into the center of the scooped-out panettone (you will not need a deep hollow in the panettone in this instance). Or omit scooping out altogether, slice the panettone, and drizzle each slice generously with warm melted chocolate.

WITH ZABAGLIONE
Instead of basic recipe, fill the scooped-out panettone with warm, freshly prepared zabaglione (see page 230) just before serving.

WITH PRALINE SAUCE
Prepare basic recipe. Then drizzle each ice-cream-filled slice with warm melted praline chocolate.

WITH BRANDY
Prepare basic recipe. Then drizzle each ice-cream-filled slice with a little brandy or liquor of your choice.

Montebianco

This recipe used Strega, an Italian herbal liquor with a bright yellow color. If you can't find it substitute with your favorite liquor or simply leave it out.

Serves 6

1 lb. (450 g) canned sweetened chestnut
   purée
4 tbsp. Strega liquor (optional)
3 cups (700 ml) heavy or whipping cream
2 tbsp. sifted confectioners' sugar
1 tsp. vanilla extract
3 large ready-made meringues, crushed

3 oz. (75 g) good-quality bittersweet
   chocolate (minimum cocoa solids content
   70%), grated
1 tbsp. best-quality unsweetened powdered
   chocolate for dusting

1½ tbsp. sifted confectioners' sugar
   for dusting
6 marrons glacés and 12 candied violets,
   to garnish

1 Mash the chestnut purée as much as possible to soften it, then mix with Strega if using. Set aside until required. Whip the cream, then sweeten with confectioners' sugar and flavor with vanilla extract. Fill the bottom of 6 glasses with a little crushed meringue and cover with a layer of whipped cream.

2 Push chestnut purée through a ricer or food mill onto the whipped cream, then sprinkle with grated chocolate. Add another layer of purée and cover with whipped cream and chocolate as before. Add another layer of crushed meringues, then cover with a final layer of whipped cream. Allow a final small amount of chestnut purée to fall over the whipped cream, then sift the powdered chocolate and confectioners' sugar, mixed together, on top to dust lightly. Chill until required. Garnish with candied violets and marrons glacés before serving.

WITH WHITE CHOCOLATE
Prepare basic recipe, replacing the chocolate with grated white chocolate and the powdered chocolate with melted white chocolate.

WITH GIANDUJA
Prepare basic recipe, replacing the grated chocolate with grated gianduja chocolate and the powdered chocolate with melted gianduja.

WITH BRANDY
Prepare basic recipe, replacing the Strega liquor with brandy.

WITH COFFEE
Prepare basic recipe, replacing the Strega liquor with the same amount of strong espresso coffee. Garnish with coffee beans.

Pears Poached in Red Wine

Serves 6

6 firm pears, peeled, left whole, with
   stalks on
½ cinnamon stick

5 tbsp. superfine sugar
1 bottle good red wine

1. Place the pears upright in a saucepan, slicing off the bottom of each one to make it stand straight and steady. Add the cinnamon stick and sugar. Pour in the wine and bring to a boil, then reduce the heat to the lowest setting. Cover the pan and simmer very slowly until the pears are soft, turning them frequently as they cook so they become completely soaked and colored by the wine.

2. Transfer to a bowl and cool, turning frequently. The longer you leave the pears in the bowl, the darker they become as they soak up the wine.

3. To serve, remove the cinnamon stick. Serve the pears on their own or with cream, ice cream, or plain mascarpone.

WITH RED WINE SYRUP
Prepare basic recipe. After simmering, drain the pears, reduce the poaching liquid to a syrup, and drizzle the syrup over the pears.

WITH WHITE WINE
Prepare basic recipe, replacing the red wine with white wine.

WITH PEACHES
Prepare basic recipe, replacing the pears with slightly unripe (hard) peaches, carefully peeled. Replace the red wine with white wine.

WITH PLUMS
Prepare basic recipe, replacing the pears with large plums, peeled if possible. (To peel them easily, blanch for 2 minutes in boiling hot water, then remove the skins before poaching.)

WITH APPLES & PEARS
Prepare basic recipe, replacing the 6 whole pears with 3 apples and 3 pears, peeled, cored, and quartered. Poach them gently with the cinnamon stick and sugar. Replace the wine with water.

Baked Peaches

Serves 6

6 large peaches, halved and stoned
6 amaretti cookies, finely crumbled
1 tbsp. butter, plus more for dish

⅓ cup (120 g) granulated sugar
1½ oz. (40 g) blanched almonds, chopped
⅔ cup (175 ml) Marsala

1. Preheat the oven to 375°F (190°C). Scoop out about half the flesh from each peach half. Mash the removed flesh with the amaretti, butter, sugar, and almonds. Dampen this mixture with a little Marsala, just enough to make a sticky texture.

2. Butter an ovenproof dish. Fill the peaches evenly with crumb mixture and arrange them in the dish. Surround the peaches with the remaining Marsala. Cover loosely with foil and bake for about 30 minutes, basting occasionally, until tender.

3. Remove the foil and raise the oven temperature for a few minutes to make the tops of the peaches slightly crisp, or slide under a broiler for a few minutes. Serve hot or cold.

WITH CHOCOLATE
Prepare basic recipe, adding a small square of good-quality bittersweet chocolate to each peach. Allow the chocolate to melt over the filling and peach.

WITH NECTARINES
Prepare basic recipe, replacing the peaches with firm pitted nectarines.

WITH PLUMS
Prepare basic recipe, replacing the peaches with large plums. You may need to use 2 plums per person, depending upon their size.

WITH APRICOTS
Prepare basic recipe, replacing the peaches with large, not too ripe apricots. You may need to use 2 apricots per person, depending upon their size.

WITH PISTACHIOS
Prepare basic recipe, replacing the blanched almonds with chopped pistachios.

Catalan Cream

Crema catalana is the Catalan version of the French dessert, crème brulée. In fact, many regions lay claim to the origin of the dessert. It is also called Crema de Sant Josep, or St. Joseph's Cream, traditionally prepared on March 19, St. Joseph's Day, the Spanish equivalent of Father's Day.

Serves 4–6

4 egg yolks
1 cup (200 g) superfine
   sugar
1 stick cinnamon

zest of 1 lemon
2 cups (475 ml) milk
1 tbsp. cornstarch

1 In a saucepan, beat together the egg yolks and ⅔ cup of the sugar until thoroughly blended and the mixture turns frothy. Add the cinnamon stick and grated lemon zest. Pour in the milk and cornstarch. Slowly heat the mixture, stirring constantly, just until thickened. Remove from heat immediately. Remove the cinnamon stick and ladle the milk mixture into 4–6 ramekins (depending on size). Allow to cool, then refrigerate for at least 2–3 hours.

2 Before serving, preheat the broiler. Remove ramekins from refrigerator and sprinkle evenly with the remaining sugar. When the broiler is hot, put the ramekins under the broiler and allow the sugar to caramelize, turning gold and brown. This may take 10 minutes or so, depending on the heat. Watch them very carefully and remove as soon as they're the right color. Serve immediately.

3 If you like, you can serve the dessert chilled, but it has more flavor when served warm from the broiler and the caramel will melt after refrigeration.

WITH NUTMEG
Prepare the basic recipe, replacing the cinnamon stick with ¼ teaspoon freshly grated nutmeg.

WITH ORANGE & LEMON
Prepare the basic recipe, replacing the cinnamon stick with a 3-in. (10 cm) strip of lemon peel, left whole, from 1 lemon. Replace the grated lemon zest with the grated zest of ½ orange.

WITH VANILLA
Prepare the basic recipe, replacing the cinnamon stick and lemon zest with the seeds removed from 1 whole vanilla pod.

WITH PISTACHIOS
Prepare the basic recipe, then add 2 tablespoons finely ground pistachios into the mixture while it is still warm, just before pouring into the ramekins for cooling and setting.

WITH CHOCOLATE
Prepare the basic recipe, replacing the lemon zest and cinnamon with 1 heaping tablespoon unsweetened cocoa powder.

Panna Cotta

This delicious Piedmontese specialty has gained popularity and fame all over Italy and beyond. The skill of the dessert lies in getting it to set without being at all rubbery, so just the right amount of gelatin needs to be used.

Serves 6

1¾ pints (850 ml) light cream
8 tbsp. confectioners' sugar
4 sheets gelatin or ½ oz. (12 g) powdered gelatin

2 tsp. vanilla extract
4 tbsp. superfine sugar
2 tsp. cold water

1 Divide the cream in half into separate saucepans. Bring each half to just under a boil. To one pan, add confectioners' sugar. To the other, add gelatin. Whisk both halves constantly until the sugar and gelatin have completely dissolved and the cream is very hot but not boiling. Pour both halves into one bowl and whisk together. Stir in vanilla extract. Cool completely.

2 While mixture cools, coat the bottom of 6 ramekins with superfine sugar sprinkled with a little water. Melt the sugar over low heat to caramelize, or caramelize the sugar and water in a small pan and then pour it into the ramekins. Make sure the caramel is only just blond, so that it will not color the set panna cotta at all. Let cool.

3 Pour the panna cotta through a sieve into a large measuring jug and then pour the mixture into the ramekins. Chill to set firmly until required. To serve, dip the ramekins into boiling water for 5 seconds, then turn out onto cold plates.

WITH COFFEE
Prepare basic recipe, substituting 3 tablespoons strong espresso coffee for 3 tablespoons cream. Omit the vanilla and caramel. To serve, drizzle 1 teaspoon cold espresso over each set panna cotta.

WITH LEMON
Omit the vanilla. Infuse the warm cream with the peel of 1 lemon. Remove it from the cream once cooled. Omit the caramel. To serve, drizzle with a little sugar syrup (melt the sugar in a pan with water until clear and syrupy) into which you have stirred 1 teaspoon finely grated lemon zest.

WITH CHOCOLATE
Prepare basic recipe, stirring 1 tablespoon powdered chocolate into the hot cream. Omit the caramel. To serve, surround with a pool of melted bittersweet chocolate.

WITH WHISKEY
Replace 2–3 tablespoons of the cream with whiskey. To serve, drizzle with 1 teaspoon whiskey.

WITH BRANDY
Prepare basic recipe, substituting 2–3 tablespoons brandy for the same amount of cream. Omit the vanilla and caramel. To serve, drizzle with 1 teaspoon brandy.

Classic Coffee & Chocolate Tiramisù

When it comes to desserts, this is the great Italian favorite. The name means "pick me up" or "lift me up," and it is supposed to be the best way to cheer up!

Serves 6

10 oz. (275 g) mascarpone or very rich cream cheese
4 extra large eggs, separated
4 tbsp. superfine sugar
2 tsp. espresso coffee

4 oz. (125 g) bittersweet chocolate, broken into very small pieces
8 tbsp. weak coffee
6 tbsp. rum, brandy, Tia Maria, or other liquor

about 20 ladyfingers
2 tsp. cocoa powder
2 tsp. instant coffee granules

1 In a large bowl, whisk the mascarpone until soft. Beat the egg yolks until pale, then whisk them into the cheese. Very gradually add the sugar to the bowl, stirring and whisking constantly. Pour in the espresso and mix thoroughly. In a separate bowl, beat the egg whites until very stiff, then fold them into the cheese mixture. Gently mix the chocolate into the mixture.

2 Mix together the weak coffee and liquor. Dip half the ladyfingers into coffee–liquor mixture one at a time, then use them to line the bottom of a serving bowl. Pour in half the chocolate–cheese mixture. Dip the remaining ladyfingers in coffee mixture, then lay them on top of the cheese layer. Pour in the remaining chocolate–cheese mixture.

3 Bang the dish down lightly to settle the layers. Mix the cocoa and coffee powders and sift over the dessert. Chill for at least 3 hours, but preferably overnight, before serving.

WITH CARAMEL
Prepare basic recipe, adding caramel between the layers. Melt 3 tablespoons sugar in a small pan with a little water and cook until dark golden brown. Once the caramel is cooled and slightly tacky, pour a small amount in swirls on top of each layer of cheese mixture as you assemble tiramisù.

WITH FRUIT & RUM
Omit chocolate, espresso, and coffee and use white rum to soak the ladyfingers. Chop fresh strawberries and mix them, along with fresh blueberries and raspberries, into the mascarpone mixture, reserving some berries to create a separate layer in the tiramisù.

WITH APPLE JUICE
Prepare berry recipe above, using apple juice to soak the ladyfingers instead of rum.

WITH NOUGAT
Prepare basic recipe, folding in chopped nougat along with the chocolate.

WITH MANGO
Prepare basic recipe, but for a tropical twist, omit coffee and espresso and mix chopped ripe mango into mascarpone mixture along with chocolate.

Turron

Turron is the Spanish version of halva. It sticks to your teeth when you eat it but crumbles when you handle it. More like a candy than a dessert, it's essential alongside a dark cup of coffee.

Makes 30 pieces

1 cup (250 ml) orange
  blossom honey
1½ cups (150 g) finely
  ground almonds

2 egg yolks
pinch ground cinnamon
zest of ½ lemon
1 egg white, stiffly beaten

1 Pour the honey into a saucepan and warm over medium-low heat to 275°F (140°C). Stir the almonds into the warm honey and remove from heat. Mix the egg yolks, cinnamon, and lemon zest into the almonds. Fold the beaten egg white into the mixture.

2 Line an 8-inch (20–cm) dish with parchment paper. Pour the mixture onto the parchment paper and smooth to a ½–inch layer. Place a sheet of parchment paper atop the mixture, then place a cutting board over the paper, and place a few items on top of the cutting board to give it some weight.

3 Allow the turron to dry for 3 days at room temperature. Cut into 1–inch squares to serve.

WITH PISTACHIO
Prepare the basic recipe, adding 1 cup (150 g) pistachios after you have folded in the egg white.

WITH WHOLE ALMONDS
Prepare the basic recipe, adding 1 cup (150 g) whole almonds after you have folded in the egg white.

WITH WHOLE ALMONDS & APRICOT
Prepare the basic recipe, adding ½ cup (75 g) whole almonds and ½ cup (85 g) chopped dried apricots after you have folded in the egg white.

WITH LAVENDER
Prepare the basic recipe, replacing the orange blossom honey with lavender honey.

Baklava

It is important that the nuts used for making this classic dessert from Turkey and Greece are as fresh as possible for the best results. Also, the honey should be thick and tasty.

Serves 6

1 lb. (450 g) chopped walnuts
1 tsp. ground cinnamon
1 x 1 lb. (450 g) package phyllo pastry
1 cup (225 g) unsalted butter, melted

1 cup (225 g) granulated sugar
1 cup (250 ml) water
1 tsp. pure vanilla extract
½ cup (120 ml) honey

1   Preheat oven to 350°F (175°C). Butter the bottoms and sides of a 9 x 13-in. (10 x 30 cm) baking pan. Toss walnuts with cinnamon and set aside. Unroll phyllo pastry. Cut whole stack in half to fit pan. Cover phyllo with a dampened cloth to keep it from drying as you work.

2   Place 2 sheets of dough in pan and brush thoroughly with melted butter. Repeat with another layer of 2 sheets to create a thick base. Sprinkle 2–3 tablespoons of nut mixture on top. Top with 2 sheets of dough, spread with butter, sprinkle with nuts, and top with 2 sheets of dough. Keep building layers until you have filled the pan.

3   Using a sharp knife, cut into diamonds or squares all the way to the bottom of the pan. You may cut into 4 long rows, then make diagonal cuts. Bake for about 50 minutes until baklava is golden and crisp. While baklava is baking, boil sugar and water until sugar is melted. Add vanilla and honey. Simmer for about 20 minutes until sauce is thickened.

4   Remove baklava from oven and immediately spoon sauce over it. Let cool. Leave it uncovered, because it gets soggy if it is wrapped. Eat on the same day, or cover with a clean cloth and use the next day, though it will keep well for 3 or 4 days.

WITH PISTACHIOS
Prepare the basic recipe, replacing the walnuts with coarsely chopped pistachios.

WITH CHOCOLATE
Prepare the basic recipe, adding a layer of melted bittersweet chocolate by drizzling it between each phyllo pastry layer with the nuts and honey.

WITH ALMONDS
Prepare the basic recipe, replacing the walnuts with a mixture of ground and slivered almonds and almond meal.

WITH MIXED NUTS
Prepare the basic recipe, replacing the walnuts with a combination of coarsely chopped pistachios, almonds, and walnuts.

Natas

Natas, the famous Portuguese custard tarts, are one of the tastiest pastries on the planet. You can find them in bakeries and delis, but try making them yourself and wow your loved ones.

Makes about 8 tarts

⅔ cup (150 ml) whole milk
4 tbsp. heavy cream
2 large free-range egg yolks
2 tbsp. light brown sugar

pinch salt
1 tbsp. cornstarch
½ cinnamon stick

½ vanilla bean, seeded
1 sheet (½ lb./225 g) puff pastry
1 tbsp. confectioners' sugar

1 In a large, heavy saucepan, combine milk, cream, egg yolks, sugar, salt, and cornstarch. Mix well until all the ingredients are smoothly combined, then add the cinnamon stick and vanilla pod and seeds. Turn on the heat to low, and stir continuously with a wooden spoon. Slowly the mixture should become thicker and hold to the back of the spoon. At this point, when it resembles a thin custard, remove it from the heat, cover, and let cool completely.

2 Meanwhile, preheat the oven to 350°F (180°C). Roll up the puff pastry into a tight roll. Slice into ¾-inch (2-cm) pieces and then roll each out into a flat round. Quickly, with your thumbs, work the rounds into the cups of a nonstick regular 12–cup muffin pan and gently press to the sides of each cup. When the pastry shells are ready, fill them two-thirds full with the custard (do not fill to the top) and dust each one with confectioners' sugar.

3 Place the muffin pan in the oven and bake for 20 minutes until the pastry is golden and the custard is set with a slight wobble. Let the tarts cool in the muffin pan. Serve cold as a tapas dessert and save the rest for a snack with a cup of coffee.

WITH CHOCOLATE
Prepare the basic recipe, stirring 2 oz. (50 g) melted dark chocolate into the finished custard mixture.

WITH CARDAMOM & ROSEWATER
Prepare the basic recipe, adding 3 crushed cardamom pods and ¼ teaspoon rosewater as you make the custard.

WITH COFFEE
Prepare the basic recipe, adding 1 tablespoon strong black espresso to the hot custard mixture.

WITH LEMON
Prepare the basic recipe, adding the zest of ½ lemon to the hot custard.

Jam Tart

This is the jam tart that is made as a teatime treat for children of all ages the length and breadth of Italy. The pastry traditionally tends to be rather sweet, but you can reduce the amount of sugar if you prefer.

Serves 6

2¾ cups (275 g) all-purpose flour
¾ cup (150 g) superfine sugar
pinch salt
3 extra-large eggs

10 tbsp. butter, softened
1 lb. (450 g) jam of your choice
grated zest of 1 lemon
butter for greasing

1 Mix the flour with all but 2 tablespoons of the sugar. Add the salt. Pile the flour-sugar mixture onto a work surface and make a hollow in the center with your fist. Break 2 eggs into the hollow and add the butter. Knead together quickly to form a smooth ball. Wrap the pastry in plastic wrap or a clean cloth and let rest in a cool place, but not the refrigerator, for about 20 minutes.

2 Preheat the oven to 400°F (200°C). Divide the dough into two sections, one larger than the other. Roll out the larger piece evenly. Butter and lightly flour a 9-in. (23 cm) tart pan. Line the pan with pastry. Fill with jam, spreading jam over the pastry evenly, then sprinkle with lemon zest. Roll out the second piece of pastry and cut it into strips. Arrange the strips over jam to form a lattice. Beat the remaining egg and brush it over the pastry lattice. Sprinkle with the remaining sugar. Bake in the preheated oven for about 30 minutes, or until the pastry is golden brown and crisp. Cool completely before serving.

WITH APPLES
Prepare basic recipe, arranging 2 peeled and sliced apples over the pastry base before covering with jam.

WITH PLUMS
Prepare basic recipe, arranging 9 large washed, pitted, and sliced plums over pastry base before covering with jam.

WITH APRICOTS
Prepare basic recipe, arranging 9 large washed and sliced fresh apricots over the pastry base before covering with jam.

WITH MARMALADE
Prepare basic recipe, replacing the grated lemon zest with the grated zest of 1 orange, and using continental-style orange marmalade instead of jam.

WITH CHESTNUTS
Prepare basic recipe, omitting the grated lemon zest. Use chestnut jam for the filling and sprinkle it with chopped toasted chestnuts before adding the pastry lattice.

Almond Cake

This deliciously nutty almond cake with a hint of amaretto liquor makes for a lovely teatime treat. Make sure the ground almonds are really fresh so that they bring plenty of moisture to the cake.

Serves 6

7 oz. (200 g) butter
3⅓ cups (350 g) all-purpose flour
2 cups (175 g) ground almonds
1 tsp. almond extract
1⅓ cups (250 g) granulated sugar
grated zest of 1 lemon
3 extra-large eggs, beaten
4 tbsp. amaretto liquor
1 cup (250 ml) milk
1 tsp. cream of tartar
1 tsp. baking soda
confectioners' sugar for dusting

1 Preheat the oven to 325°F (160°C). Using some of the butter, grease a 12-in. (30 cm) round cake pan thoroughly, then dust with some of the flour.

2 Melt the remaining butter and let it cool. Sift the remaining flour into a large mixing bowl. In a small bowl, mix the ground almonds with almond extract. Stir the almonds, sugar, and lemon zest into the flour. Then mix in the eggs, melted butter, and amaretto. Beat the mixture thoroughly. Stir the cream of tartar and baking soda into the warm milk, then pour this mixture into the cake mixture and beat again.

3 Pour the batter into the prepared pan and bake for about 1 hour or until a toothpick inserted into the center of the cake comes out dry and clean. Serve the cake warm or cold, dusted with confectioners' sugar.

WITH CHOCOLATE
Prepare basic recipe, replacing the lemon zest with 2 tablespoons semisweet chocolate chips.

WITH DRIED FIGS
Prepare basic recipe, adding a handful of coarsely chopped dried figs when you add eggs, melted butter, and amaretto.

WITH DRIED APRICOTS
Prepare basic recipe, adding a handful of coarsely chopped dried apricots when you add the eggs, melted butter, and amaretto.

WITH PRUNES
Prepare basic recipe, adding a handful of coarsely chopped pitted prunes when you add the eggs, melted butter, and amaretto.

WITH PISTACHIO
Prepare basic recipe, replacing half the ground almonds with the same amount of ground pistachios.

Tuscan Rice Cake

The rich, eggy, sticky quality of this very traditional Tuscan rice cake makes it delicious and incredibly filling. It is like a homemade version of those little oval rice cakes you can buy at all Tuscan cafés and patisseries, called simply budino, which translates as "pudding." This is a very substantial cake, so a little will go a long way. Don't worry about how liquid the mixture seems when you pour the mixture into the pan; the cake will set, but it should remain wet and sticky, although firm enough to slice neatly.

Serves 6 generously

¾ cup (150 g) short-grain rice
4 cups (1 liter) milk
butter for greasing
2 tbsp. semolina

9 extra-large eggs
1¼ cups (250 g) superfine sugar
3 tbsp. brandy
grated zest of 1 lemon

1 Put the rice and about two-thirds of the milk into a saucepan. Simmer for 10 minutes, then drain, reserving the milk, which will have absorbed some of the starch from the rice. Butter a 14-in. (35-cm) round cake pan thoroughly, and sprinkle with the semolina. (Do not use a loose-bottomed pan, because the liquid will ooze away.) Turn the pan upside down and shake gently to remove any loose semolina.

2 Preheat the oven to 350°F (175°C). Beat the eggs in a large bowl until foaming and very pale yellow. This will take about 20 minutes. Add the sugar gradually, beating constantly, then add the brandy and lemon zest. Stir thoroughly, then add the cooked rice and all the remaining milk, including the milk reserved from cooking rice.

3 Pour the resulting, very wet mixture into the cake pan. Bake for about 50 minutes, or until a skewer inserted in the center comes out clean. The cake should be well set and golden brown. Serve when cooled.

WITH CANDIED PEEL
Prepare basic recipe, adding about 4 tablespoons mixed chopped candied peel to the beaten eggs along with the cooked rice.

WITH WALNUTS
Prepare basic recipe, adding about 4 tablespoons coarsely chopped walnuts to the beaten eggs along with cooked rice. For an extra nutty taste, toast the walnuts briefly before chopping them.

WITH ALMONDS
Prepare basic recipe, adding about 5 tablespoons chopped blanched almonds to the beaten eggs along with the cooked rice. You can change the texture of the cake further by using ground almonds instead of chopped.

WITH PISTACHIO
Prepare basic recipe, adding about 4 tablespoons coarsely chopped pistachios to the beaten eggs along with the cooked rice.

WITH MARSALA
Prepare basic recipe, replacing the brandy with Marsala.

Churros Con Chocolade

Churros are sausage-shaped donuts that are meant for plunging in the thick chocolate sauce served with them. They're a tradition all day and are also eaten for breakfast.

Serves 4

⅔ cup (150 ml) water
4 tbsp. vegetable oil, plus
    more for deep-frying
½ cup (55 g) flour
pinch of salt
2 eggs

¼ cup (55 g) granulated
    sugar
2 oz. (50 g) chocolate
⅔ cup (150 ml) heavy
    cream

1   Place the water in a saucepan with 4 tablespoons oil and bring to a boil. Mix the flour with the salt and gradually add it to the boiling water. Stir well with a wooden spoon over low heat until the mixture sticks together and leaves the sides of the pan. Remove from the heat and then beat in the eggs.

2   Add enough vegetable oil to a large, heavy saucepan to come halfway up the sides, and heat it to 350°F (180°C). Spoon the churros mixture into a pastry bag fitted with a large star-shaped tip. Pipe 7- or 10-cm (3- or 4-inch) lengths of dough directly into the hot oil and cook for 3 minutes until crisp and golden. Spoon the churros onto a plate lined with paper towels and sprinkle with the granulated sugar. Repeat until all the churros mixture is used up.

3   To make the chocolate dip, gently warm the chocolate and cream together in a small saucepan. When the mixture is smooth, remove it from the heat and transfer to a small bowl. Serve with a pile of the hot churros.

WITH CINNAMON
Prepare the basic recipe, adding 1 teaspoon ground cinnamon to the granulated sugar.

WITH CHILI POWDER
Prepare the basic recipe, adding a pinch of chili powder to the chocolate sauce.

WITH DULCE DE LECHE
Prepare the basic recipe, replacing the chocolate sauce with 3–4 tablespoons of dulce de leche.

WITH ORANGE
Prepare the basic recipe, adding the zest of 1 orange to the chocolate sauce.

Italian Chocolate Cake

Everybody loves chocolate cake, and this one is light and delicious and perfect with whipped cream or sweetened mascarpone, or, of course, with vanilla ice cream.

Serves 6

½ lb. (225 g) good-quality bittersweet chocolate
10 tbsp. butter, cubed

5 extra-large eggs, separated
1 cup (200 g) superfine sugar
1 tsp. baking powder

2 tbsp. cocoa powder
1 cup (100 g) all-purpose flour
confectioners' sugar for dusting

1 Grease a 9-in. (23-cm) loose-bottomed cake pan and line the bottom with waxed paper. Preheat the oven to 350°F (175°C). Chop the chocolate and melt it in a heatproof bowl set over a pan of simmering water. When it has melted, stir in the butter. Meanwhile, beat the egg whites until stiff, then slowly fold in the sugar. In a separate bowl, mix the baking powder with cocoa powder and flour.

2 Remove the chocolate from the heat, cool until just tepid, and stir in the beaten egg yolks, taking care not to scramble the eggs in the chocolate, which will happen if the chocolate is still too hot. Then gently fold the mixture into beaten egg whites. Finally, sift in the flour and cocoa mixture and fold in carefully with a large metal spoon. Turn the batter into the prepared cake pan and bake for 40 minutes. Let the cake cool in the pan, then ice with plain white or chocolate icing or a combination of the two, or simply dust with icing sugar.

WITH COFFEE
Prepare basic recipe, adding 2–3 teaspoons strong espresso coffee to the melted chocolate along with the butter.

WITH WALNUTS
Prepare basic recipe, adding 1 handful coarsely chopped walnuts after mixing in the egg yolks.

WITH MILK CHOCOLATE
Prepare basic recipe, replacing the bittersweet chocolate with best-quality milk chocolate.

WITH GIANDUJA
Prepare basic recipe, replacing the bittersweet chocolate with best-quality gianduja chocolate.

WITH PISTACHIO
Prepare basic recipe, adding 2 handfuls coarsely chopped pistachios after mixing in the egg yolks.

Egyptian Sweet Couscous

Among the variations of couscous, this recipe from Egypt is unrivaled for the sweet-toothed palate. It's traditionally served with a cold glass of milk or a cup of heavy Arabic coffee.

Serves 6

2 cups (450 ml) fruit juice, strawberry, raspberry, blueberry, or cranberry
2 tbsp. rose water
1 cup (225 g) couscous

3 tbsp. melted sweet butter
¼ cup (25 g) almond meal
¼ cup (25 g) finely ground pistachios

½ cup (60 g) confectioners' sugar
½–1 tbsp. ground cinnamon
½ cup (60 g) pomegranate seeds

1 In a saucepan, bring fruit juice and rose water to a boil. Add couscous, stir well, cover, remove from heat, and let stand 15 minutes. Fluff with a fork. Rub melted butter into the grains thoroughly. Mix in the almond meal and pistachios.

2 Mound on a serving platter and sprinkle with mixture of confectioners' sugar and cinnamon.

3 Serve at room temperature. Garnish with pomegranate seeds.

WITH CANDIED ALMONDS
Prepare the basic recipe, then garnish with candied (Jordan) almonds, scattered over the top.

WITH CANDIED CITRUS
Prepare the basic recipe, replacing the rose water with orange blossom water, and adding 3 tablespoons finely chopped candied orange to the nuts.

WITH FRUIT COMPÔTE
Prepare the basic recipe, then serve it with a little warm mixed fruit compôte.

WITH CANDIED PINEAPPLE
Prepare the basic recipe, adding cubes of candied pineapple to the cooked couscous before adding the rest of the ingredients.